A COMMENTARY ON THE EFFECT OF THE

EQUAL RIGHTS AMENDMENT ON STATE LAWS AND INSTITUTIONS

prepared for

The California Commission on the Status of Women's
Equal Rights Amendment Project

by

Anne K. Bingaman

Anita Miller, Project Director; 926 J Street, Suite 1014;
Sacramento, California   95814

254471

A COMMENTARY ON THE EFFECT OF THE
EQUAL RIGHTS AMENDMENT ON STATE LAWS AND INSTITUTIONS

Table of Contents

PREFACE

The California Commission on the Status of Women has been
funded by the Rockefeller Foundation to make a national study
of the societal impact of conformance of laws to the Equal Rights
Amendment, with the goal of promoting public understanding of the
issues involved. Several assumptions underlie the formulation
of this Project: (1) Widespread discrimination on the basis of
sex exists in all aspects of our national life and is reinforced
by a network of legal protections; (2) The ERA will set forth
with unequivocal clarity the principle that equality of rights
under the law shall not be denied or abridged on account of sex
and mandate legal change at every governmental level; (3) The
resultant legal changes will have broad societal impact, with the
major institutions such as marriage, family, government, education, and commerce undergoing substantial change as a direct
result of requirements to bring federal, state, and local laws
into conformance with the ERA; and (4) The process of social
change may be facilitated by a wide public knowledge of the
issues involved and the alternatives which exist. Assuming, then,
the existence of legal backing for sex discrimination, the
approaching ratification of the ERA, the far-reaching effects of
its implementation, and the possibility of orderly social change,
the Commission has developed a Project which will assist in the
process of change.

The Project has a dual dimension. It includes code reviews
and the development of guidelines for model codes in the areas of
family, employment, education, and criminal justice to be used
as models for conformance in all states. But pinpointing areas
of necessary legal change is in itself a preface to the examination of the impact of such change on selected key societal
institutions. This second dimension of the Project is meant to
generate an understanding of the interaction of social and legal
change in order to develop models for legal change which will
simultaneously provide required conformance to the ERA, make
adequate provision for orderly institutional change, and give due
recognition to human needs.

Fundamental change of the proportion implied here need not
be accompanied by chaos if systematic and well-thought-out
approaches are used rather than hasty and simplistic ones. The
Commission's Project seeks to move beyond the inadequacies of a
piecemeal approach by addressing the totality of the problem.
For example, property law, whether community or common, is in-
extricably involved with law in the field of probate, divorce or
dissolution, pensions, retirement, credit, domicile, child
support, welfare, and taxes. Of equal complexity is the matter
of societal impact of revisions in property law. The impact upon

the institution of the family is significant, involving not only law but human reactions. Changes in the center of family power, psychological implications of power shifts, changes in self-image for males and females, and changes in attitudes need to be considered, along with changes for the judiciary in handing down decisions within a different framework.

It is the Commission's belief that multi-disciplinary attention to the effect of change on major societal institutions can keep the issues of conformance clearly laid out before the public while the process of meeting human need is studied, refined, and genuinely reflected in the law. To further the development of thought in some crucial legal and social areas, the Commission asked national leaders from a variety of disciplines to contribute articles to a book soon to be published, Impact ERA: Limitations and Possibilities. The legal dimension of the Project has resulted in the publication of ERA Conformance: An Analysis of the California State Codes and now, A Commentary on the Effect of the Equal Rights Amendment on State Laws. At the present time the Project is moving toward the publication of an exhaustive ERA bibliography. Hopefully, these studies identify important issues in the entire process of legal and social revision of which we should all be aware.

More specifically, the Commission is publishing this Commentary in the hope that it will serve several purposes. First, we hope that it will prove useful as a comprehensive, and comprehensible, guide for concerned people around the country who want to understand why the Equal Rights Amendment is needed, how it will be interpreted by the courts after it is passed and its effect on major areas of law in their own states. The Commentary therefore begins with an explanation of the fourteenth amendment equal protection clause and its interpretation by the United States Supreme Court in cases involving statutes which treat women and men differently solely because of their sex--whether for occupational, tax, social security or other purposes. The remainder of chapter one lays the basis for the rest of the Commentary by explaining the legal theory of the Equal Rights Amendment which is applied throughout.

Chapters two through six deal respectively with the effects of the Amendment on state criminal laws and penal institutions; education; family laws; state labor laws; and state laws governing property owned by married persons. These state laws and institutions are matters of great importance in the daily lives of each of us. They affect such basic matters as the quality of the education our children receive; the property we ourselves legally own if we are married; and the amount of property we own in the event of divorce and at death. All of us must understand the present laws and institutions which affect us in order to understand the need for, and effect of, the Equal Rights Amendment.

Secondly, we hope that this volume will prove useful to
professionals around the country who will take part in the
major task of revising the laws in their own states after the
Amendment is passed. Because it is intended as a general guide
to the major problems of state law which the Amendment will
address, minor or unusual problems have not been treated here.
However, we believe that this work offers a beginning for an
analysis of the effect of the Amendment on state laws; to date,
such a resource has not been available in a single reference
work.

To increase the usefulness of the Commentary to those who
are interested in further study of the problems discussed here,
we have collected all major law review articles written since
1967 which deal with sex discrimination in state laws. These
references are grouped immediately following a narrative
discussion of the particular problem to which each pertains.
The possible solutions included here are meant only as
suggestions; they should not be viewed as definitive answers to
what are often very difficult policy questions.

We are deeply indebted to the members of an advisory
symposium held in Palo Alto on ERA implementation whose
collective thoughtfulness generated the idea for this book:
Janell Anderson, teacher of political science at California
State University, Sacramento; Ruth B. Cowan, professor of
political science at New York City Community College of C.U.N.Y.
and President of the Women's Caucus of the American Political
Science Association; Catherine East, Executive Secretary of the
Interdepartmental Committee on the Status of Women, Department
of Labor; Jo Freeman, assistant professor of political science
at State University College of New York at Purchase and a
prolific writer and lecturer on feminism; Anne S. Miner,
Affirmative Action Officer of Stanford University; Larene Paul,
International Representative with the Communication Workers of
America; Kathleen Peratis, Director of the Women's Rights Project
of the American Civil Liberties Union; Barbara Shack, Assistant
Director of the New York Civil Liberties Union; and Lenore J.
Weitzman, assistant professor of sociology at the University of
California, Davis, and Director of the Divorce Law Research
Center for the Study of Law and Society in Berkeley.

Special acknowledgment, however, must go to Anne K. Bingaman,
associate professor of law at the University of New Mexico Law
School and presently a Ford Foundation Fellow studying marital
property rights, for the development of the idea and the prepara-
tion of these materials in record time. Anne was active in the
efforts to achieve ratification of the Equal Rights Amendment
to the New Mexico State Constitution in 1972 and in 1972-73
served as the Chairperson of the State Bar Committee appointed
by the New Mexico Legislature to rewrite New Mexico's community
property statutes to conform to the State ERA. She is currently
serving as a consultant to the Equal Credit Opportunity Task
Force of the Federal Reserve Board, drafting regulations to

implement the federal Equal Credit Opportunity Act passed
by Congress in 1974.

It is particularly true of this work that it could not have
been written without the dedicated assistance of several people
whom we and Anne would like to take this opportunity to thank:
Professor Pamela B. Minzner of the University of New Mexico Law
School for her careful scrutiny of the manuscript; Ellen Souberman
and Marcia Huaco, students at the University of New Mexico Law
School, for their research and rewriting for the manuscript;
and Virginia White for her general indispensability to the
entire project.

The Commission is especially grateful to Harriet Shepler,
who typed the final manuscript not only with unusual competence
but also with due respect for the limitations of time and a rare
gift for good cheer and equanimity in the face of often harried
circumstances.

Finally, and most importantly, the Commission hopes that
those who read this Commentary will come away from it as
astounded as we are at the number of inequities which state
laws and institutions now impose on persons solely because of
their sex, and as convinced of the great need in American
society for the Equal Rights Amendment. We believe, as we hope
you do, that the Equal Rights Amendment, if taken seriously,
will provide the impetus for innovative legislative solutions
to problems which have been with us for centuries.

Much lies ahead.

Anita Miller, Director

Equal Rights Amendment Project

California Commission on the Status
    of Women

926 J Street, Suite 1014

Sacramento, CA 95814

August 1975

vii

Chapter One

THE EQUAL RIGHTS AMENDMENT AND THE CONSTITUTION

Table of Contents

2

THE EQUAL RIGHTS AMENDMENT

Proposed Amendment XXVII

(Proposed by Congress on March 22, 1972)

Section 1. Equality of rights under the law shall not be denied or abridged by the United States or by any State on account of sex.

Section 2. The Congress shall have the power to enforce, by appropriate legislation, the provisions of this article.

Section 3. This amendment shall take effect two years after the date of ratification.

INTRODUCTION

The Equal Rights Amendment offers a legal solution to legal, social and cultural problems in our society. Because the ERA will create law--a new Amendment to the United States Constitution--and because it will have distinctly legal effects on existing state laws and institutions, an understanding of the legal need for the Amendment and the way in which the courts will or may interpret it is basic to understanding the role the Amendment will play.

Therefore, this chapter explains in some detail the history of the Supreme Court's treatment, under the fourteenth amendment equal protection clause, of statutes and governmental actions based solely on the sex of the persons affected. When that history is understood, the need for the Amendment as a matter of law will be clear.

The chapter then sets forth both the possible theories the Supreme Court may use in applying the Amendment to cases which come before it and the theories which have been adopted throughout this work to analyze the Amendment's effect on major areas of state law and state institutions.

THE NEED FOR A CONSTITUTIONAL AMENDMENT

Equal Protection Doctrine in the United States Supreme Court

Ratified in 1868, the fourteenth amendment to the United States Constitution contains the famous equal protection clause which provides:

> Nor (shall any state) deny to any person within its jurisdiction the equal protection of the laws.

In its interpretation of the equal protection clause, the United States Supreme Court traditionally has applied at least two tests: the "minimum scrutiny" or "reasonableness" test; and the "strict scrutiny" test. Each will be discussed below.

"Minimum Scrutiny" or the "Reasonableness" Test

While the equal protection clause's guarantee may appear to require that all laws apply "equally" to all persons, in fact in most cases the clause only requires that the legislature have a "reasonable" basis for the classifications it uses in a statute. Under "minimum scrutiny," the Court will uphold a legislative act if two tests are met: (1) the purpose of the act is a valid one; and (2) the classifications made--or the persons to which the act applies--are "reasonably" related to the purpose for which the act was passed.

Under the minimum scrutiny test, the first requirement is almost invariably met: state governments and legislatures have extremely broad "police" powers under which they may enact a wide variety of laws. As for the second requirement under minimum scrutiny--that the classifications made be "reasonably" related to the purpose of the statute--if the Court can itself imagine any rational basis for the classifications made in a statute, the act will not be held to violate equal protection.

The result of the application of this extremely lenient standard of review is almost self-fulfilling. Because the Court can almost always hypothesize reasons which provide at least a minimum rational basis upon which a state legislature might have acted in passing a particular law, a state statute is almost always upheld against an equal protection attack, if a genuine minimum scrutiny test is applied. Because of this result Justice Holmes once labeled equal protection "the last refuge of the hopeless litigant."

"Strict Scrutiny" Test for "Suspect Classifications" or "Fundamental Interests"

In the last thirty years, the Court has developed a second test under the equal protection clause known as the "strict scrutiny" test. If this test is held to be applicable in a particular case, the burden of proof shifts to the state. This means the state must demonstrate that: (1) it had a "compelling state interest" for passing the law; and (2) the classification of persons to whom the law applies was necessary to accomplish the state's extremely important, or "compelling," purpose.

Strict scrutiny was first ennunciated by the Court in 1942 in Skinner v. Oklahoma, 316 U.S. 535; however, it was not fully accepted as a recognized constitutional doctrine until the mid-1950's, after the Court in Brown v. Board of Education, 347 U.S. 483 (1954), applied the test to racial classifications.

Just as the minimum scrutiny test almost always assures that a statute will be upheld if it is applied, application of the strict scrutiny test is tantamount to assurance that the challenged law will be stricken. In cases litigated under the strict scrutiny test, the only racial classification ever upheld was that made in sending Japanese-Americans to concentration camps during World War II. In the case of Korematsu v.

U.S., 323 U.S. 214 (1945), the Court said that the government had demonstrated the necessary "compelling state interest" because of the urgency of war; but most commentators believe that the decision was incorrect. Thus, if strict scrutiny is applied, the law in question will almost always be found to violate equal protection.

Equal Protection Doctrine and Sex Discrimination Cases

Until the Supreme Court's decision in Reed v. Reed, 404 U.S. 71 (1971), the Supreme Court had never held that a statutory classification based on sex was unconstitutional. In fact, applying the minimum scrutiny test to the statutes involved in two famous earlier cases, Goesaert v. Cleary, 335 U.S. 464 (1948), and Hoyt v. Florida, 368 U.S. 57 (1961), the Court had held that legislative classifications based solely on sex were constitutional.

In Goesaert, the Michigan legislature had passed a statute which prohibited all women from serving as barmaids unless they were the wives or daughters of male bar owners. The statute was challenged by the Goesaerts, a mother and daughter who owned a bar and had made their livelihood by operating it. In determining whether the legislative classification used was reasonable, Justice Frankfurter said that the Michigan legislature might have rationally believed that women tending bar would be in danger unless a male relative--husband or father--were in the bar to protect them. This possible purpose, which was completely unsupported by any factual evidence,[1] served as the minimum "rational" basis which was sufficient to uphold the statute under the equal protection clause. In other words, the classification used, sex alone, was a "reasonable" one. This case is but one example of the almost automatic results which flow from application of the minimum rational basis, or minimum scrutiny, test.

In Hoyt v. Florida, a woman who had been convicted by an all-male jury of murdering her husband with a baseball bat in a fit of rage over his adultery challenged Florida's jury selection statutes as an unconstitutional denial of equal protection. The statutes in question required all men to serve on juries, but automatically exempted all women unless

---

1. In fact, it is well documented, and was argued to the Court in Goesaert, that the all-male Bartenders Union had embarked on a successful campaign in 1945 to have state statutes enacted which prohibited women from tending bar. See B. Babcock, A. Freedman, E. Norton and S. Ross, Sex Discrimina-and the Law 93,n. 2 (1975).

they went through a registration process; as a result, juries in Florida were comprised of less than 5% women. The woman convicted in Hoyt believed that women on the jury might have been more sympathetic to her motivations than was the all-male jury. As late as 1961, when Hoyt was decided, the Supreme Court had no difficulty in finding that the Florida legislature clearly had a reasonable basis for imposing jury duties and giving exemptions from duty solely on the basis of a prospective juror's sex. The Court said:

> We cannot conclude that Florida's statute is not
> based on some reasonable classification. . . .
> Despite the enlightened emancipation of women from
> restrictions and protections of by-gone years, and
> their entry into many parts of community life
> formerly reserved to men, women are still regarded
> as the center of home and family life. We cannot
> say that it is constitutionally impermissible for
> a state . . . to conclude that a woman should be
> relieved from the civic duty of jury service unless
> she herself determines that such service is consistent
> with her own responsibilities. (368 U.S. 57, 61-62)

Thus, the gross overgeneralization based solely on sex used in the statute was held to be a "reasonable" classification which did not deny equal protection.

Until 1971, then, the Court had never held a classification based on sex to violate the equal protection clause. Applying the minimum scrutiny or "reasonableness" standard, it had always found sex-based classifications justified under the particular circumstances of the legislation in question.

During the 1960's, however, commentators and legal scholars had great hope that the Court would declare sex to be a "suspect" classification just as race had been in Brown v. Board of Education. Such a holding, they thought, would automatically invalidate any statute which used sex alone as a basis for classification. It was this hope which kept sincere supporters of equal rights from unifying behind the Equal Rights Amendment. With the Court's sex discrimination decisions in 1971, those hopes were dashed: supporters of equal rights realized that if the goal were to be realized, it would have to come through constitutional amendment.

The 1971 Decisions: Williams and Reed

In 1971, two cases challenging statutes which made sex-based distinctions were brought to the United States Supreme Court.

In the first of those cases, <u>Williams v. McNair</u>, 401 U.S. 951 (1971), <u>mem. aff'g</u> 316 F. Supp. 134 (D.S.C. 1970), the Court affirmed without opinion a lower court decision upholding the maintenance in South Carolina's educational system of all-women's and all-men's colleges in addition to sex-integrated institutions. The lower court found that such classifications by sex in a public school system had a "reasonable" basis and did not violate the right to equal protection.

After this disappointing result, many national organizations wrote <u>amicus curiae</u> ("friend of the Court") briefs urging the Court to take the opportunity presented by <u>Reed v. Reed</u>, also before the Court in 1971, to declare that sex was a "suspect" classification, thus requiring the state to demonstrate a "compelling" interest in order to justify using sex alone as a ground for classification in state legislation.

At issue in <u>Reed v. Reed</u> was an Idaho law which provided a statutory preference for men which probate courts were to follow when they appointed administrators of estates. The Reeds were divorced and were involved in litigation to determine who should be appointed administrator of their deceased child's estate. The Idaho Supreme Court upheld the probate court's appointment of Mr. Reed as the administrator of the estate, validating the statute against an equal protection attack. The U.S. Supreme Court reversed this decision; it did not, however, apply the strict scrutiny test, but purported to apply the minimum scrutiny or "reasonableness" test. According to the Court in <u>Reed</u>, the Idaho statute did not meet even that very lenient test, and was therefore unconstitutional.

In fact, as many commentators have since pointed out, had the Court truly applied the "reasonableness" test it had used in past decisions, the statute in <u>Reed</u> would have been upheld. Certainly, it would have been as easy for the Court to hypothesize that the Idaho legislature had a rational basis for believing that men were more experienced in business affairs, and thus were better qualified to serve as administrators of estates than were women, as it had been for the Court in <u>Goesaert</u> to suppose that the Michigan legislature might believe that women were in physical danger tending bar unless a male relative was close at hand. The fact that this result was not reached, although the minimum scrutiny test was purportedly applied, has led many students of the Court to believe that where sex is concerned, the Court will apply a stricter standard than minimum scrutiny but one less strict than that which would be applied if sex were declared a "suspect" classification. <u>See</u>, for an exposition of this view, the articles cited in reference nos. 1 and 2 below.

When the decision in Reed came down, the many supporters of equal rights who had hoped that the Court would place sex, along with race, in the "suspect" classification category realized that the Court would not follow that route easily or quickly. It was only then that efforts began in earnest to secure ratification of the Equal Rights Amendment. After an intensive lobbying effort, Congress passed the Amendment on March 22, 1972.

Later Court decisions have shown that the Amendment would be necessary even if the Court were to decide that sex is a "suspect" classification. To understand why, it is necessary to review the Court's decisions in sex discrimination cases since 1971 in some detail.

The Decisions Since Reed

The history of sex discrimination cases in the Supreme Court since Reed v. Reed has been an erratic one. In 1972, two cases involving sex-discriminatory statutes came before the Court. In the first, Forbush v. Wallace, 401 U.S. 970 (1972)mem. aff'g 341 F. Supp. 217 (M.D. Ala. 1971), the Court affirmed without opinion a lower court decision which held that an Alabama regulation requiring married female applicants for drivers' licenses to use their husbands' surnames, rather than their own birth names, was "reasonable" and did not violate the equal protection clause.

Also in 1972, however, the Court decided the case which has remained the high-water mark of sex discrimination cases in the Supreme Court, Frontiero v. Richardson, 411 U.S. 677 (1972). In that case, the Court, in an eight to one decision, struck down an Air Force regulation which required husbands of female Air Force officers to prove that they were in fact dependent upon their wives for support before gaining dependency benefits, while automatically giving all wives of male Air Force officers the same benefits. For supporters of equal rights, however, even more important than the result was the fact that four of the nine justices declared their belief that sex was a "suspect" classification and should be treated as such in all future cases. While four justices were not, of course, a majority of the Court, they did seem to

represent substantial sentiment in support of applying the
strict scrutiny test to all sex-based classifications.[2] Thus,
1972 produced disappointing results in Forbush, and hopeful
results in Frontiero.[3]

At the time, it was believed that the Court would apply the
"compelling state interest" test as strictly in examining sex-
based classifications as it had previously in examining race
classifications. As the 1974 decision in Kahn v. Shevin was
to show, however, that belief was probably incorrect.

---

2. That belief was further aided by the fact that the
four justices who concurred in the result, but did not agree
that sex was a "suspect" classification, based their reasoning
in large part on the fact that the Equal Rights Amendment was
in the process of being ratified by the states. This, they
felt, should prevent the Court from stepping in at that
particular moment in history and declaring sex a suspect
classification.

3. The Court also decided Stanley v. Illinois, 405 U.S.
645 in 1972, a case involving the constitutionality of an
Illinois statute under which unwed mothers were presumed to
be fit to have legal custody of their children unless proven
not to be, but unwed fathers were conclusively presumed to be
unfit for custody; their children automatically were placed
in foster homes. The Court held this statute violative of a
natural father's equal protection rights.

Thus, Stanley was decided under the equal protection clause,
but most commentators believe that the case really turned on the
fourteenth amendment's guarantee of procedural due process, the
right to a hearing before the state may deprive a person of
certain rights. Because only equal protection had been
argued by the plaintiff lawyer in the courts below, however,
the Court was forced to use that clause rather than the more
appropriate due process clause in writing its decision.

Thus, while Stanley v. Illinois is technically a sex
discrimination case decided on equal protection grounds, it
probably is a procedural due process case, and therefore is
not discussed in the text.

No cases involving the equal protection clause and sex discrimination were decided by the Court in 1973. 1974, however, brought four major sex discrimination cases, two decided under the equal protection clause and two under the due process clause of the fourteenth amendment.[4]

In both of the cases decided on equal protection grounds, statutes creating sex-based distinctions were upheld. The first, Kahn v. Shevin, 416 U.S. 351 (1974), involved a Florida statute which provided a $500 property tax exemption available to all widows, without regard to need or income, but not to widowers. Justice Douglas--who had agreed in Frontiero v. Richardson that sex was a "suspect" classification--wrote for the 6-3 majority and applied the minimum scrutiny test to the Florida statute. Douglas reasoned that because of past economic discrimination against women in jobs and salaries, it

---

4. The two cases decided on due process grounds were Cleveland Board of Education v. LaFleur and Cohen v. Chesterfield County School Board, 414 U.S. 632 (1974). In both of those cases, teachers challenged the constitutionality of school district rules which required maternity leaves to begin four to five months before expected childbirth. The Court said that arbitrarily fixed maternity leaves were "conclusive presumptions" concerning the physical ability of pregnant teachers to continue work and, as such, were unconstitutional because they did not allow individual physical differences to be taken into account.

Although the teachers won in both cases, the Court, by using a due process rather than an equal protection approach, in effect treated pregnancy as a unique problem rather than as one comparable to any other temporary physical disability. Therefore, under the due process approach taken in these cases, school boards can still continue to require teachers to prove their capacity to continue work or return to work, while not requiring employees with other temporary disabilities to make similar showings.

Because the major issue in the consideration of the Equal Rights Amendment has been the applicability of equal protection to sex discrimination issues, the due process approach taken in LaFleur and Cohen will not be discussed here.

For a discussion of the approach taken by the Court in these cases, see Note, "Irrebuttable Presumptions: An Illusory Analysis," 27 Stan. L. Rev. 449 (1974).

The issue of pregnancy and mandatory maternity leave under the Equal Rights Amendment is discussed more fully below in Section on restrictive labor laws for women of the chapter on Labor Laws.

was rational, said Douglas, for the Florida legislature to attempt to rectify that discrimination by a form of benign discrimination now--in this case a property tax exemption available to any woman who had lost her husband, but to no man who had lost his wife, regardless of his economic circumstances.

Justice Brennan and Marshall, in dissent, reiterated their view in Frontiero that sex was a "suspect" classification which triggered application of the strict scrutiny test. Applying that test, they asked first whether the state could show a "compelling state interest" for the classification. What is interesting, and even somewhat frightening, about Brennan and Marshall's approach is that they viewed the same past economic discrimination against women emphasized by Douglas in the majority opinion as the sufficiently compelling state interest which would justify the statute's present discrimination against men.

Thus, although the majority and dissenters purported to apply two very different constitutional standards--minimum scrutiny versus strict scrutiny--both viewed the fact of past economic discrimination as either a "rational" or a "compelling" state interest for giving the tax exemption to women as a class, regardless of economic circumstance. Turning next to the "less drastic means" analysis required by strict scrutiny, Brennan and Marshall stated that the exemption was overbroad because it included wealthy widows as well as poor ones, and that the statute therefore ultimately violated equal protection.

Kahn v. Shevin demonstrates two things. First, a majority of the Court is willing to uphold very broad "benign" sex discrimination in favor of women, a result not possible under the ERA.[5] Second, the decision shows the dangers of the strict scrutiny or compelling state interest test in actual application to sex discrimination claims. If the rationale of Brennan and Marshall's dissent in Kahn v. Shevin were applied in other cases, a new rubric could be substituted to uphold sex-discriminatory statutes. Under the guise of "remedying past discrimination," protective labor legislation as well as other statutes and governmental actions which in fact might ultimately work not to benefit women but to harm them, can be justified. Further, statutes which harm men can be upheld.[6]

---

5. See section on "benign quotas" of this chapter for a discussion of the constitutionality under the Equal Rights Amendment of affirmative action programs to benefit women.

6. See conclusions to this section below for a more complete explanation of ways in which this rationale may work to the detriment of women.

13

It is clear that the Florida tax exemption validated by
the majority in Kahn v. Shevin, and which even Brennan and
Marshall would have upheld had it not been drawn so broadly,
would be unconstitutional under the Equal Rights Amendment.
Thus, Kahn v. Shevin is further evidence of the need for the
Equal Rights Amendment, because even the most consistent
supporters of equal rights on the Court were willing to apply
the "compelling state interest" test required under strict
scrutiny in a far more lenient manner in a sex-discrimination
case than the Court has ever applied that test in a case
involving racial discrimination.[7]

The second sex-discrimination case decided by the Supreme
Court in 1974 was Geduldig v. Aiello, 417 U.S. 484 (1974). At
issue there was the constitutionality of a California
unemployment insurance statute which excluded from its coverage
all disabilities related to pregnancy. The majority of the
Court held that the statute did not discriminate on the basis
of sex, but merely on the basis of one physical condition,
pregnancy--albeit a condition unique to one sex. Justice
Stewart's footnote 20 in the majority opinion of Geduldig v.
Aiello was the only discussion by the majority of the sex-
discrimination issue.

In a strong dissent, Justices Brennan, Douglas and Marshall
recognized that Title VII of the Civil Rights Act of 1964
requires pregnancy to be treated as any other temporary
disability and reiterated their view that sex was a "suspect"
classification which was subject to strict scrutiny. The
dissenters explicitly viewed the majority opinion as an
"apparent retreat" from Reed and Frontiero. The effect of the
Equal Rights Amendment on the Aiello decision is discussed extensively below in the section on the exclusion of pregnancy from
disability plans in the chapter on Labor Laws.

In 1975, four cases dealing in some way with sex discrimination were decided by the Court. In three of them, sex-
discriminatory statutes were stricken; one upheld, in a 5-4
decision, a sex-based distinction in a Navy promotional statute.

In Taylor v. Louisiana, 95 S. Ct. 692 (1975), the Court
implicitly overruled Hoyt v. Florida by holding unconstitutional
a jury system which required all men to register to serve but
which automatically exempted all women. While the Taylor

---

7. See section on strict scrutiny of this chapter, below,
for a full explanation of the "compelling state interest" test
in statutes making racial classifications and a comparison
to Kahn v. Shevin.

opinion rested on a defendant's sixth amendment right to trial
by a jury drawn from a fair cross-section of the community,
and not on express sex discrimination founds, footnote 17 of
the opinion is interesting. The Court recites the extensive
role of women and mothers in the U.S. labor force and thereby
disputes the assertion upon which the result in Hoyt v.
Florida rested--"that woman is still regarded as the center
of home and family life."[8] The Taylor Court said that the
labor statistics showed

> the evolving nature of the structure of the family
> unit in American society . . . /and/ they certainly
> put to rest the suggestion that all women should be
> exempt from jury service based solely on their sex
> and their presumed role in the home.[9]

It is apparent that the Court's consciousness was raised
in the fourteen years between Hoyt v. Florida and Taylor v.
Louisiana. The Hoyt defendant was a woman, who certainly could
claim possible prejudice from having been convicted by an all-
male jury likely to be unsympathetic to her defense of temporary
insanity to the charge of murdering her husband; the defendant
in Taylor v. Louisiana was a male convicted of rape, who could
not possibly claim prejudice from a lack of women on the jury.
Both the facts of the two cases and the Court's language show
that the Supreme Court's view of sex discrimination has
evolved in a positive direction, but the change has not come
quickly.

In Schlesinger v. Ballard, 95 S. Ct. 572 (1975), a bare
majority of the Court, applying the minimum scrutiny test,
held that a statute under which male Navy officers were allowed
three years less time to achieve promotion or receive a
mandatory discharge than were female officers was constitutional.
Looking to the statutory "promotion or discharge" scheme
created by Congress, the majority concluded that Congress might
have allowed women longer to achieve promotion because they had
fewer opportunities for promotion based on combat and sea duty.

The four dissenting Justices, however, severely criticized
the Court's willingness to apply only minimum scrutiny to a sex-
based statutory classification, and argued that even that
lenient test had not been met because there was no indication
that Congress had in fact intended to compensate women officers
when it enacted the discriminatory statute.

---

8. Hoyt v. Florida, 368 U.S. at 62 (1961).

9. Taylor v. Louisiana, 95 S. Ct. 692, at 700 n. 17 (1975).

The third case decided in 1975 was Weinberger v. Wiesenfeld, 95 S. Ct. 1225 (1975). There, the sex-based distinction in the Social Security Act, which gave survivors' benefits to mothers but not to fathers of dependent children whose deceased spouses had paid into Social Security before their deaths, was held unconstitutional under the fifth amendment due process clause, which imposes the same equal protection restrictions on the federal government that the fourteenth amendment equal protection clause imposes on state governments. The statutory scheme, said the Court, made sex-based distinctions which could not be rationally sustained and were therefore stricken. In Wiesenfeld, the Court applied a "reasonableness" test to the classification; the Justices first looked to the purpose of the statute and then determined whether the classification was a rational means of achieving that purpose. While Wiesenfeld is encouraging in that it struck down a sex-discriminatory statute, it certainly does not apply a strict scrutiny test.

In the last sex-discrimination case of 1975, Stanton v. Stanton, 43 U.S.L.W. 4449 (April 15, 1975), the Court reversed a decision of the Utah Supreme Court, declaring unconstitutional a Utah statute which established the age of majority as eighteen for girls and twenty-one for boys. Although the Court explicitly stated that Reed v. Reed controlled its decision in Stanton, it also noted:

> We therefore conclude that under any test--
> compelling state interest, or rational basis, or
> something in between--/the Utah statute/ . . .
> does not survive an equal protection attack.
> (43 U.S.L.W. 4449, 4452)

Today, then, when sex-based statutory classifications are challenged in the Supreme Court, the Court may deal with the challenge in a variety of ways. These range from Justice Brennan's and Marshall's position that sex is a "suspect" classification; to an intermediate standard of review which is greater than true minimum scrutiny but less than strict scrutiny, as in Reed v. Reed and Wiesenfeld; to the position that sex-based classifications are subject only to minimum scrutiny, as in Geduldig v. Aiello. Thus, those who claim that a constitutional amendment is not needed because the fourteenth amendment guarantees "equal protection of the laws" either have not read or do not understand the Supreme Court's opinions which apply the equal protection clause to instances of sex discrimination. Even the brief summary of those cases offered here makes it clear that supporters of equal rights cannot rely on the Court to declare sex a "suspect" classification under the fourteenth amendment equal protection clause--and that even if it did, as Kahn v. Shevin shows, a compelling state interest could still be found to justify sex discrimination in statutes or governmental actions. The Amendment, then, offers the only certain means for achieving the goal of equal legal rights for men and women.

Beyond the constitutional reasons, the Amendment is needed as an impetus for broad-scale legal reforms which a Supreme Court decision alone could never provide: litigation is a slow, expensive process which achieves genuine law reform only in time measured by decades. For those who doubt this, the Supreme Court's decision in Brown v. Board of Education and its tragic aftermath during the long years of non-implementation--including recent events in the public schools of Boston--need only be remembered. Passage of the Equal Rights Amendment can only be regarded as an urgent necessity if "equal justice under law" for women and men is to be a reality in our lifetimes.

References

1. For analyses of the Reed v. Reed decision which argue that in that case the Court applied a higher standard of review than the "minimum scrutiny" which it purported to apply, see:

a. Gunther, "Foreword: In Search of Evolving Doctrine on a Changing Court: A Model for a Newer Equal Protection in the Supreme Court, 1971 Term," 86 Harv. L. Rev. 1, 29-34 (1972); and

b. Tribe, "Foreword: Toward a Model of Roles in the Due Process of Life and Law," 87 Harv. L. Rev. 1, 118-24 (1973).

2. Ginsburg, "Comment on Reed v. Reed," 1 Women's Rights L. Reptr. 7, 8 (Spring 1972).

3. For a comprehensive discussion of the development of the "rational basis" and "strict scrutiny" standards of review under the equal protection clause see Note, "Developments in the Law--Equal Protection," 82 Harv. L. Rev. 1065 (1969).

4. The leading article on the Equal Rights Amendment and the need for it is Brown, Emerson, Falk and Freedman, "The Equal Rights Amendment: A Constitutional Basis for Equal Rights for Women," 80 Yale L. J. 871 (1971).

5. Johnston and Knapp, "Sex Discrimination by Law: A Study in Judicial Perspective," 46 N.Y.U. L. Rev. 675 (1971).

6. Rawalt, "The Equal Rights Amendment for Men and Women Is Needed," 59 Women Law. J. 4, 6 (1973).

7. For an analysis of Kahn v. Shevin, see B. Babcock, A. Freedman, E. Norton and S. Ross, Sex Discrimination and the Law 124 (1975).

8. Eastwood, "The Double Standard of Justice: Women's Rights under the Constitution," 5 Val. L. Rev. 281 (1971).

9. Note, "Sex Discrimination and Equal Protection: Do We Need a Constitutional Amendment?," 85 Harv. L. Rev. 1499 (1971).

10. Citizen's Advisory Council on the Status of Women, The Proposed Equal Rights Amendment to the United States Constitution (1970). This publication may be obtained from the Women's Bureau of the Department of Labor, Washington, D.C. 20210.

11. Dorsen and Ross, "The Necessity for a Constitutional Amendment," 6 Harv. Civ. Rights Civ. Lib. L. Rev. 216 (1971).

12. Note, "Constitutional Law: The Equal Protection Clause and Women's Rights," 19 Loyola L. Rev. 542 (1973).

13. Note, "Recent Developments in the Area of Sex-based Discrimination--The Courts, the Congress and the Constitution," 20 N.Y.U. L. F. 359 (1974).

14. Note, "Sex Discrimination in the 1970's: The Supreme Court Decisions," 6 Tex. Tech. L. Rev. 149 (1974).

15. For comments on Geduldig v. Aiello, Kahn v. Shevin and Weinberger v. Wiesenfeld, see 13 J. of Family Law 867 (1974).

16. Note, "Sex Discrimination and Equal Protection: An Analysis of Constitutional Approaches to Achieve Equal Rights for Women," 38 Albany L. Rev. 66 (1973).

17. Note, "Toward Sexual Equality? An Analysis of Frontiero v. Richardson," 59 Ia. L. Rev. 377 (1973).

18. Note, "Evaluating Sex Classifications: The Search for Standards," 23 Cath. U. L. Rev. 599 (1974).

THE STANDARD OF REVIEW UNDER THE EQUAL RIGHTS AMENDMENT

As we have seen, a majority of the Supreme Court has never held that the strict scrutiny test applies under the equal protection clause to determine the constitutionality of statutes which make classifications based on sex. In recent cases, the

Court majority has purported to apply the minimum scrutiny test; however, many commentators believe that in fact an intermediate standard between minimum and strict scrutiny is being used.

Clearly, the Equal Rights Amendment would require at the least that the Court apply a standard of strict scrutiny in reviewing statutes which make sex-based classifications. However, if the Court takes the route indicated by both the legislative history of the Amendment and the scholarly commentary it has engendered, it will apply a standard even higher than strict scrutiny--one of absolute prohibition of sex-based classifications, with certain well-defined exceptions. These two possible standards of review are discussed separately below.

Absolute Prohibition of Sex-based Classifications

Brown, Emerson, Falk and Freedman, in "The Equal Rights Amendment: A Constitutional Basis for Equal Rights for Women," 80 Yale L. J. 871 (1971), set forth the theory of the Amendment expressly adopted in the Congressional debates which led to its passage in 1972 and widely accepted since. In that article, the authors state that strict scrutiny would not be permitted as an interpretation of the Equal Rights Amendment. They say:

> /I/t follows that the constitutional mandate must be absolute. The issue under the Equal Rights Amendment cannot be different but equal, reasonable or unreasonable classification, suspect classification, fundamental interests, or the demands of administrative expediency. Equality of rights means that sex is not a factor . . . (80 Yale L. J. 871 at 892).

The only exceptions the authors make to the principle of absolute equality between the sexes in all laws and governmental actions are those of the right of privacy and certain applications of the "unique physical characteristics" test, discussed separately below.

If a challenged statutes does not come under either of these qualifying principles, it would be prohibited under the Amendment regardless of any "compelling state interest" put forward in support of the law. That, at least, is the theory upon which the leading supporters of the Amendment in Congress acted in adopting the Amendment and which the Yale article sets forth.

The Yale article is itself a part of the legislative history of the Amendment, having been placed in the Congressional Record by Senator Birch Bayh, the leading proponent of the Amendment in the Senate. It was distributed to all House members by Congresswoman Martha Griffiths, the Amendment's leading proponent in the House and was mentioned repeatedly in Senate floor debates on the Equal Rights Amendment.[10] Even Senator Ervin, the leading opponent of the Amendment, stated that the Yale article was "primary legislative history" and called it "one of the best guides to a general interpretation of the Equal Rights Amendment."[11] There can be no question, therefore, that Congress relied heavily upon the interpretation of the amendment put forward in the Yale article. That congressional reliance is extremely important, because the Supreme Court traditionally emphasizes and defers to the understanding Congress had when it passed laws and constitutional amendments. Therefore, both the congressional reliance on the Yale article, and the importance of the article itself as an authoritative guide and the most far-reaching and complete analysis of the Amendment yet to appear, make it likely that the interpretation contained in it will be followed by the Supreme Court when the Amendment is passed. For that reason, this summary of the effect of the Amendment on various areas of state law has relied heavily on the interpretation of the Amendment which it sets forth.

Strict Scrutiny

As noted earlier, the Court has adopted the strict scrutiny standard of review under the fourteenth amendment equal protection clause to assess classifications based on race. In this area, the Court has only once found the necessary "compelling state interest" to justify a governmental distinction based solely upon the race of the persons affected; the case was Korematsu v. United States, 323 U.S. 214 (1945), described above. If the same extremely strict standard of scrutiny which the Court applies in the area of racial discrimination were applied to sex-based classifications, the strict scrutiny test would possibly be tantamount to an absolute prohibition of statutory distinctions based on sex.

---

10. See 117 Cong. Rec. 35012 (1971) and 118 Cong. Rec. 9083 (1972).

11. 118 Cong. Rec. 9096 (1972); Senate Committee on the Judiciary, Equal Rights for Men and Women, S. Rep. No. 92-689, 92nd Cong., 2nd Sess., Minority Views of Mr. Ervin at 35.

However, Justices Brennan and Marshall's dissenting opinion in Kahn v. Shevin, 416 U.S. 351 (1974), described above, gives reason to believe that the Court might well view sex-based classifications much more leniently than it does classifications based on race. In that case, Justices Brennan and Marshall, found in the prior history of wage and employment discrimination against women as a class, the necessary "compelling state interest" for a tax exemption available only to widows. This prior discrimination, they said, justified the attempt by the State of Florida to remedy it now by providing special benefits for women as a class. As noted by leading scholars of the Amendment:

> It is important that courts and legislatures compensate the victims of discrimination for their losses. However, the paradox of remedies for sex and race discrimination is that often they must take sex and race into account. In individual cases, the need to remedy this situation is sufficiently acute, and the factual evidence of who suffered how much loss as a result of discrimination sufficiently strong, that remedial sex and race classification is appropriate. . . . In contrast, Brennan's hypothetical law /in his Kahn v. Shevin dissent/involves sex averaging on such a grand scale that it undermines the concept of individual treatment without regard to sex. In effect it substitutes discrimination against men for discrimination against women rather than substituting individual treatment for overbroad sex classification.

> Such overclassification by sex is unjust. It is also a dangerous precedent. It creates the possibility that the rationale of remedying past discrimination will replace the rationale of "protecting" women as constitutional justification for statutory sex classifications which, in the guise of benefiting women, actually discriminate against them. /B. Babcock, A. Freedman, E. Norton, and S. Ross, Sex Discrimination and the Law 124 (1975)./

Justice Brennan's opinion in Kahn v. Shevin is disappointing because it is he, more than any other Justice, who in other opinions has been particularly sensitive to problems of sex discrimination. For Justice Brennan to find a "compelling" state interest in a law which points so broadly, by discriminating against all males in favor of all females, is disheartening. The strict scrutiny test, it seems, is not as strict as one would hope in claims of sex discrimination.

Conclusions

Although it cannot be predicted with certainty what
standard the Supreme Court will use to interpret the Equal
Rights Amendment in the first cases which come before it after
the Amendment's passage, it seems likely that the absolute
prohibition approach contained in the Yale article will be
followed. It should be recognized, however, that it is
possible that the Court will not adopt this interpretation. If
it does not, and adopts instead the strict scrutiny test under
which "compelling state interests" may justify legislative
distinctions based on sex, some of the results which the Yale
analysis and this Commentary state to be legally required by
the Amendment may not be so required. For instance, if the
Court allowed a state to make a showing of a "compelling state
interest" for maintaining segregated men's and women's prisons,
it is possible--especially given the comparatively lenient
standard of Justices Brennan's and Marshall's dissent in Kahn
v. Shevin--that a state could successfully argue that improved
rehabilitation and diminished danger to women prisoners were such
compelling justifications that prisons could constitutionally
remain segregated after the Amendment's passage. Such a result
would be unconstitutional if the absolute approach adopted in
the remainder of this Commentary were used.

Therefore, readers should be aware that the results given
here as legally required by the Amendment are those results
which flow from the analysis of the Amendment contained in the
Yale article. It is believed, for reasons stated earlier, that
that approach is preferable to the strict scrutiny test and is
supported by the legislative history of the Amendment in
Congress. If, however, strict scrutiny is used instead, the
Amendment probably will accomplish less than is predicted here:
how much less cannot be determined, because, particularly after
Kahn v. Shevin, no one now knows what interests the Court might
find to be "compelling state interests" under a strict scrutiny
test.

THE STATE ACTION CONCEPT AND THE EQUAL RIGHTS AMENDMENT

It has long been settled that the fourteenth amendment of
the United States Constitution applies only to "state action."
The state action concept developed under the fourteenth amendment because of the wording of significant parts of that
amendment. The equal protection clause provides, for example,
that no "state shall deny . . . the equal protection of the laws."
Thus, the Court has held that the equal protection clause does
not apply to private discrimination, but only to discrimination
by state governments, whether statutory or through the action

of government officials, or by private entities which can be said to be so "significantly involved" with the state that their actions are tantamount to actions of the state. Finding state action, therefore, has the effect of expanding the fourteenth amendment to apply not only to actions of state governments, but to some nominally private individuals. For instance, racial discrimination by the proprietors of a privately-owned restaurant was found to be state action, and hence prohibited by the equal protection clause, where the restaurant premises were leased from the city and located in a building devoted to public parking. See Burton v. Wilmington Parking Authority, 365 U.S. 715 (1961).

The language of the Equal Rights Amendment which incorporates the state action concept is emphasized in the following quotation of the Amendment:

> Equality of rights under the law shall not be denied or abridged by the United States or by any state on account of sex.

Thus, the Equal Rights Amendment will apply only to the actions of government and those private institutions which are so intertwined with the government that they can be said to be acting for the state. It will not apply, just as the fourteenth amendment does not apply, to actions or activities of wholly private persons or groups.

Although it cannot be said with certainty that the state action cases developed under the fourteenth amendment will be applied under the Equal Rights Amendment, at the very least it is fair to say that those cases will have great influence. The following discussion, therefore, will briefly explain the major test applied by the Supreme Court to determine whether private institutions can be said to be acting for the state and are, therefore, subject to the fourteenth amendment. That test will then be applied to major private institutions which some have argued will come within the Equal Rights Amendment.

The major test applied by the Supreme Court to determine whether a private entity can be said to be acting for the state is that of "significant state involvement." Although the test has been criticized by almost all scholars as having no predictive value for determining how the Court will decide when faced with new and unanticipated fact situations, it can be said that under this test the Court generally looks to the degree of contact and involvement of state government with the private institution in question. In cases litigated to date, such contacts have included state leases of property to a restaurant known to discriminate racially (Burton v. Wilmington Parking Authority, 365 U.S. 715 (1961); the reassignment of a

municipal park to private trustees because the terms of the
gift of the park required the city to discriminate by race
/Evans v. Newton, 382 U.S. 296 (1966)7; and state passage of
a constitutional amendment, which could be overturned only by
a two-thirds vote of the electorate, under which private
persons were authorized to discriminate racially in the sale
of housing /Reitman v. Mulkey, 387 U.S. 369 (1967)7. From a
brief description of these cases, it is obvious that the
situation involved in each of them is unique, and the Court's
conclusions are very difficult indeed to apply to completely
different sets of facts.

However, the lower courts have struggled to apply the
"significant state involvement" cases in widely different
situations. Factors generally looked to include state regulation of the institution in question; tax exemptions; funding;
or some other state involvement which enhances the ability of
the private entity to operate and therefore to discriminate.
When enough state involvement is found in any given case--
although it is difficult to say precisely how much is "enough"--
the private entity will be held subject to the requirements of
the fourteenth amendment.[12]

---

12. The second major test relevant to the question of state
action under the fourteenth amendment is the "public function"
test. In certain cases, the Court has said that where a private
entity is performing a governmental or public function, it is
subject to the requirements of the fourteenth amendment. Cases
which have applied the "public function" test have included a
case in which a wholly-owned company town, which provided housing
and all other necessary services for its residents, discriminated
against a particular religious sect by not allowing its members
to go door to door to proselytize residents of the town, Marsh v.
Alabama, 326 U.S. 501 (1946). Another "public function" case held
that a shopping center open to the public could not discriminate
against labor picketers, Amalgamated Food Employees Union v.
Logan Valley Plaza 391 U.S. 308 (1968). However, in a recent case,
the Supreme Court undercut the reasoning of Logan Valley Plaza
by holding that a large shopping center which was open to the
public could ban anti-war leafletters from the privately-owned
property. See, Lloyd Corp. v. Tanner, 407 U.S. 551 (1972).

In all areas in which a question might arise as to the scope
of state action under the Equal Rights Amendment, however, it is
very unlikely that the "public function" test will be used. It
has never been suggested in the fourteenth amendment cases that
the "public function" test could be used to find that private
educational institutions, churches, private single-sex clubs,
banks, savings and loans, insurance companies, or places of public
accommodation were subject to the fourteenth amendment. Thus, the
only state action test relevant to the doctrine under the ERA is
the "significant state involvement" test discussed in the text.

The state action concept is critically important to an understanding of the reach of the Equal Rights Amendment. Will, for instance, private educational institutions be held to be "significantly involved" with the state and therefore subject to the Equal Rights Amendment? May private churches or religious organizations be subjected to the Amendment? Banks? Insurance companies? Private single-sex clubs? Places of public accommodation? The state action doctrine, as it develops after passage of the Equal Rights Amendment, will determine to which private entities the Amendment applies. No answer can be given with certainty at this point, but a brief indication of the status of these institutions under the state action doctrine of the fourteenth amendment can be outlined.

Private Educational Institutions

As discussed more fully below in the chapter on Education, the lower courts have uniformly held that private educational institutions are not subject to the requirements of the fourteenth amendment, regardless of the fact that they receive large sums of money from state and federal governments and tax exemptions of a very substantial nature. Private educational institutions which have been held exempt from the requirements of the fourteenth amendment include Columbia University, Tulane University, the University of Denver and several other large and well-known schools. Some have suggested that the Equal Rights Amendment will be interpreted to apply to very large, private educational institutions. Although that is a possibility, it seems remote given the history of the fourteenth amendment cases. In any case, the Amendment certainly will not apply to small or medium-sized private educational institutions. (See reference no. 3, below.)

Religious Institutions

Because the first amendment prohibits the "establishment of religion" by the federal government or by any state government, there is much less state involvement with religious groups and churches than with private educational institutions. The only significant involvement of the state with religious institutions consists of the granting of tax exemptions for property used for churches. In a recent case, the U.S. Supreme Court held that the mere granting of a state tax exemption to church property was not such significant state involvement as to constitute the establishment of religion which the first and fourteenth amendments proscribe. See Walz v. Tax Comm'r. of the City of New York, 397 U.S. 664 (1970).

Some opponents of the Equal Rights Amendment have claimed that churches which today exclude women from their ministries would be subject to the requirements of the Amendment and would therefore have to change their religious beliefs and allow women to become ministers after its passage. Several factors make this claim demonstrably false. First, the Walz case and the insignificant state and federal involvement with religious institutions in general mean that under traditional state action concepts, churches would be exempt from the Amendment.

However, another clause of the first amendment is also relevant here. It prohibits the state and federal governments from interfering in any manner with the "free exercise" of religious beliefs. Thus, the free exercise clause of the first amendment would prohibit the application of the Equal Rights Amendment to a particular religious organization's beliefs, even if the institution were, hypothetically, considered to be acting for the state.[13]

It is absolutely clear, therefore, that the Equal Rights Amendment will not apply to private religious institutions and will not require any particular religious organization to admit women to its ministry.

Banks and Savings and Loan Associations

The business activities of banks and savings and loan associations have never been held to constitute state action and therefore have not been subject to the requirements of the fourteenth amendment; it is most unlikely that such institutions would be held to the requirements of the Equal Rights Amendment.

---

13. Reynolds v. United States, 98 U.S. 145 (1878), held that a federal law prohibiting the practice of bigamy in the then territory of Utah was not invalid as a restraint on the free exercise of religion of the Mormons, who were believers in polygamy. The Reynolds court held that, while government could not interfere with religious beliefs about marriage, it could regulate marriage as a civil institution. Qualifications for the ministry or priesthood, on the other hand, are solely matters of religious concern with which the state and federal governments may not interfere under the free exercise clause.

However, two federal statutes are worthy of note here. First, Title VII of the Civil Rights Act of 1964, which is discussed extensively below in the chapter on Labor Laws, prohibits all banks and savings and loan associations in the United States from discriminating on the basis of sex in employment. Thus, a prohibition against sex discrimination in employment in these institutions has already been provided by federal law.

Second, the recently enacted Equal Credit Opportunity Act, effective October 28, 1975, prohibits any creditor in the United States from discriminating on the basis of sex or marital status in the granting of credit or in any other aspect of credit transaction.[14] Therefore, the major reason for any attempt to place banks and savings and loan associations under the requirements of the fourteenth amendment has been obviated by passage of the Equal Credit Opportunity Act.

Thus, while it is very doubtful that the Equal Rights Amendment would be interpreted to apply to these private institutions, federal laws enacted by Congress under other provisions of the United States Constitution have already made banks and savings and loan associations subject to important prohibitions regarding sex discrimination.

Insurance Companies

No insurance company activity has yet been held to constitute state action,[15] but suits which have attempted to do that have proceeded on the theory that the heavy state regulatory power over insurance companies renders states "significantly involved" with the operations of those companies. Because of recent Supreme Court decisions indicating a reluctance to extend the state action doctrine,[16] it seems unlikely that state action will be found. Therefore, it is probable that under the current trend of state action case law, insurance companies will not be held subject to the requirements of the Equal Rights Amendment.

---

14. Equal Credit Opportunity Act, 15 U.S.C. Secs. 1691 et seq. (Supp. Pamphlet No. 1, Feb. 1975); Proposed Regulation, 12 C.F.R. Secs. 202.1 et seq., 40 Fed. Reg. 18183 (1975).

15. In one case, Stern v. Mass. Indemnity and Life Ins. Co., 365 F. Supp. 433 (E.D. Pa. 1973), the suit was settled after the district court refused to dismiss the complaint.

16. Recent decisions in which the Supreme Court has refused to find state action include Moose Lodge v. Irvis, 407 U.S. 163 (1972); Lloyd Corp. v. Tanner, 407 U.S. 551 (1972); Columbia Broadcasting v. Democratic National Committee, 412 U.S. 94 (1973); and Jackson v. Metropolitan Edison Co., 95 S. Ct. 449 (1974).

However, it should be recognized that the practices of
insurance companies--e.g., whom they will insure, premium
rates, cancellations of insurance--are largely unregulated
today. Because the Amendment will not, in all likelihood, be
held to apply to private insurance companies, it will not
remedy what is presently a very serious problem for many
women. Therefore, in order to reach the present sex-discriminatory practices in the insurance industry, a federal statute or
a series of state statutes must be enacted specifically to
regulate the insurance industry.

Private Single-Sex Clubs

Many private single-sex clubs and organizations exist in
the United States, some with very little or no state involvement, others with varying degrees of state involvement in their
activities. Such clubs include the American Assocation of
University Women; the Kiwanis and Rotary Clubs; Elks and Moose
Lodges; Masonic Lodges; Knights of Columbus; the V.F.W; Little
League; sororities and fraternities; and literally thousands
of other private, single-sex clubs or organizations. Where
attempts are made to subject such organizations to the requirements of the fourteenth amendment's prohibition against racial
discrimination or the Equal Rights Amendment's prohibition
against sex discrimination, the first amendment's guarantee of
the right to freedom of association must be taken into account.

In Moose Lodge v. Irvis, 407 U.S. 163 (1972), the Supreme
Court, in a 6-3 decision, refused to hold that the racially
discriminatory practices of the Lodge were unconstitutional
simply because the Lodge held a liquor license issued by the
state. The license was not enough, the Court said, to subject
the Lodge to the requirements of the fourteenth amendment. Even
Justice Douglas, who dissented, recognized that the first
amendment creates a "zone of privacy," saying:

> The associational rights which our system honors
> permit all white, all black, all brown and all
> yellow clubs to be formed. (407 U.S. 179-180)

The first amendment also protects the right of persons to
form private all-male or all-female clubs, as long as those
clubs are not "significantly involved" with the state. Thus,
while the precise contours of the state action doctrine as it
may apply under the ERA to a particular private, single-sex
club cannot be defined today, it can be said with certainty
that organizations which receive no tax exemptions; do not hold
liquor or other types of licenses; and do not use government

28

facilities for meetings or other activities are not today subject to the fourteenth amendment and will not be subject to the Equal Rights Amendment.[17] Most private clubs, then, will not be subject to the Equal Rights Amendment and may continue to remain single-sex if they so choose.

Public Accommodations

Many restaurants, bars, nightclubs, hotels, apartments and other places ostensibly open to the general public are closed to one sex. Litigation attempting to strike down sex discrimination in public accommodations under the fourteenth amendment has been relatively rare to date. However, one federal district court decided, in Seidenberg v. McSorleys' Old Ale House, Inc., 317 F. Supp. 593 (S.D.N.Y. 1970), that a liquor license held by a bar open to all members of the general public who were male significantly involved the state in the bar's operation. Thus, the bar was held to the standards of the fourteenth amendment, which the district court said prohibited sex discrimination in this context.

It will be remembered, of course, that in Moose Lodge v. Irvis, decided in 1972, the United States Supreme Court refused to hold that ownership of a liquor license issued by the state constituted the "significant state involvement" which would subject the Moose Lodge to the requirements of the fourteenth amendment's ban on racial discrimination. Given this holding, is the federal district court's decision in Seidenberg likely to be extended after passage of the Equal Rights Amendment?

While the answer cannot be certain, it is possible that it will be. Leading commentators on the state action doctrine have analyzed it as involving, essentially, a balancing by the Court of the competing interests at stake. Thus, as noted earlier, the members of the Moose Lodge have a constitutional right of their own to assert in opposition to the claim that they must not racially discriminate--the first amendment right of privacy and free association. The Moose Lodge decision, then, can be viewed as the Supreme Court's balancing of the members' right to associate with whomever they choose, on whatever grounds, against the country's and individual black's interest in ending racial discrimination, expressed in the fourteenth amendment equal protection clause. Under this view

---

17. For a more thorough discussion of the state action concept as applied to private single-sex clubs, see the section on the application of the ERA to educational institutions in the chapter on Education, below.

of Moose Lodge, the majority holding is an expression of the belief that the Lodge members' first amendment rights were important ones to protect.

The interests which can be claimed by the operator of an establishment which invites all members of the general public in--except those of one sex or race--are much less compelling than those which can be claimed by members of a truly private club. When a restaurant, bar or other public accommodation will admit anyone at all who is of the "right" sex or race, but absolutely no one of the "wrong" sex or race, the first amendment claim of the right of privacy and free association is weak indeed.

This difference in the balance of competing interests is one way in which the "sit-in" cases of the 1960's can be read. Although the Court majority relied on narrow, technical grounds of state law for a decision that a restaurant open to the public could not refuse to serve blacks, while serving all whites, Justice Douglas, in his concurrence, urged the Court to recognize expressly that the first amendment right of privacy and free association does not extend to discrimination in places of public accommodation:

> The property involved is not . . . a man's home or his yard or even his fields. Private property is involved, but it is property that is serving the public. . . . We should not hold that property voluntarily serving the public can receive state protection when the owner refused to serve some solely because they are colored. (Bell v. Maryland, 378 U.S. 226 at 252 (1964).

Thus, it is possible that even given the Moose Lodge decision, places of public accommodation which are licensed by the state could be held to be so significantly involved with the state that their activities would constitute state action for purposes of the Equal Rights Amendment. If that is in fact what happens after the Amendment's passage, places of public accommodation will be required to serve both sexes equally.

Even if that does not happen, however, it should be recognized that state legislation or city ordinances may be passed, before or after the Amendment, to prohibit sex discrimination by places open to the general public. See reference no. 7 below for citation to a list of states and cities which have already enacted such ordinances.

Conclusion

This summary treatment of the state action concept has outlined the relevant aspects of that doctrine and its application in important areas under the fourteenth amendment. If, as seems likely, the fourteenth amendment cases are applied to determine the dimensions of state action under the Equal Rights Amendment, the predictions made here as to which private organizations will or will not be held subject to the requirements of the Equal Rights Amendment will be valid. Answers, however, will only be obtained--just as those answers we now have in the fourteenth amendment area were obtained--through case-by-case litigation after passage of the Amendment.

References

1. For a sampling of the scholarly commentary which criticizes the complexity of the state action doctrine under the fourteenth amendment, see:

    a. Lewis, "Burton v. Wilmington Parking Authority--A Case Without Precedent," 61 Col. L. Rev. 1458 (1961); and

    b. Williams, "The Twilight of State Action," 41 Tex. L. Rev. 347 (1963).

2. For other articles concerning the state action doctrine, see:

    a. Black, "Foreword: State Action, Equal Protection and California's Proposition Fourteen," 81 Harv. L. Rev. 69 (1967); and

    b. Karst and Horowitz, "Reitman v. Mulkey: A Telophase of Substantive Equal Protection," 1967 Sup. Ct. Rev. 39.

3. Gallagher, in "Desegregation: The Effect of the Proposed Equal Rights Amendment on Single-Sex Colleges," 18 St. Louis U.L.J. 41 (1973), suggests that because tax exemptions and public funds may not be allowed to large private universities which discriminate on the basis of sex, such institutions will integrate voluntarily in order to obtain these benefits.

4. For a discussion of the possibility that the Equal Rights Amendment will be found to apply to very large private educational institutions, although not to small private educational institutions, see the discussion of state action contained in Brown, Emerson, Falk, and Freedman, "The Equal Rights Amendment: A Constitutional Basis for Equal Rights for Women," 80 Yale L. J. 871, 907 (1971).

5. If the insurance industry is either subjected to the Equal Rights Amendment or treated in a statute barring sex discrimination, the questions of the use of sex-based mortality tables and premium rates based on the sex of the insured will have to be resolved. See Note, "Sex Discrimination and Sex-based Mortality Tables," 53 B.U.L. Rev. 624 (1973).

6. Stearns v. V.F.W., 500 F. 2d 788 (D.C. Cir. 1974), held that the fact that the Veterans of Foreign Wars (V.F.W.), a private, all-male organization, had been chartered by Congress, did not constitute state action for purposes of the fourteenth amendment. However, the Court remanded the case to the trial court to determine whether other aspects of government involvement with the V.F.W. were sufficient to constitute state action. See Note, "Discriminatory Membership Policies in Federally Chartered Nonprofit Groups," 72 Mich. L. Rev. 1265 (1974).

7. B. Babcock, A. Freedman, E. Norton and S. Ross, Sex Discrimination and the Law 1057 (1975) contains an excellent discussion of sex discrimination in places of public accommodation, with a list of states and cities which have recently enacted statutes or ordinances prohibiting such discrimination.

STATUTES WHICH ARE "NEUTRAL ON THEIR FACE
BUT DISCRIMINATORY IN IMPACT"

It may be said generally that statutes which are drawn in terms of sex will be absolutely prohibited after passage of the Equal Rights Amendment. Thus, statutes such as the now unconstitutional jury selection laws which explicitly required all males to serve, but automatically exempted all females, also would have been invalidated by the Equal Rights Amendment. The following chapters in this Commentary are concerned largely with the analysis of statutes which are expressly drafted and applicable according to sex.

There are two exceptions to the principle of absolute prohibition of classifications based on sex. The first is the right of privacy qualification, discussed in the next section; that right will permit either statutes or governmental institutions to make distinctions based solely on sex where necessary to preserve an individual's right to personal privacy in matters relating to bodily functions. The second exception involves the "unique physical characteristics" test, discussed separately below. That test will, in certain narrowly defined circumstances, permit laws to apply by their terms to one sex alone if those laws deal with the necessary result of physical characteristics found in only one sex.

Aside from the relatively limited situations which will satisfy either the right of privacy qualification to the Amendment or the "unique physical characteristics" test, all statutes or other forms of state action subject to the Amendment must be completely sex-neutral. Thus, the Amendment will allow statutes to be drafted and governmental actions to be taken according to functions performed by persons of either sex, but not by explicit reference to sex itself. Under this principle, regulations of school districts or government agencies which prescribed leaves of a specified duration for childrearing, a function which could be performed by either sex, would have to be drafted in completely sex-neutral terms so that leave would be available to males and females alike.

In some instances, however, laws which are drafted in completely sex-neutral terms may, in particular circumstances, bear more heavily on one sex than upon the other. Such laws are described throughout this Commentary as laws "neutral on their face, but discriminatory in impact." One of many possible examples of a seemingly sex-neutral rule which would weigh more heavily on one sex than on the other would be a high school's maintenance of only one team in each sport fielded by the school, with participation on each team limited to 20 persons. In a high school of 2,000 students, which had 10 athletic teams limited to 20 persons each, it is obvious that women students, because of their smaller size and limited athletic training, would be effectively precluded from participating in the state-sponsored athletic program of that school. Such a school rule, although sex-neutral by its terms, would in fact discriminate against the right of women students to participate in high school athletics on an equal basis with men. Thus, this hypothetical rule is an example of one which is "neutral on its face, but discriminatory in impact."18

---

18. Supreme Court cases which have held statutes unconstitutional under the fourteenth amendment as laws "neutral on their face, but discriminatory in impact" include: Gaston County v. United States, 395 U.S. 285 (1969); Lane v. Wilson, 307 U.S. 268 (1939); Gomillion v. Lightfoot, 364 U.S. 339 (1960); Green v. County School Board, 391 U.S. 430 (1968); United States v. Jefferson County Board of Education, 372 F. 2d 836 (5th Cir. 1966), cert. denied, 389 U.S. 840 (1967); Sherbert v. Verner, 374 U.S. 398 (1963).

In Griggs v. Duke Power Co., 401 U.S. 242 (1971), the Court held that Title VII prohibited an employer from imposing a test for certain jobs where the employer could not demonstrate that the test was related to skills needed for the job and the test had a disportionate impact on blacks. In such a setting, the Court said, the test was "neutral on its face, but discriminatory in impact" and therefore violated the prohibition against racial discrimination in employment contained in Title VII.

Another example of such a rule is the imposition by state statutes of criminal penalties for nonpayment of child support. While such a rule is sex-neutral by its terms, in fact, in 95% of the cases women are given custody of children, with men usually ordered to pay child support. Thus, a statute which provides criminal penalties and imprisonment for failure to pay child support bears much more heavily on men than upon women, and as such must be strictly scrutinized as a law "neutral on its face, but discriminatory in impact." Throughout this analysis, repeated reference will be made to such laws or rules. The concept is essential to implement fully the Equal Rights Amendment.

It should be noted, however, that in a recent case the United States Supreme Court cast doubt upon whether this interpretation of the Amendment, put forward in 1971 by the authors of the Yale article, will be accepted by the Court. In Jefferson v. Hackney, 406 U.S. 535 (1974), the Court refused to recognize as "neutral on their face, but discriminatory in impact" laws which demonstrably affected persons of whom nearly 90% were Mexican-American or black and of whom less than 15% were Anglo-Saxon; the Court said that mere percentages will not serve to trigger use of the strict scrutiny test under equal protection.

If this recent case is extended in later cases, it is possible that the analysis presented in this Commentary of laws "neutral on their face, but discriminatory in impact" will not be accepted by the Supreme Court. In order to provide a view of the most far-reaching effects the Amendment could possibly have--while recognizing that the Supreme Court may interpret the Amendment less broadly than its language and history would permit--this analysis has assumed that statutes and regulations "neutral on their face, but discriminatory in impact" will be unconstitutional under the Equal Rights Amendment. However, only subsequent litigation under the fourteenth amendment and under the Equal Rights Amendment after its passage can finally determine the scope of the doctrine.

THE RIGHT OF PRIVACY QUALIFICATION TO THE AMENDMENT

The authors of the Yale article, as well as the proponents of the Amendment in Congress, recognize the right of privacy doctrine recently developed by the Supreme Court as a major qualification to the Amendment. The Senate Report on the Amendment stated that:

/T/he constitutional right of privacy established by the Supreme Court in Griswold v. Connecticut . . . would . . . permit under the Equal Rights Amendment a

separation of the sexes with respect to such places
as public toilets, as well as sleeping quarters of
public institutions.[19]

The right of privacy as a constitutional right was first
recognized by the United States Supreme Court in Griswold v.
Connecticut, 381 U.S. 479 (1965); in that case the Court held
that a couple's right of privacy in the marital relationship
prevented the State of Connecticut from imposing laws concerning
their use of contraceptive devices. Similarly, in Eisenstadt
v. Baird, 405 U.S. 438 (1972), the right of privacy was held to
protect an unmarried person's right to receive contraceptive
information; that case struck down a state law prohibiting
unmarried persons from receiving such information. Most
importantly, in Roe v. Wade, 410 U.S. 113 (1973), and Doe v.
Bolton, 410 U.S. 179 (1973), the Court held that it was the
right of privacy which protected a woman during the first
trimester of pregnancy from interference by the state in her
decision as to whether to have an abortion.

Although to date the right of privacy has only been applied
in cases involving contraception and abortion, those cases are
relevant to an analysis of the reach of the right of privacy
under the Equal Rights Amendment; they involve recognition by
the Court of an individual's right to control his or her bodily
processes without interference by the state. Thus, in the
context of the Equal Rights Amendment, the right of privacy
would protect an individual's right to perform personal bodily
functions, such as sleeping, showering and disrobing, without
intrusion by members of the opposite sex due to the integration
of dormitories, living facilities, locker rooms or other physical
facilities belonging to the state where such personal functions
are customarily performed. By relying so heavily on the
constitutional right of privacy in cases of such far-reaching
importance and national impact as the Roe and Doe abortion cases,
the present Court has lent strong support to the belief that it
will in fact use the right to decide the relatively less
important questions of the constitutionality of sexually-
segregated public bathrooms and dormitories under the Equal
Rights Amendment.

Thus, both the Court's very recent reliance on the doctrine
and the express recognition of the right of privacy in
Congressional debate and in the Yale article make it likely, if

---

19. See Senate Comm. on the Judiciary, Equal Rights for
Men and Women, S. Rep. No. 82-689 92nd Cong., 2nd Sess. 12, 14
(1972).

not certain, that the right will be recognized as an acceptable
qualification to the Equal Rights Amendment after its passage.

References

    1. For the Yale article's exposition of the significance
of the right of privacy in interpreting the Equal Rights Amendment, written before Eisenstadt v. Baird, Roe and Doe were
decided, see Brown, Emerson, Falk and Freedman, "The Equal Rights
Amendment: A Constitutional Basis for Equal Rights for Women,"
80 Yale L. J. 871, 900 (1971).

    2. It should also be noted that the privacy qualification
was discussed and explicitly recognized as applicable to the
Equal Rights Amendment throughout the Committee hearings and
floor debates in both the Senate and the House. See, Equal
Rights for Men and Women, 1971, Hearings on S. J. Res. 35, 208 and
Related Bills Before Subcommittee, No. 4 of the House Comm. on
the Judiciary, 92nd Cong., 1st Sess. 402-6 (1971).

    For the Senate hearings recognizing the right of privacy,
see Equal Rights 1970, Hearings on S. J. Res. 61 and S. J. Res.
231 Before Senate Comm. on the Judiciary, 91st Cong., 2nd Sess.
303-4 (1970).

    For floor debates in which the right of privacy was
recognized, see 117 Cong. Rec. 35809 (1971) (remarks of
Congressman Ashley).

    For Senate debates recognizing the right of privacy, see
118 Cong. Rec. 9336 (1972) (remarks of Senator Gurney).

    3. An early recognition by a federal court of the right
of privacy, prior to the Supreme Court's recognition of it, is
contained in Ford v. Storey, 324 F. 2nd 450 (9th Cir. 1963),
cert. denied, 376 U.S. 939 (1964).

    4. Comment, "The Equal Rights Amendment and the Right of
Privacy," 23 Emory L. J. 197 (1974).

LAWS RELATING TO "UNIQUE PHYSICAL CHARACTERISTICS"
FOUND IN ONLY ONE SEX

    The absolute standard of the Equal Rights Amendment
proposed in the Yale article and in the legislative history of
the Amendment is also qualified by the "unique physical
characteristics" principle. Under this test, physical--but not
emotional, psychological, or social--factors found in one sex
alone may be used as the basis for particular legislation.
Common examples of laws which by their terms could constitutionally

be applied to one sex only are laws dealing with wet nurses or sperm donors. Laws or regulations allowing only women to take employment leaves for childbearing, as opposed to childrearing, also would be constitutional. Further, as discussed in the section on community property systems in the chapter on Marital Property Laws, laws which distinguish between men and women in order to establish the paternity of children would also be permissible as laws based upon a "unique physical characteristic"-- the unique ability of women to bear children and their consequent positive identification at the child's birth. The principle would permit fathers, who are more difficult to identify, to be treated separately in a statutory procedure for determining paternity.

Beyond these obvious and uncomplicated examples, the area which may cause the most litigation and possible problems under the "unique physical characteristics" test is that of pregnancy. Because only women are capable of becoming pregnant, there are a multitude of ways in which states may, by statute or other forms of state action, attempt to justify what are in fact sex-discriminatory laws on the basis of women's unique ability to bear children.

One such example, treated briefly below in the section on student conduct in the chapter on Education, may be found in the rule requiring the expulsion of pregnant students, a practice common in public schools today. After passage of the Equal Rights Amendment, a school board might argue that such a regulation was justified under the "unique physical characteristics" principle because only female students can become pregnant. Such an argument is unquestionably spurious; the "unique physical characteristic" in question, pregnancy, has absolutely no relationship to any legitimate interest of the school board and should not be accepted as a subterfuge for what is in fact a sex-discriminatory regulation.

When pregnancy, or any other "unique physical charactertistic" found in only one sex, is put forward as the justification for what may in fact be a sex-discriminatory rule, strict scrutiny will be required to determine its constitutionality under the Equal Rights Amendment. The Yale article establishes six factors which should be examined in strictly scrutinizing the defense that a "unique physical characteristic" requires a law, rule or regulation which affects only one sex.

For clarity, each of the six factors will be set forth below, followed by an analysis of a now common regulation which school boards might seek to justify as constitutionally permissible after passage of the Amendment because it deals with a "unique physical characteristic": the expulsion of pregnant students on the grounds that they disrupt classes and harm other students' morals.

First: the proportion of the members of one sex who actually have the characteristic in question. A relatively small number of women high school students are pregnant.

Second: the relationship between the characteristic and the problem sought to be solved by dealing only with persons who have that characteristic. There is little relationship between the characteristic of being pregnant and the problems sought to be solved by the school board, disruption in the classroom or morals of other students. All high school students today are well aware that girls over the age of puberty can become pregnant.

Third: the proportion of the problem which is sought to be solved which can be properly attributed to the unique physical characteristic. Only a tiny proportion of the problem of classroom disruption or students' morals can be attributed to the presence of pregnant students in classes.

Fourth: the proportion of the problem which is eliminated by the solution. Very little, if any, of the problems of classroom disruption or sexual activity among teenagers would be solved by expelling all pregnant students from high school.

Fifth: the availability of "less drastic alternatives"-- less drastic for the person restricted; more limited in the number of persons or opportunities affected; or alternatives not based on sex at all. Less drastic alternatives are clearly available. Pregnant students could be put in special classes if they are genuinely disruptive or truly harmful to other students' morals, although both justifications are difficult to countenance.

Sixth: the importance of the problem being solved as compared with the cost of the least drastic solution. Although classroom disruption and students' morals are important problems, it is impossible to see how they are significantly affected by expelling pregnant students from school. If their removal is considered necessary, however, the cost of establishing separate classes for them is minor.

Thus, application of the six tests identified in the Yale article to one common situation in which pregnancy is used as a screen for what is in fact sex discrimination shows that pregnant students should not be expelled from school under the Equal Rights Amendment on the ground that pregnancy is a "unique physical characteristic" of women students. It is critically important to the interpretation of the Amendment that any justification based on a "unique physical characteristic" be strictly scrutinized and not accepted at face value without careful analysis. If strict scrutiny is not applied to all such justifications, pregnant women may be severely harmed by

38

regulations which are in fact sex-discriminatory but which are explained on the ground that only women are capable of becoming pregnant. After passage of the Amendment, it will be up to the courts and litigants to ensure the careful scrutiny of such regulations.

References

1. Brown, Emerson, Falk and Freedman, "The Equal Rights Amendment: A Constitutional Basis for Equal Rights for Women," 80 Yale L. J. 871, 893-897 (1971).

2. Bartlett, "Pregnancy and the Constitution: The Uniqueness Trap," 62 Calif. L. Rev. 1532 (1974).

REJECTION OF THE SEPARATE-BUT-EQUAL DOCTRINE
UNDER THE EQUAL RIGHTS AMENDMENT

In 1954, the Supreme Court in Brown v. Board of Education, 347 U.S. 483 (1954) struck down the separate-but-equal doctrine as it applied to race relations. From that time forward, it has not been legal for any state to maintain racially segregated facilities, whether they are schools, beaches, restrooms, or other places open to the public.

The use of the separate-but-equal doctrine under the Equal Rights Amendment has been authoritatively rejected by the authors of the Yale article, as well as by Congress in passing the Amendment, because, in fact, separate rarely is equal. Were that doctrine to be maintained under the Amendment, a gaping hole would be torn in its guarantee of the legal equality of the sexes. As will be seen in the discussion of conditions and programs in men's and women's prisons in the chapter on Criminal Laws and Penal Institutions, women's prisons are today almost universally separate from men's; however, they are never equal in training and vocational rehabilitation programs, educational opportunities, recreational opportunities and the like. Similarly, men's prisons are not equal to women's in physical comforts. It is only the physical integration of men's and women's prisons that will ensure the equality for the sexes which passage of the Equal Rights Amendment will affirm as the law of the land. Allowing a doctrine of separate-but-equal to exist under an Equal Rights Amendment will in fact only serve to perpetuate unequal physical facilities provided by the state for the sexes.

Similarly, in the field of education, after passage of
the Amendment, states will not be allowed to maintain separate-
but-equal schools for the sexes. Again, although men's and
women's schools are often separate, they are rarely equal. The
only way to ensure equality of education for both men and women
is to ensure that each sex has the same opportunity to obtain
precisely the same education--not a sexually separate one, but
a sexually integrated one.

If the separate-but-equal doctrine is not rejected, decades
upon decades of litigation will ensue before the Amendment's
guarantee of equality for the sexes under the law is fulfilled.
To avoid the prospect of such a drastic undercutting of the
Amendment's central purpose, this Commentary has rejected use
of the separate-but-equal doctrine.

Reference

See Brown, Emerson, Falk and Freedman, "The Equal Rights
Amendment: A Constitutional Basis for Equal Rights for Women,"
80 Yale L. J. 871, 901 (1971), for a rejection of the use of the
separate-but-equal doctrine under the ERA.

BENIGN QUOTAS AND COMPENSATORY AID FOR WOMEN
UNDER THE EQUAL RIGHTS AMENDMENT

Under the Yale article's analysis of the absolute approach
to the Equal Rights Amendment, no "compelling state interest"
could ever be sufficient to justify sex-based distinctions.
Thus, if a state school of engineering decided to institute a
"benign quota" system and admit 50% women, although only 10% of
the applicants to that school were women, such a program would
be unconstitutional under the Equal Rights Amendment. It is in
this area that the differences between an absolute approach and
a "strict scrutiny" approach are most sharply defined. Under
the absolute approach, no justification can be put foward by
the state to explain its admission of women under different
standards than those established for men or an admissions policy
based on the percentage of students of each sex it wished to
enroll: to do so would deny men the equality of rights which
the Amendment guarantees.

Under the strict scrutiny approach, however, it is possible
that a state could argue, much as Justices Brennan and Marshall
did in their dissent in Kahn v. Shevin, above, that discrimination against men was necessary in order to remedy the effects of
past societal discrimination against women. Thus, if the strict

scrutiny approach to the Equal Rights Amendment is applied
rather than the absolute one, it is possible that affirmative
action programs which set different standards for women than for
men would be constitutional. Under the absolute approach,
however, which has been adopted throughout this analysis, such
programs would be unconstitutional.

Although there is a suggestion in the Yale article that in
individual cases a court could order affirmative action as a
remedy. if a sufficiently strong showing of discrimination is
made, that principle has not yet been fully developed in the
literature explaining the Equal Rights Amendment, and the reach
of that concept is unclear.   Reference no. 2 below contains a
further discussion of this particular problem. For purposes of
this Commentary, it has been assumed that neither benign quotas
nor compensatory aid will be allowable under the absolute
interpretation of the Equal Rights Amendment, since such programs
discriminateagainst men solely on the basis of their sex.

References

1. See Brown, Emerson, Falk and Freedman, "The Equal Rights
Amendment: A Constitutional Basis for Equal Rights for Women,"
80 Yale L. J. 871, 902 (1971).

2.   The authors of the Yale article cite the case of Swann v.
Charlotte-Mecklenburg Board of Education, 402 U.S. 1 (1971), for
the proposition that:

> /w/here damage has been done by a violator who acts
> on the basis of a forbidden characteristic, the
> enforcing authorities may also be compelled to take
> the same characteristic into account in order to undo
> what has been done. This form of relief is a common
> feature of laws seeking to eliminate discrimination,
> whether the restriction imposed be absolute or not.
> 80 Yale L. J. 871, 904, n. 58 (1971).

This statement apparently means that if women plaintiffs prevailed
in a suit against state officials under the Equal Rights Amendment
for a specific alleged violation of the Amendment, a court could
order the state officials found in violation to remedy their
conduct by taking sex into account in some manner. The Swann
case cited in the Yale article involved a busing order intended
to remedy the effects of past official discrimination against
black students by the school board; the only remedy available was
to take the race of students into account in establishing student
populations in schools. Note, however, that the remedy suggested
in Swann is a narrow and specific one which is directed at a

specific, intentional and proven violation perpetrated by the same officials who are charged with remedying the violation by taking the characteristic into account.

That situation is very different from broad-scale affirmative action programs which attempt to remedy injustice against one race or sex in the society at large. However, the specific contours of the Swann case and compensatory aid in the context of the Equal Rights Amendment can only be developed after the Amendment's passage.

3. Hillman, "Sex and Employment under the Equal Rights Amendment," 67 Nw. U. L. Rev. 789, 834-840 (1973), discusses whether the Equal Rights Amendment will prevent affirmative action programs in employment. This question also is one which will have to be litigated after the effective date of the Amendment in order to settle it authoritatively.

THE ROLE OF CONGRESS AND THE STATES IN LEGISLATING AFTER
PASSAGE OF THE EQUAL RIGHTS AMENDMENT

The Right of the States to Legislate under the Amendment

Section 2 of the Equal Rights Amendment provides:

The Congress shall have power to enforce, by appropriate legislation, the provisions of this article.

This language is substantially identical to similar provisions found in the 13th, 14th, 15th, 19th, 23rd, 24th and 26th Amendments to the United States Constitution. However, some opponents of the Amendment have tried to argue that because section 2 of the Amendment mentions only Congressional power to enforce the Amendment, states will lose the power to revise or deal with vast areas of law now regulated only by them, including family and marital property laws, labor laws, criminal laws and educational matters discussed in the remainder of this Commentary.

Those who so contend are ignorant of a basic and central theory of the United States Constitution, that the federal government has only the powers expressly granted to it by the Constitution. Thus, article I of the United States Constitution, which establishes the Congress and, in section 8, enumerates the subjects upon which Congress has power to legislate, contains express grants of power to Congress to legislate on those subjects. As amendments to the Constitution were added, it was necessary to state expressly in each successive amendment that

"Congress shall have the power to enforce this article by appropriate legislation." It is for that reason, and that reason alone, that so many amendments to the Constitution contain express grants of power to Congress to legislate.

The Constitution places the states in precisely the opposite position. While the national government has only the powers expressly granted to it, all powers not so granted are reserved to the States. That was understood at the time of the adoption of the Constitution in 1787, and it was reiterated in the tenth amendment, adopted in 1791, which provides:

> The powers not delegated to the United States by the Constitution, nor prohibited to it by the States, are reserved to the States respectively or to the people.

It is abundantly clear, therefore, from the underlying theory of the United States Constitution; the express grants of power contained throughout the Constitution itself and in the amendments; and the wording of the tenth amendment, that section 2 of the Equal Rights Amendment was absolutely necessary, as a matter of constitutional law, to give Congress the power to legislate under it. The states have the power to legislate concerning matters of state law because that power was retained by the states, as the tenth amendment affirms.

The legislative history of the Amendment reflects this basic fact of United States constitutional theory. In one version of the amendment, put forward in 1970 and 1971, section 2 was drafted to provide:

> Congress and the several states shall have power, within their respective jurisdictions, to enforce this article by appropriate legislation.[20]

Proponents and opponents of the Amendment alike criticized that version of section 2 as an exceedingly poor constitutional draft. Professor Paul Freund of the Harvard Law School, a well-known and long-time opponent of the Equal Rights Amendment, stated his belief that the proposed language--"within their respective jurisdictions"--restricted Congressional power more than that

---

20. H. J. Res. 35, 92nd Cong., 1st Sess., 1971; H. J. Res. 231, 92nd Cong., 1st Sess., 1971; S. J. Res. 61, 91st Cong., 1st Sess., 1970.

found in any other amendment or elsewhere in the Constitution and should not be adopted.[21] Dean Pollack of the Yale Law School, a proponent of the Amendment, also criticized the language. It was therefore deleted, and the present language, found in section 2 as passed by Congress and proposed for ratification by the states, was adopted.

The stated concern, then, of some opponents of the Amendment--that it will cause a vast shift of power to the federal government and will remove from the states their traditional power to legislate in certain areas--is simply unfounded.

The Morgan Case and Congress' Use of Its Powers to Legislate

Some opponents of the Amendment have also claimed that the language of section 2 will, because of the Supreme Court's interpretation, in Katzenbach v. Morgan, 384 U.S. 641 (1966), of identical language contained in the fourteenth amendment, give the Congress great new powers to legislate on matters of state law which it does not now possess, even if the states do have concurrent power also to legislate in such areas. To understand why that contention is legally incorrect, it is necessary to understand the holding of the Morgan case.

Morgan involved the constitutionality of the 1965 Voting Rights Act, which contained a section prohibiting the states from placing restrictions concerning English literacy on the right to vote in state elections. The particular section in question had been put in the Act on the floor of the Senate by Senators Javits and Kennedy of New York in order to give Puerto Ricans living in New York City the right to vote in state elections; many of them had been educated in Puerto Rico and could read Spanish, but were illiterate in English. Thus, the section inserted in the Act required states to allow persons to vote in state elections who had been educated through the sixth grade in American flag schools, regardless of whether the language used in those schools was English and regardless of whether the voter could speak or read the English language. The section was challenged on the theory that Congress had not been granted the power to legislate in matters concerning the qualifications for voting in state, as opposed to federal, elections.

---

21. For comments on the inadvisability of wording section 2 as proposed in 1970 and 1971, see Hearings on S. J. Res. 61 and S. J. Res. 231 Before Senate Comm. on the Judiciary, 91st Cong., 2nd Sess. 80, 208 (1970); and Equal Rights for Men and Women, 1971, Hearings on S. J. Res. 35, 208 and Related Bills Before Subcommittee No. 4 of the House Comm. on the Judiciary, 92nd Cong., 1st Sess. 143 (1971).

In an extremely far-reaching decision, the Supreme Court upheld the Congressional statute. The Court said, among other things, that Congress possessed the power to legislate concerning voting qualifications in state elections under its power to define the meaning of equal protection. This power, the Court said, was derived from section 5 of the fourteenth amendment, which is identical in language to section 2 of the Equal Rights Amendment, and was as broad as Congress' power to legislate under the necessary and proper clause contained in article I of the Constitution.

Opponents who claim that section 2 of the Equal Rights Amendment will give Congress great new powers to legislate because of the Morgan decision apparently do not grasp the import of the Morgan holding itself. If Congress can define equal protection as prohibiting distinctions in state voting laws based on English literacy, it can certainly define equal protection to prohibit all distinctions in state laws based on sex. Thus, under a literal reading of the Morgan decision, Congress already has the power to legislate for the states in all matters of law, state or federal, in which sex-based distinctions are made.

Therefore, Congressional passage of the Equal Rights Amendment, far from being a frightening expansion of federal power, is a demonstration of Congressional respect for the states. The Morgan case, which some opponents of the Amendment claim makes section 2 of the Amendment so potentially harmful, in fact--read as literally as the opponents read it--gives Congress the power to enact all necessary equal rights legislation, both state and federal, without passing any constitutional amendment at all. In this context, then, passage of the Amendment by Congress in 1972--some six years after Morgan--is the most convincing proof of Congressional respect for the states' position and authority.

References

1. For a very small sampling of the scholarly commentary which the Morgan case engendered, see:

a. Burt, "Miranda and Title II: A Morganatic Marriage," 1969 Sup. Ct. Rev. 81; and

b. Cox, "Foreword: Constitutional Adjudication and the Promotion of Human Rights," 80 Harv. L. Rev. 91 (1970).

Chapter Two

CRIMINAL LAWS AND PENAL INSTITUTIONS

Table of Contents

48

INTRODUCTION

Large numbers of people in this country have never had to deal with the criminal justice system; thus, they are unaware of how it works and of the extraordinarily detrimental impact it has upon many people's lives. As with every other institution in society, the prisons, jails and juvenile detention homes have not escaped the damaging effects of sex-discriminatory policies and practices. In fact, the examples of sex discrimination practiced by these institutions are perhaps more intense and shocking than those found anywhere else. This chapter describes the existing conditions in penal institutions across the country and suggests major and beneficial reforms which the Equal Rights Amendment would require.

Another group of people with whom most of us are unfamiliar are patients in state mental institutions. There, women also suffer the effects of discrimination in the initial commitment process, in the kind of treatment they receive, and in the standards applied for their release.

Finally, this chapter discusses sex-discriminatory aspects of criminal laws themselves. Historically, women have been the victims both of statutes designed to protect them, such as rape laws, and of those under which they were prosecuted, such as prostitution laws. Again, the Amendment will require that sex-discriminatory criminal statutes be re-written and that police, district attorney and court practices be thoroughly revised.

The Equal Rights Amendment will have an immense and beneficial impact on state criminal laws and penal institutions, both areas which our society has neglected for too long.

SEX-DISCRIMINATORY ASPECTS OF THE CRIMINAL JUSTICE SYSTEM

Pre-trial Release Practices

Legal problem: It is well documented that women arrested and charged with crimes are released on bond on their own recognizance much more frequently than are men charged with similar crimes. The Equal Rights Amendment, which is applicable not only to state and federal laws, but also to the practices of officials of the state and federal governments, will make such sex-discriminatory practices unconstitutional.

Possible solutions: Those who have studied the entire pre-trial release system in the United States and noted the sex-discriminatory aspect mentioned above do not recommend that the problem of discrimination be remedied by refusing to release women as freely before trial as they are now released. Rather, the Vera Institute has recommended in a lengthy report, as have many others critical of the present system, that the entire system of bond, bail and pre-trial release in the United States be drastically reformed.

While it is recognized that this recommendation will not be easy to implement, the criminal justice system's handling of persons charged with crime before trial has been a major problem for many years. This area is one example of the way in which the Equal Rights Amendment, if taken seriously and truly complied with, can possibly be the most important impetus for broad-scale reform and improvement of the law in our history.

References

1. Note, "Bail Reform and the Constitutionality of Pre-trial Detention," 55 Va. L. Rev. 1223 (1969).

2. Nagel and Weitzman, "Women as Litigants," 23 Hastings L.J. 170, 198 (1971).

3. Note, "The Bail System and Equal Protection," 2 Loyola L. Rev. 71 (1969).

4. Galigan, "Working Paper on Bail," 38 Mod. L. Rev. 59 (1975).

5. For the studies upon which the Vera Institute's recommendation is based, see: Freed and Wald, Bail in the United States (1965); Goldfarm, Ransom: A Critique of the American Bail System (1965); Ares, Rankin and Sturz, "The Manhattan Bail Project: An Interim Report on the Use of Pre-trial Parole," 38 N.Y.U. L. Rev. 67 (1963).

Administration of Jury Selection Laws

Legal problem: Nagel and Weitzman, in "Women as Litigants," summarize several studies concerning the influence of the sex of members of a jury on the verdict reached by that jury. They conclude that, on the whole, jurors tend to "favor" persons of their own sex whom they are asked to judge. Thus, a predominantly female jury will tend to treat a female defendant more leniently than would a predominantly male jury, while a predominantly male jury will tend to favor male defendants.

Possible solutions: In January, 1975, the Supreme Court in Taylor v. Louisiana, 95 S. Ct. 692, reversed its holding in Hoyt v. Florida, 368 U.S. 57 (1961). Hoyt had held that states could constitutionally require all men to serve on juries, while allowing women to take the affirmative step of signing up on a jury list if they wanted to serve, a practice which naturally resulted in many fewer female than male jurors.

With the reversal of Hoyt, it might seem that states could equalize their jury service rules either by requiring all persons of both sexes to serve on juries unless excused for cause or by allowing all persons of both sexes to volunteer for jury duty. However, adoption of a completely voluntary jury service system might operate as a system "neutral on its face, but discriminatory in impact." Since almost all adult men are employed, but only about 60% of adult women work outside the home, such a system might tend to produce juries which were predominantly female. A better approach, therefore, would be to require all persons to sign up for jury service, subject to being excused for cause by a judge.

What will be important under the Equal Rights Amendment is not the facial neutrality of the suggested system, but its administration. The judges charged with deciding whether to excuse jurors for cause must administer the system fairly and without bias toward relieving either women or men for essentially sex-based causes. For instance, if, under revisions in jury selection laws made pursuant to Taylor v. Louisiana, men and women alike are automatically put on jury rolls, but a particular judge automatically excuses everyone with a job, juries so selected would tend to be more heavily female than male. Such a practice would work to the detriment of male defendants. On the other hand, if all persons with young children to care for were automatically relieved of jury duty, while no others were, juries would tend to be more heavily male than female, and female defendants would be disadvantaged.

To avoid the effects on jury verdicts of unintentional, personal rules for excusing jurors, it is suggested that, in light of Taylor v. Louisiana and the Nagel and Weitzman study, a uniform code be drafted to establish a jury selection procedure and guide for judges.

References

1. Nagel and Weitzman, "Women as Litigants," 23 Hastings L.J. 170, 192-197 (1971).

2. Note, "Twelve Good Persons Are True," 9 Harv. Civ. Rts-Civ. Lib. L. Rev. 561 (1974).

52

3. Note, "Federal Courts--Juries--Exclusion of Women,"
58 Ky. L.J. 572 (1970).

4. Some commentators have found that women charged with
crime tend to be more readily acquitted by juries than men.
See Jurow, "New Data on the Effect of a 'Death Qualified' Jury
on the Guilt Determination Process," 84 Harv. L. Rev. 567 (1971).

Sentencing of Women Convicted of Crime

Two problems arise in the sentencing of women convicted of
crime. One is the type of statute under which they are sentenced.
The other is the statistically proven fact that where sentencing
statutes provide for equal treatment of men and women offenders,
women receive shorter sentences than men convicted of the same
crime. These two problems will be discussed separately below.

Sentencing Statutes

Legal problem: Many states still have laws in effect which
impose different sentences on women and men convicted of the
same crime. One variety of such laws is the "indeterminate
sentencing statute." These statutes often remove a sentencing
judge's discretion as to the minimum and maximum terms to be
imposed upon a woman convicted of a crime and mandate certain
"indeterminate" sentences up to a maximum set by statute. A
male convict, on the other hand, is usually sentenced under a
statute which imposes fixed minimum and maximum terms and which
also gives the sentencing judge discretion to reduce the
maximum term imposed. The theory of "indeterminate sentencing
statutes" is that women are more likely candidates for "rehabilitation" and thus may benefit more than male offenders from
longer incarceration.

Because in most cases parole may be applied for after a
prisoner has served one-third of his or her minimum sentence,
indeterminate sentencing statutes, which contain no minimum
sentence but require an undetermined term up to a certain
maximum, may have one of two effects. Because no minimum term
has been established in her case, a woman may spend longer in
jail than a man, who having served his minimum, might be
paroled earlier. On the other hand, the woman may apply for and
receive parole earlier than the man, since she has no minimum
sentence and therefore no set portion to serve before she can
apply for parole.

Two recent cases, Commonwealth v. Daniels and State ex rel.
Robinson v. York, cited in reference no. 1 below, have held
indeterminate sentencing statutes for women to be violations of

the fourteenth amendment equal protection clause. Such
statutes would certainly violate the Equal Rights Amendment.

Many states have other types of sentencing statutes which
mandate different sentencing for men and women convicted of the
same crime. These include statutes which do set minimum and
maximum terms for women offenders, but give the judge no discretion in setting different minimum or maximum terms; the statutes
for male offenders, however, give a judge broad discretion to
tailor the minimum and maximum terms to his view of the
seriousness of the particular crime. Yet another variety of
differential sentencing statutes for men and women flatly
imposes higher maximums for women than men convicted of the same
crime.

Without question, a sentencing statute which makes any
distinctions whatsoever based on the sex of the offender will
be unconstitutional under an Equal Rights Amendment. They are
probably unconstitutional today under the fourteenth amendment.

Possible solutions: The obvious solution to the problem
of state statutes which make sex-based distinctions in sentencing
is to revise them by either including men in the statutes
applicable to women or including women in the statutes applicable
to men. Preference cannot be decided without analyzing
individual statutes because they vary greatly in details.

While this step is undoubtedly necessary and desirable, a
further reform in sentencing statutes in the United States would
greatly strengthen our criminal justice system. The United
States is one of the few major nations in the Western world
which, as a whole, makes no provision for appellate review of
criminal sentences. Sentencing judges have absolute and
uncontrolled discretion to mete out whatever sentences seem to
them appropriate--which is why, under our system, one judge may
develop a reputation as a "hanging judge," while another may be
known for leniency. An offender's fate should not depend on the
personality of the judge assigned to sentence him or her any
more than it should depend on the offender's sex.

A few states have already made appellate review of criminal
sentences available. Connecticut has a sentence review panel
and Illinois has an appellate review procedure; New Mexico is
adopting a state Supreme Court rule which provides for a sentence
review board. The general revision of criminal codes which will
take place after passage of the Equal Rights Amendment would
provide an ideal opportunity to make this much needed change in
American jurisprudence.

54

References

1. Commonwealth v. Daniels, 430 Pa. 642, 243 A. 2d 400 (1968); State ex rel. Robinson v. York, 281 F. Supp. 8 (D. Conn. 1968).

2. K. Davidson, R. Ginsburg and H. Kay, Sex-based Discrimination 893-906 (1974).

3. Comment, "Sex Discrimination in Sentencing Criminal Offenders Is Unconstitutional," 50 N. D. L. Rev. 359 (1974).

4. Comment, "Disparate Sentencing Schemes for Males and Females Declared Unconstitutional," 23 Cath. U.L. Rev. 389 (1973).

5. Comment, "Sex and Sentencing," 26 S.W. L.J. 890 (1972).

6. For a detailed review of the types of sentencing statutes in existence in the United States in 1960, see Note, "Statutory Structure for Sentencing Felons to Prison," 60 Colum. L. Rev. 1134 (1960).

7. For examples of sex-neutral sentencing statutes which would satisfy the requirements of an Equal Rights Amendment, and at the same time vastly improve the complex sentencing statutes now in effect in many states, see:

   a. Model Penal Code, Secs. 6.01 and 6.06 (Proposed Official Draft, 1962); and

   b. Model Sentencing Act, drafted by the Council of Judges of the National Council on Crime and Delinquency (2nd ed. 1971).

8. Tappan, "Sentencing Under the Model Penal Code," 23 Law and Contemp. Prob. 528 (1958).

9. Note, "The Model Sentencing Act," 18 Crime and Delinq. 335 (1972).

10. Temin, "Discriminatory Sentencing of Women Offenders: The Argument for ERA in a Nutshell," 11 Am. Crim. L. Rev. 355 (1973).

11. For articles concerning the need for appellate review of criminal sentences, see:

   a. Note, "Appellate Review of Primary Sentencing Decisions: A Connecticut Case Study," 69 Yale L.J. 1453 (1960); and

b. The articles cited in reference nos. 4 through 8 in the next section.

Sentencing Practices

Legal problem: After studying California statistics, widely acknowledged as the most complete in the nation, the National Commission on Violence concluded that female offenders benefit after arrest from the "chivalry" factor at work in the American penal system. The California statistics show that in 1970, the ratio of males to females arrested was 6 to 1; the ratio of males to females actually incarcerated was 21 to 1. Even allowing for the fact that women are arrested more frequently than men for non-violent crime, the Commission concluded that judges treat women more leniently than men.

Nagel and Weitzman, in the study cited in reference no. 2 below, also concluded, after a comprehensive review of sentencing statistics, that judges more often put women offenders on probation. Where sentencing statutes are sex-neutral, they give women shorter sentences than men convicted of the same crime.

Because the action of an officer of the state is state action for purposes of the Equal Rights Amendment, and thus falls within its prohibition, perpetuation of such sentencing practices will be unconstitutional after the Amendment's passage.

Possible solutions: Nagel and Weitzman, after noting the sex-discriminatory sentencing practices described above, concluded that the solution to the problem is not simply to begin locking up more women. Rather, because it is widely recognized today that most prisons harden prisoners' attitudes toward crime and society, they suggest that inequality in sentencing practices should be remedied by a thorough review of the desirability of all sentencing to prisons as we know them today. Greater use of halfway houses, work release, probation and other devices for male and female offenders would, they suggest, equalize the present criminal sentencing practices and, at the same time, improve this acknowledged deficiency in our criminal justice system.

A second solution to this problem is that suggested earlier in connection with sex-discriminatory sentencing statutes--appellate review of sentencing decisions. If appellate review were widely available, males sentenced to unduly long terms could appeal those sentences under the equal protection clause and the Equal Rights Amendment with some hope of relief, a possibility almost never available today.

The reality of sentencing practices and the discrimination against men produced by an attitude of paternalism toward women offenders should be widely recognized. Recognition of this inequality should spur reform of the entire sentencing procedure and a review of the role which prison sentences actually play in dealing with the problem of crime.

References

1. National Commission on Violence, Crimes of Violence: A Staff Report, Vol. 13, at 845, cited in B. Babcock, A. Freedman, E. Norton and S. Ross, Sex Discrimination and the Law 938 (1975).

2. Nagel and Weitzman, "Women as Litigants," 23 Hastings L.J. 17, 171-181 and 198 (1972).

3. Comment, "Sex and Sentencing," 26 S.W. L.J. 890 (1972).

4. For a sample of the many articles which have recommended appellate review of sentencing decisions, see:

a. ABA Project on Minimum Standards for Criminal Justice, Standards Relating to Appellate Review of Sentences (Approved Draft 1967);

b. Weigel, "Appellate Revision of Sentences: To Make the Punishment Fit the Crime," 20 Stan. L. Rev. 405 (1968);

c. Hruska, "Appellate Review of Sentences," 8 Am. Crim. L.Q. 10 (1969); and

d. Thomas, "Appellate Review of Sentences and the Development of Sentencing Policy: The English Experience," 20 Ala. L. Rev. 193 (1968).

5. Note, "Appellate Review of Sentences and the Need for a Reviewable Record," Duke L.J. 1357 (1973).

6. Note, "Appellate Review of Sentencing," 33 La. L. Rev. 559 (1973).

7. Note, "Appellate Review of Sentencing: A New Dialogue?," 45 U. Colo. L. Rev. 209 (1973).

8. As a way of making appellate review of sentencing a meaningful remedy, one author has suggested that sentencing judges be required to justify for the record each sentence handed down. Disparities in treatment of similarly situated offenders could thus be documented. See Thomas, "Sentencing-- The Case for Reasoned Decisions," 1963 Crim. L. Rev. 243.

Parole

Two possible problems under the Equal Rights Amendment are present in the parole process. One is the standard applied by parole boards in making decisions to grant or deny parole. The other is possible unequal enforcement of the conditions imposed on male and female parolees. Each will be discussed separately below.

Standards for Granting Parole

Legal problem: Parole boards in the United States today operate in great secrecy. In most states, an applicant for parole has no right to present his or her case to the board personally, and has no right to have an attorney present at the board's hearing. In most instances, the only records kept are the final decisions, which contain no supporting reasons for the board's action in a particular case. Further, there is no right to appeal from a denial of parole. Parole is, in legal theory, a "privilege," not a "right." Therefore, denial of the privilege of parole is a final action. The prisoner's only remedy is to wait until enough time lapses to entitle him or her to file another application. While such a process might seem harsh, on first glance it does not appear to be in violation of the Equal Rights Amendment.

The equal rights problem becomes apparent only when one becomes aware of further statistics. As noted earlier, one woman is arrested for every six men. By the time sentencing occurs, that ratio has widened to 21 to 1. Among prisoners actually serving time in state or federal prisons, the gap widens even further. In 1970, there were 34 men in prison for every woman. The "chivalry" factor, pointed up by the National Commission on Violence in the sentencing process, appears to remain in the parole granting process. Although no statistics from parole boards are available to verify it, there is a very real possibility that women are treated more leniently by parole boards than men convicted of the same crime. If that is true, passage of an Equal Rights Amendment will render the application of different parole standards to men unconstitutional.

Possible solutions: Two new procedures would go far toward solving the problem of sex discrimination in the granting of parole. The first would be to open parole hearings to prisoners and to give applicants for parole the right to be represented by attorneys at the hearings. When a prisoner's freedom is the issue at stake, it is fatuous to label parole a "privilege" and therefore deny him or her the due process rights which apply to all other stages in the criminal process. A record of the hearing should be maintained and boards should be required to state their reasons for decisions on parole applications, whether favorable or unfavorable. Only with records and stated reasons for decisions will it be possible to determine whether the standards applied by parole boards are sex-discriminatory.

Secondly, a right of appeal should exist in all cases where parole is denied. Appeals of parole denial, along with stated reasons for the denial and open records of the parole board's treatment of other similarly situated offenders are the only obvious means by which sex discrimination, if it exists in the granting of paroles, may be remedied.

It is recognized that what is suggested here is a drastic change from present law and would impose substantial additional costs on the states' administration of their penal systems.[1] In recognition of those substantial costs, perhaps a special Board of Appeals could be established for parole matters only, with an expedited procedure which would lower costs both to the state and prisoners. Also, records could be kept on video-tape or audio-tape, not transcribed by court reporters, both to save appeal time and to lower costs. Finally, because of the more effective representation prisoners would gain from this procedure, states could justifiably allow applications for parole to be made less frequently than they are now.

If the matter is considered important enough, ways can be devised to establish an open parole hearing system, the records of which could be used to appeal to a higher body. To truly effectuate the Equal Rights Amendment in this area, as well as to greatly improve the administration of criminal justice in this country, revision of present parole practices and standards is an essential step.

References

1. Singer, "Women and the Correctional Process," 11 Am. Crim. L. Rev. 295, 296 (1973).

2. Haft, "Women in Prison: Discriminatory Practices and Some Legal Solutions," 8 Cl. Rev. 1, 4 (1973).

3. Stout, "Women in Probation and Parole," 19 Crime and Delinq. 61 (1973).

---

1. Because the equal protection clause requires states to provide indigent persons with counsel, free counsel for indigent prisoners would have to be supplied for parole hearings and appeals if this route were taken.

Conditions of Parole

Legal problem: Quite obviously, an Equal Rights Amendment
will require that the stated conditions of parole be the same
for men and women parolees, as is generally the case today.
The Equal Rights Amendment will also require that those parole
conditions be equally enforced between men and women parolees,
which is probably not done today.

As an example, consider one common condition of parole
in the United States, a rule that a parolee not live with a
member of the opposite sex. While no statistics are kept which
show reasons for revocation of parole and the sex of the person
whose parole was revoked, it seems possible, because of the
sexual double standard which still prevails in our society,
that this condition of parole, and others which are linked to
sex stereotypes, are enforced more often against women than
against men parolees. If this is true, such a practice will
violate the Equal Rights Amendment.

A second area in which it is possible that violations of
the Equal Rights Amendment will occur is in the determination
of "fitness" to recover custody of children placed in a foster
home while the parolee was in prison. The determination of
whether a parent, either a mother or a father, is "fit" to
regain custody of children is made initially by a parole
officer. While there is a right to a hearing if custody is
denied, many parolees probably never learn of this right. If
parole officers apply different standards to determine whether
mothers and fathers are fit to regain custody of their children,
the Equal Rights Amendment will be violated. The sexual double
standard, which often governs child custody decisions after
divorce, may be applied in this context also. A female
parolee's sexual relations with a man may be considered
sufficient reason to deny her custody of her children while a
male parolee's sexual relations with a woman would be considered
normal conduct.

Again, the complete lack of statistics in this area make
these violations only possibilities--but it is speculation
grounded in documented experience with the application of the
sexual double standard in other areas.

Possible solutions: The great problem in the area of
unequal enforcement of parole conditions is that absolutely no
statistics are available; no records are kept from which it may
be determined whether conditions of parole are being enforced
more strictly or differently against one sex than the other.
Thus, the essential prerequisite for knowing what the Amendment
will require in this area is knowledge of what is actually
occurring. To accomplish this, states and the federal
government should keep records of the reason for revocation of

parole, and should note on such records the sex of the parolee.

Secondly, if such records do show that rights under the Equal Rights Amendment are being violated by stricter enforcement of parole conditions against one sex, a remedy must be provided. The obvious one, as in sentencing and parole standards, is to provide an appeal from parole revocations. Again, because of cost factors, a special board might be established to deal only with parole revocation questions.

As an alternative, if after study it is believed that the most serious inequalities in the revocation of parole occur because of the application of a sexual double standard, the problem might be remedied by simply removing all questions of sexual conduct from parole revocation standards, unless the conduct were a crime serious enough to be prosecuted, such as prostitution or rape. If normal, non-criminal sexual relations were not in any way the subject of parole conditions, it is possible that the major inequities in the enforcement of parole conditions would be removed.

References

1. Haft, "Women in Prison: Discriminatory Practices and Some Legal Solutions," 8 Cl. Rev. 1, 4 (1973).

2. Stout, "Women in Probation and Parole," 19 Crime and Delinq. 61 (1973).

SEX-DISCRIMINATORY ASPECTS OF THE TREATMENT OF JUVENILES

Jurisdictional Statutes for Juvenile Courts

Legal problem: Until very recently, several states gave juvenile courts jurisdiction of girls under eighteen and of boys under sixteen. However, in the last two years, all but one such statute has been repealed. The one remaining is New York's runaway statute, which provides that a runaway girl of eighteen must be returned to her parents but only a runaway boy of sixteen must be so returned. This statute will violate the Equal Rights Amendment and is probably already unconstitutional under the equal protection clause.

Possible solutions: All state statutes pertaining to juveniles should be read carefully to be sure that they contain no differential age limits for boys and girls.

References

1. Davis and Chaires, "Sex Discrimination in Juvenile Law," 7 Ga. L. Rev. 494, 498 (1973).

2. See Matter of Patricia A., 31 N.Y. 2d 83, 335 N.Y.S. 2d 33 (1972), holding that New York's "Persons in Need of Supervision" (PINS) age differential for males and females was unconstitutional under the equal protection clause.

3. Gold, "Equal Protection for Juvenile Girls in Need of Supervision in New York State," 17 N.Y.U.L.F. 570 (1971) concerning the constitutionality of New York's PINS statute.

Standards of Misconduct for Which Juveniles Are Incarcerated

Legal problem: Many states have statutes which allow judges to send juveniles to reformatories for "willful disobedience" or similar misconduct. Under such statutes, stricter standards of conduct are often applied to juvenile girls than boys. A Connecticut study showed that while only 18% of the boys in its reformatories were there for conduct which would not be criminal if committed by an adult, fully 80% of the girls in Connecticut reformatories had been committed for non-criminal conduct. A similar study in New Jersey showed that over 80% of the girls in its reformatories were "criminals without crimes." They had been committed for such offenses as running away from home, being incorrigible or ungovernable by parents, being truants, being promiscuous, engaging in sexual relations, and becoming pregnant. These statistics undoubtedly reflect prevalent attidues about sex roles in our society, which render aggressive, anti-parental or overt sexual conduct in girls sufficient reason for commitment to reformatories; similar behavior in boys in rarely considered serious enough to justify incarceration.

Experience in New York and other states demonstrates that girls are more likely than boys to be committed to reformatories solely for sexual activity. Although a New York Court, in Matter of Patricia A., 31 N.Y. 2d 83 at 88, 335 N.Y.S. 2d 33 at 37-38, 286 N.E. 2d 432 at 437 (1972), explicitly discussed and declared unconstitutional the application of a sexual double standard in incarcerating minors, the practice of committing girls to reformatories solely for their sexual activity is still common in many states. The Equal Rights Amendment will not permit the application of different standards of conduct to boys and girls in committing them to reformatories.

62

Possible solutions: The most far-reaching and effective change which has been suggested in this area is the limitation of the conduct for which any juvenile, male or female, could be committed to a reformatory to behavior which violates criminal law. Essentially, this would eliminate the Children-In-Need-of-Supervision (CHINS) category from the juvenile code; it is the CHINS offenses which are the most ill-defined and subject to sex-discriminatory interpretation.

A less radical change in the area of juvenile misconduct and commitment is simply to specify concretely the kinds of behavior which the CHINS classification includes. This would mean eliminating such vague designations as "incorrigible," which, as indicated above, operate in a sex-discriminatory manner to incarcerate many more girls than boys for less serious offenses.

Even if no changes are made in CHINS statutes, since statistics exist showing the reasons for which boys and girls are committed to reformatories, and since the Supreme Court has declared that juveniles are entitled to the same due process rights as adults, attorneys for girls should appeal reformatory sentences imposed on sex-discriminatory grounds after passage of the Equal Rights Amendment.

References

1. Singer, "Women and the Correctional Process," 11 Am. Crim. L. Rev. 295, 298 (1973).

2. Lerman, "Child Convicts," 8 Transactions 35 (1971).

3. Haft, "Women in Prison: Discriminatory Practices and Some Legal Solutions," 8 Cl. Rev. 1 (1974).

4. For a description of the Supreme Court's decisions in Gault and Kent concerning the constitutional rights of juveniles, see Davis and Chaires, "Equal Protection of Juveniles: The Present Status of Sex-based Discrimination in Juvenile Court Laws," 7 Ga. L. Rev. 494 (1973).

Length of Terms to Which Boys and Girls Are Sentenced

Legal problem: New York's Youthful Offenders Act is one example of a statute found in many states. It provides that juveniles who commit a crime may, in the discretion of the judge, be sentenced to a state prison under the criminal code; or they may be treated as juveniles and sentenced under the Act, which sets a uniform indeterminate term of up to four years for all youths, regardless of the crime or offense involved. Thus, if a judge chooses, a juvenile may receive a longer sentence in a reformatory than the maximum term imposed by the criminal statute which he or she violated.

While the Youthful Offenders Act is neutral on its face, experience under the now-unconstitutional Wayward Minors Act in New York suggests that judges may impose an indeterminate four-year reformatory term, rather than a lesser prison sentence, more frequently when the offender is a girl. Thus, girls in New York, and undoubtedly in many other states also, probably spend a longer time in reformatories for crimes for which similarly-situated boys are sentenced to shorter terms in prison.

In general, the justification for longer reformatory terms is that reformatories rehabilitate juveniles by providing work and training programs; see cases cited in reference no. 3 below. Further, the conduct of juveniles sentenced under the provisions of juvenile court acts does not become part of the youth's permanent record. Thus, arguably there are advantages received by girls who are sentenced to longer terms in reformatories which are not available to those boys sentenced to shorter terms in prison.

Because of the dual aspect of the benefits and burdens of the problem described here, both boys and girls can claim that their rights under the Equal Rights Amendment are violated by such sentencing practices. Girls can argue that reformatories are not significantly better than prisons and that incarceration in any state institution amounts to loss of freedom. They may therefore claim that a longer sentence, regardless of where it is served, violates the Equal Rights Amendment.

Boys can argue, as two boys did with success in Lamb v. Brown, 456 F. 2d 18 (10th Cir. 1972), that they are denied equality when sentenced to prison instead of reformatories because of the rehabilitative aspect of reformatories and the lack of a criminal record.[2] Thus, depending on the circumstances,

---

2. Lamb v. Brown involved the constitutionality of an Oklahoma statute which defined a "child" as a girl under eighteen of a boy under sixteen. "Children," as defined in the statute, were entitled to treatment as juveniles. Two seventeen-year old boys sentenced to prison for car theft challenged the constitutionality of the age/sex differential in their Oklahoma juvenile court act. The Court of Criminal Appeals of Oklahoma denied their claim /see Lamb v. State, 475 P. 2d 829 (1970)/, but the 10th Cir. Court of Appeals upheld it in Lamb v. Brown, above. Although Lamb v. Brown involved a sentencing statute which contained an explicit age/sex differential, what is suggested here is that the rationale for the decision extends to sentencing practices which differentiate between disposition of boys and girls solely on the basis of sex.

either sex might justifiably claim a denial of equal rights under the sentencing practices described here.

Possible solutions: The only solution which will satisfy the Equal Rights Amendment is to sentence boys and girls equally to prisons or reformatories. Sentencing practices based on the premise that girls are more subject to rehabilitation than boys will be unconstitutional under the Amendment.

References

1. K. Davidson, R. Ginsburg and H. Kay, Sex-based Discrimination 906-908 (1974).

2. For a more complete listing of sex-discriminatory sentencing statutes for juveniles than was possible in this summary description of the problem, see Davis and Chaires, "Equal Protection for Juveniles: The Present Status of Sex-based Discrimination in Juvenile Court Laws," 7 Ga. L. Rev. 494, 506 (1973).

3. If no sex-discrimination issue is present, there is virtually no avenue open for a successful challenge to statutes which allow a youth to be committed to a reformatory for a longer term than would be served in prison for the same conduct. It has uniformly been held that as long as there is different or special treatment given juveniles in reformatories, juvenile commitment statutes with longer maximum terms than might be imposed in prison are constitutional. See, for example, State v. Pitt, 253 A. 2d 672 (1969); and Cunningham v. United States, 256 F. 2D 457 (1958).

Standards for Parole from Reformatories

Legal problem: The studies referred to earlier demonstrate that 80% of the girls in reformatories were committed for conduct which is not a violation of the criminal law; in contrast, only 18% of boys were incarcerated for non-criminal conduct. Other studies, however, show conclusively that girls nevertheless spend a longer time in reformatories than boys. In 1964, a nationwide survey showed that the average length of girls' stays in reformatories was 10.7 months, compared to an average stay for boys of 8.2 months. A 1971 Connecticut study supported these findings: there, girls stayed in reformatories an average of 7 months, boys an average of 5 months. In New York, a similar report showed that girls stayed in reformatories an average of 12 months, boys an average of 9.3 months.

Thus, while girls are generally committed to reformatories for less serious offenses than boys, they tend to remain in reformatories longer. Informed observers explain this seeming paradox as another example of paternalistic attitudes toward girls and women who come in contact with the criminal system. Girls are thought to require more protection and to be more susceptible to rehabilitation, so they are sent to reformatories for less serious conduct than boys. On the other hand, once there, authorities seem to believe both that they are more educable than boys and that they might become pregnant if released during idle summer months; so they keep girls longer.

One hopeful possibility for reform might be to set a fixed and shorter term for either boys' or girls' commitment to reformatories, such as six months or one year, with automatic release, unless a judge, for good cause, committed the youth to another term of like duration. Such a practice would ensure release of all juveniles within a legislatively-established period of time, unless reformatory officials could demonstrate to a court's satisfaction good reasons for keeping a youth longer. The reasons for a second period of detention should, of course, be clearly established by statute and not left to the discretion of reformatory officials or judges.

Given the statistics showing that the average length of most reformatory stays for boys and girls alike is less than one year, a fixed term of six months would provide more meaningful reform in this area than would an established term of one year.

References

1. Singer, "Women in the Correctional Process," 11 Am. Crim. L. Rev. 291, 299 (1973).

2. A number of states already have statutes which limit the term of commitment of a juvenile adjudicated delinquent. For example, in New Mexico, Sec. 13-14-35, N.M.S.A. (1953), imposes a one-year limitation; and in New York, The Family Court Act, in Sec. 757, limits probation to two years, while Sec. 758 limits commitment to three years.

Girls' and Boys' Reformatory Conditions and Programs

The published work which describes the discrepancies between state reformatories for boys and girls suggests that many of the differences between them are similar to the differences between men's and women's prisons and stem from the same sex-stereotyped attitudes. Girls, for instance, are typically trained in cooking, cleaning, sewing and other domestic chores; boys receive training in woodwork, welding, baking and vocationally-related skills. Boys are thought to need less privacy than girls, and so are kept in large dormitories; girls are given very small, private rooms. Sports and physical activities are provided for boys; girls typically receive so little exercise that they gain weight in girls' reformatories. All state reformatories for youths are now completely sex-segregated.

The Equal Rights Amendment will require that reformatories which are now sexually segregated be integrated, except for sleeping, showering and dressing quarters. For a more complete discussion of these issues in connection with men's and women's prisons, see the following section. Further, of course, all educational, recreational, and vocational programs must be opened to both boys and girls without regard to sex.

Because areas in which reformatory conditions and programs will violate the Equal Rights Amendment closely parallel those in which conditions and programs in men's and women's prisons will violate the Amendment, needed changes in reformatories will not be separately discussed here. However, any general revision of state juvenile codes should not ignore the question of sex-integration of reformatories or the need for equal conditions and programs for boys and girls. Such problems should be investigated in every state and specifically addressed in statutes revised to conform to the Equal Rights Amendment.

References

For an excellent description of the differing conditions, rules and programs in Connecticut's girls' and boys' reformatories which appear to be fairly representative of those in many states, see Rogers, "For Her Own Protection. . . Conditions of Incarceration for Female Offenders in the State of Connecticut," 7 J. Law and Soc. Ass., 223, 230 et seq. (1972).

SEX-DISCRIMINATORY ASPECTS OF ADULT PENAL INSTITUTIONS

Physical Integration of Men's and Women's Prisons

Legal problem: Thirty-five of fifty adult state penal institutions in the United States today have completely separate facilities for men and women prisoners. In the fifteen states in which females are housed with male inmates, the women are kept in a separate corner of the institution and are not allowed to participate in the full range of activities open to male prisoners.

The Yale article on the Equal Rights Amendment, and the Congressional debates and legislative history indicate that states may not apply the Amendment by providing separate-but-equal facilities for the sexes. This interpretation has been widely accepted because "separate" is in fact rarely "equal." Rejection of the doctrine will prevent condoning the almost universal situation where separate, but unequal, facilities are maintained.

As will be seen from the discussion which follows, women's prisons, which are separate today, are decidedly unequal and in most respects inferior to the prisons provided for men. This inferiority stems largely from the vast disparity in the number of men and women inmates. In 1971, for example, there were 191,619 men and 6,219 women incarcerated in state and federal prisons.[3]

Because of this great difference in the number of prisoners of each sex, states believe that it is too expensive to duplicate programs routinely provided for men for their very small women's prisons. Particularly in the case of state prisons, then, "separate" is not "equal" now, and never will be unless the number of women in prison rises beyond imagination. The only feasible means of resolving the many disparities and inequities found today in any survey of conditions in men's and women's prisons is to physically integrate the institutions. Such an approach is not only consistent with the theory of the Equal Rights Amendment, but, as will be seen, represents the only practical solution to the many inequalities found in women's prisons today.

Three questions will arise from the requirement that men's and women's prisons be physically integrated. The first is the role of the right of privacy qualification of the Amendment and its effect on the maintenance of separate sleeping, showering and dressing quarters for men and women prisoners. The second is whether guards must be of the same sex as the prisoners with whom they are charged. Finally, when prisons are sexually integrated, must the prisons which now house male inmates be upgraded to the generally higher physical conditions now prevalent in women's prisons or may women prisoners be placed in the less comfortable men's prisons? Each of these questions will be discussed separately below.

---

3. *Statistical Abstract of the United States* 164 (1974).

Possible solutions: Regarding the right of privacy in sleeping, showering and dressing quarters, the Yale article on the Equal Rights Amendment states clearly, as does the legislative history of the Amendment in Congress, that the right of privacy in performing personal bodily functions is an acceptable qualification of the Equal Rights Amendment. The right of privacy is a young, but well-accepted constitutional doctrine which has been used repeatedly by the U.S. Supreme Court in the last ten years. See Griswold v. Connecticut, 381 U.S. 479 (1965); Eisenstadt v. Baird, 405 U.S. 438 (1972); Roe v. Wade, 410 U.S. 113 (1973); and Doe v. Bolton, 410 U.S. 479 (1973). These cases led the Congress to believe that the Court would accept the current mores of our society in interpreting the Amendment and recognize that personal bodily functions, such as showering, disrobing for sleep and sleeping are customarily performed only in the presence of members of one's own sex. Thus, while all public areas of penal institutions must be sexually integrated after the effective date of the Amendment, including those used for eating, work, education and recreation, those areas used for sleeping and showering should be allowed to remain sexually segregated under the right of privacy qualification.

Regarding the requirement that guards be the same sex as their prisoners, the right of privacy qualification to the Equal Rights Amendment should allow states to use only female guards to search female prisoners and only females to guard women inmates who are showering or asleep. However, all public areas of the prisons, as well as those sexually segregated areas which are not being used by inmates for personal bodily functions, may be guarded by persons of either sex. In fact, in many states today male guards are used in public areas of women's prisons for security reasons.4

Regarding the equalization of men's and women's prisons ("up" or "down"?), it must be pointed out that, because men outnumber women in the prison population today by some 34 to 1, women's prisons are usually quite small and are often physically more comfortable than men's prisons. How will the physical integration of men's and women's prisons required by the Equal Rights Amendment be accomplished with existing physical facilities?

---

4. Except insofar as sex is a "bona fide occupational qualification" (BFOQ) under Title VII because of the right of privacy qualification discussed in the text above, a state prison's refusal to hire guards on grounds of sex violates Title VII of the Civil Rights Act of 1964 and will also violate the Equal Rights Amendment.

For a more complete discussion of Title VII and the state's duties as an employer, see generally the chapter on Labor Laws.

Although where feasible, the courts generally prefer to
equalize "up" to a higher level, that is probably not practical
given the small size of the more comfortable women's prisons.
Theoretically, it would be possible for states to build new and
more comfortable prisons in which to house both men and women
prisoners; but the cost of such a building program will make it
prohibitive in most states. Thus, the Amendment will probably
be realized by housing women inmates in the now-extant men's
prisons and using the present women's facilities as honor units
for prisoners of both sexes who have demonstrated good behavior
or are about to be released.

Where the number of women prisoners integrated into a
formerly all-male prison is extremely small, it is possible
that an issue under the eighth amendment's guarantee of freedom
from cruel and unusual punishment, including physical abuse
while incarcerated, could arise. For instance, if two women
were placed in a prison of 800 men, the possibility of physical
danger, and the eighth amendment right to be protected from it
while in prison, would conflict with the requirements of the
Equal Rights Amendment. While such a case is unlikely because
most states have enough women prisoners to make such an
occurrence a remote possibility, if the question does arise, the
eighth amendment right would probably take precedence over the
requirements of the ERA.

The question is noted here because the eighth amendment
is uniquely applicable to state prisons and the Equal Rights
Amendment must be applied in a manner consonant with it.

References

1. For an explanation of the right of privacy qualification of the Amendment and an exposition of the view that it
includes the right to be searched only by a guard of one's own
sex, see Brown, Emerson, Falk and Freedman, "The Equal Rights
Amendment: A Constitutional Basis for Equal Rights for Women,"
80 Yale L. J. 871, 901 (1971).

2. See Rep. Martha Griffith's remarks to the effect that
the right of privacy was to be incorporated and used in interpreting the Amendment in Hearings Before Sub. 4 of House Comm'n
on the Judiciary, 92nd Cong., 1st Sess., 47 (1971).

3. For a thorough discussion of the requirements of the
Amendment as it applies to state and federal prisons, the
physical integration of prisons and the eighth amendment, see
Note, "The Sexual Segregation of American Prisons," 82 Yale L.J.
1229, 1261-1266 (1973).

4. Singer, "Women in the Correctional Process," 11 Am. Crim. L. Rev. 291 (1973).

5. Note, "Women's Prisons: Laboratories for Penal Reform," 1973 Wis. L. Rev. 210.

6. For a thorough discussion of the right of privacy qualification of the Amendment, as well as an exposition of the reasons that the separate-but-equal doctrine should be rejected in interpreting the ERA, see Brown, Emerson, Falk and Freedman, "The Equal Rights Amendment: A Constitutional Basis for Equal Rights for Women," 80 Yale L. J. 871, 900-907 (1971).

7. See the section on the right of privacy qualification in chapter one, The Equal Rights Amendment and the Constitution, above. The discussion there summarizes the arguments put forth in the Yale article and discusses the leading cases on the right of privacy.

Isolation of Women Prisoners from Families

Legal problem: Because of the extremely small percentage of women in the total prison population, eight states today do not maintain any facilities whatsoever for women inmates. Instead, they send them to the states which do maintain women's prisons and pay for their incarceration on a per capita basis. Even in states which have women's prisons, there is rarely more than one, while there may be several men's prisons. This means that women may be incarcerated several hundred miles from family and friends and thus virtually isolated. The present isolation of women prisoners would violate the Equal Rights Amendment.

Possible solutions: After passage of the Equal Rights Amendment, men's and women's prisons will be required to be physically integrated. Admission to a particular state prison (where the state maintains more than one such facility) will probably have to be determined on some sex-neutral basis, such as good conduct or educational or vocational interests. Thus, the sexual integration of prisons required by the Equal Rights Amendment will automatically correct the current isolation of women prisoners in American penal institutions.

Although it would appear that after the Amendment's effective date, a state could determine admissions to prison solely on the basis of conduct, educational interests or seriousness of the crime committed, it is possible to imagine situations in which such an admissions policy might be a rule "neutral on its face, but discriminatory in impact."

Statistics demonstrate that 80% of women prisoners are mothers. A high percentage of the prisoner-mothers may also be the only parents or legal guardians of their children. Therefore, admitting prisoners who are mothers to one of several state prisons based on factors which do not take into account their need to be physically close to their children might be a practice which would weigh more heavily upon women than upon men prisoners.

If this hypothetical situation is demonstrably the case, states could fashion a sex-neutral rule in this area allowing prisoners of either sex who were the sole parents or guardians of their children to choose the basis upon which their admission to prisons be made, such as physical location or other factors. Such a rule would permit those parents who valued proximity to their children above vocational opportunities or the type of penal institution in which they were incarcerated to choose that option. Other prisoners who so desired would be allowed to choose the advantages of a more remote, but educationally or more physically desirable state institution. In many instances, the choice between educational or vocational opportunities and proximity to family will be a difficult one. However, each prison would be required to offer all prisoners vocational and educational opportunities in conformity with the discussion in the following section.

References

1. Haft, "Women in Prison: Some Discriminatory Practices and Some Legal Solutions," 8 Cl. Rev. 1, 3 (1974).

2. For a case brought by the ACLU against the State of Hawaii's practice of sending all women convicts to other states' prisons on the mainland, see Park v. State, National ACLU Women's Rights Project Docket No. W.R. 4202. A district court decision, reported at 356 F. Supp. 783 (D. Hawaii 1973), allowed the complaint to be amended to include a charge of sex discrimination.

3. Note, "The Sexual Segregation of American Prisons," 82 Yale L. J. 1229, 1232 (1973).

4. Note, "Prisoner-Mother and Her Child," 1 Cap. U. L. Rev. 127 (1972).

5. Note, "Women's Prisons: Laboratories for Penal Reform," 1973 Wis. L. Rev. 210.

Vocational Rehabilitation Opportunities

Legal problem: The current sexual segregation of prisons in the United States carries with it the segregation of vocational rehabilitation and work training programs. What this usually means is that male inmates are given considerable opportunities for vocational training, while women inmates are often trained only in domestic chores. One recent article, cited in reference no. 1 below, noted that at several state prisons women are given vocational training only in house-cleaning. A state may not maintain "rehabilitation" programs which reflect stereotyped notions about the proper roles of the sexes after passage of the Equal Rights Amendment. The ERA will unquestionaly require that vocational rehabilitation opportunities be open to all inmates without regard to sex.

Possible solutions: Again, physical integration of men's and women's prisons in the United States will have a major and beneficial impact on vocational rehabilitation opportunities; an important factor in the current lack of vocational training opportunity for women is the small number of women prisoners and their distance from the training programs conducted for male inmates.

However, while all vocational rehabilitation programs must be open to persons of both sexes, prison administrators cannot simply open auto mechanics and welding courses to women inmates and do nothing more in order to comply with the Amendment. They must recognize the current jobs preferred by and available to most women, and make realistic vocational train-ing available in professions in which women inmates can and want to work after parole. Further, maintaining one course of possible interest to women prisoners, such as hairdressing, will not satisfy the Amendment where eight or ten offerings are made which are of interest predominantly to male inmates. The vocational training opportunities must be genuinely equal in light of the current job preferences of women and the fields in which they are most likely to be employed after parole.

References

1. Note, "Women's Prisons: Laboratories for Penal Reform," 1973 Wis. L. Rev. 210.

2. Note, "The Sexual Segregation of American Prisons," 82 Yale L. J. 1229, 1242 and Appendix II (1973).

Educational and Work Release Programs

Legal problem: In a number of states, because the
population of women prisoners is small and prison administrators are reluctant to sexually integrate prison programs,
women prisoners are denied the academic programs available to
male prisoners. In a great many more states, work release
programs which are routinely made available to male prisoners
are denied women prisoners. The Equal Rights Amendment will
require that all prison programs be offered equally to
prisoners of both sexes.

Possible solutions: Once more, the physical integration
of men's and women's prisons will prove of benefit in making
expensive academic programs equally available to men and
women prisoners.

As for work release programs, there is presently no good
reason why they are not uniformly available to women.
Unquestionably, the Equal Rights Amendment will require prison
administrators to allow women prisoners who meet sex-neutral
standards for admission to work release programs to enter those
programs on the same basis as male prisoners.

References

1. Concerning academic programs in men's and women's
prisons today, see Note, "The Sexual Segregation of American
Prisons," 82 Yale L. J. 1229, 1241 (1973).

2. Note, "Denial of Work Release Programs to Women: A
Violation of Equal Protection," 47 So. Cal. L. Rev. 1453 (1974).

Honor Farms and Halfway Houses

Legal problem: The result of the small number of women
in prison in the United States and the reluctance of many
prison administrators to sexually integrate prison facilities
has been to deny women the benefits of honor farms and halfway
houses in many state prison systems. Such practices will, of
course, violate the Equal Rights Admendment.

Possible solution: The Equal Rights Amendment's requirement that all state prison facilities be sexually integrated
will solve the problem which now exists for many women
prisoners. All physical facilities of state prisons, including
honor farms and halfway houses, must be equally available to

prisoners of both sexes, with admission standards established on a completely sex-neutral basis.

Reference

The National ACLU has filed a suit requesting that women in Maryland's prisons be given equal access to the state's honor farm and halfway houses. See Grosso et al. v. Lally et al., U.S.D.C. (D. Md.) Cir. No. Y-74-447, ACLU Women's Rights Project Docket No. 4206.

Recreational Facilities and Programs and Team Sports

Legal problem: Because of the small size of the female prison population, and probably also because of sex-stereo-typed notions about the interests of female prisoners, many state prisons make available only a limited range of physical activities to women prisoners, while maintaining extensive team sports and gymnasium facilities for male prisoners. The Equal Rights Amendment will require that a similar range of physical recreation facilities and activities be made available to men and women prisoners.

Many prisons now maintain male teams for baseball, basket-ball and other sports which compete with local nonprison teams. A question will arise in the area of teams maintained by state prisons similar to that posed by teams supported by public schools. Will the Amendment allow separate men's and women's teams to be fielded? May only one team, open to both men and women who qualify, be maintained? Or will the Amendment require prisons to maintain at least two teams so that the physically less strong women prisoners will have a realistic chance of competing on the second string?

Finally, although male prisoners now enjoy a much wider variety of physical sports and activities than women prisoners, women are often taken outside the prison for swimming in local pools or movies; such outside recreation is possible because of the small number of women in most state prisons. Obviously, giving privileges to go to outside recreational activities solely on the basis of sex will violate the Amendment.

Possible solutions: The physical integration of men's and women's prisons which the Amendment will require will solve many of the existing problems for women prisoners who desire and need athletic programs and facilities. After passage of the ERA, any programs and facilities for athletics will have to be open to men and women prisoners without regard to sex.

The question of team sports and the basis for team selection is as difficult as it is in the public school area. See the section on athletic teams in the chapter on Education, and the references contained there for an analysis of the solutions offered by authors in that field.

It should be noted, however, that if a state prison fields only one team in a particular sport, such a practice is likely to be one "neutral on its face, but discriminatory in impact," since most women will not have the necessary physical skills or be strong enough to qualify for a first-string team in competition with men. Prisons, then, must maintain a minimum of two teams, at least one of which a reasonable number of women prisoners can qualify for.

The ERA will require, of course, that decisions as to which prisoners can participate in recreational events outside the prison, such as attendance at movies or public swimming pools, be made on a sex-neutral basis, such as good behavior, and be available to prisoners of both sexes.

Reference

Note, "The Sexual Segregation of American Prisons," 82 Yale L. J. 1229, 1239 (1973).

Prison Rules and Regulations

Prisoners' Dress

Legal problem: In most state prisons, male prisoners are required to wear standard prison uniforms, while female prisoners are allowed to wear clothes of their own choosing which they bring to prison with them. Prison administrators believe that uniforms have an important psychological effect and tend to induce a lack of identity and self respect. The Amendment will require, of course, that male and female prisoners be treated alike with regard to wearing apparel.

Decoration of Cells

Legal problem: Most state prisons do not allow male prisoners to use personal bedspreads, curtains or other decoration for their cells. Women prisoners, on the other hand, are allowed to freely decorate their cells as their personal tastes dictate. This difference is explainable both by sex-stereotyped notions and by the much more frequent searches of cells in men's prisons; administrators believe personal decorations in the cells of male prisoners would hinder search procedures.

Use of Prison Law Libraries

Legal problem: In many state prisons, use of law and other library facilities is accorded only to male inmates. Women prisoners are either not allowed to use the libraries at all, or are given quite limited access to them.

Visitors and Visiting Hours

Legal problem: Many prisons allow female inmates shorter hours for visitors than male prisoners, and some do not allow children to visit female inmates, although 80% of female prisoners are mothers. The explanation given for this is a lack of staff to supervise visiting and a general feeling that because of the leniency with which the criminal justice system generally treats women, those who do get to prison are more likely to be hardened criminals than their male counterparts. Any such differential treatment based on the sex of prisoners will, of course, violate the Equal Rights Amendment.

Possible solutions: Where prison rules and regulations differ solely according to the sex of prisoners, the ERA will require that prison administrators re-think and re-write those rules to be sex-neutral. Prison administrators have three choices: (1) to deny to all prisoners benefits now accorded only one sex, such as dress or cell decoration; (2) to extend any benefits now accorded only one sex to both sexes equally; or (3) to allow benefits to be earned on a sex-neutral basis, such as good behavior, or to establish different rules according to the security of the institution. While no answers can be provided here as to which rules will be unconstitutional after passage of the Equal Rights Amendment, each such rule must be closely examined to determine how it may be applied equally to both male and female inmates.

References

1. Note, "The Sexual Segregation of American Prisons," 82 <u>Yale L. J.</u> 1229, 1238 (1973).

2. Rogers, "For Her Own Protection . . . Conditions of Incarceration for Female Offenders in the State of Connecticut," 7 J. Law and Soc. Ass'n. 223 (1972).

3. Singer, "Women in the Correctional Process," 11 Am. Crim. L. Rev. 295, 302 (1973).

Availability of Prison Services

Religious Services

Legal problem: Because of the larger size of men's prisons, many have regular religious services and full-time chaplains available to counsel prisoners. The much smaller women's prisons do not usually have either regular services or a religious staff available for personal counseling.

Medical Services

Legal problem: The extremely small population of women's prisons has made it economically impractical for most states to equip them with medical facilities, or to have full-time doctors on call. Most state men's prisons do have such facilities.

Possible solution: Because these problems, like so many arising from the differential staffing and programs in men's and women's prisons, are primarily due to the small number of prisoners at women's prisons, the physical integration of women into men's prisons, required by the ERA, will solve the problems of availability of religious and medical services for female inmates.

Reference

Note, "The Sexual Segregation of American Prisons," 82 Yale L. J. 1229, 1236 (1973).

Abortion Rights of Female Prisoners

Legal problem: Since the Supreme Court decisions in Roe v. Wade, 410 U.S. 113 (1973) and Doe v. Bolton, 410 U.S. 479 (1973), it has been the right of adult women in the

United States, in consultation with their physicians, to have abortions during the first two trimesters of pregnancy; this right is subject only to the state's right to make reasonable restrictions on the place where abortions may be performed during the second trimester and by whom any abortion is performed.

No published study has been made since Roe and Doe of the practice of state prisons with regard to furnishing women prisoners the same right to abortion guaranteed other female citizens of the United States. However, it was clear from studies done before those decisions were handed down that state prisons often denied abortions to women prisoners, even when the abortion was specifically requested and was legal under state law.

Such a practice by state prison officials clearly violates the 1973 decisions in Roe and Doe. As part of any wide-scale effort to ensure the rights of women prisoners, every step should be taken to assure that female inmates are informed of their right to obtain an abortion if they so choose. They must further be told of the prison's duty to pay for abortions as it would pay for any other needed medical care, including delivery of a full-term child.

Reference

Singer, "Women in the Correctional Process," 11 Am. Crim. L. Rev. 292, 302 (1973).

Failure to Classify Women Prisoners by Seriousness of Offense

Legal problem: Once again, due to the very small number of women in prison, they are rarely, if ever, classified and incarcerated according to the seriousness of the offense committed; such classification is routine practice with male prisoners. As a result, first offenders, and in some states, misdemeanants are placed in the same prison with women serving long terms for serious offenses. Although there is some disagreement among prison administrators as to the desirability of this practice, most seem to believe that younger and less experienced prisoners are damaged by long exposure to older women who are multiple offenders.

Possible solution: When women's prisons are integrated with the physically larger men's prisons, some degree of classification of women prisoners will be possible. Women will then become eligible for honor farms and halfway houses, institutions now generally available only to men; even small populations of women prisoners, for example 30, can be divided into two or more groups according to age and seriousness of offense. In this area also, then, the physical integration of men's and women's prisons required by the ERA will be of substantial benefit to female inmates.

References

1. Note, "The Sexual Segregation of American Prisons," 82 Yale L. J. 12-29, 1234 (1973).

2. See Commonwealth v. Stauffer, 214 Pa. Super. 113, 251 A. 2d 718 (1969) for a case ordering a woman convicted of a misdemeanor sent to a county jail rather than a penitentiary to avoid having her mix with women who had committed more serious crimes. Males who committed misdemeanors were regularly sent to county jails, not the state penitentiary.

Isolation of Women in County Jails

Legal problem: Singer, in the reference cited below, notes that half the women incarcerated on any one day in the United States are in county jails, not state prisons. In numerical terms, then, of the 16,000 women in confinement on any one day, 8,000 are held in the more than 3,500 county jails around the country. There are, on an average, just over two women in every county jail in the United States.

These statistics demonstrate that women in county jails are even more isolated than women in prison. In fact, many women in county jails are in effect held in solitary confinement because women prisoners are always sexually segregated from male inmates. While the genesis of this situation is understandable, it often imposes severe hardships on individual women who are held in county jails awaiting trial. In one celebrated recent case in North Carolina, a woman prisoner, Joanne Little, now on trial for killing a male guard who allegedly raped her, was held in solitary confinement for 81 days while serving a sentence for robbery; there simply were no other women in the Beufort County Jail at that time. In terms of the sheer number of women affected by the penal system, this problem ranks as one of the more important.

Possible solutions: Since most county jails have poor facilities, many prisoners spend most of their time in their cells. Because women must, under the right of privacy qualification of the Equal Rights Amendment, be given cells separate from male prisoners, it would appear that the only solution consonant with the Amendment, the woman prisoner's right to privacy, her right to be held in the locale of her crime, and her right not to be held in solitary confinement without good cause, is to give a single woman prisoner in a county jail a choice as to whether she wishes to remain where she is, alone, or wishes to be transferred to a neighboring county jail where she can have the company of other women prisoners while awaiting trial or serving a sentence.

Reference

Singer, "Women in the Correctional Process," 11 Am. Crim. L. Rev. 292, 300 (1973).

SEX-DISCRIMINATORY ASPECTS OF THE MENTAL INSTITUTIONALIZATION OF WOMEN

Commitment to State Mental Institutions

Legal problem: State statutes providing for civil commitment to state mental institutions are written in vague and ambiguous terms which leave great leeway for individual psychiatrists' opinions as to the desirability of commitment. Such statutes give great latitude, as well, for relatives-- often husbands attempting to gain custody of children, or parents who are in some way punishing a misbehaving daughter-- to make use of civil commitment for purposes other than treat- ment of the patient. Statutes which courts are asked to apply in committing patients to state mental institutions typically provide such standards as "a danger to herself or others"; or "having a disorder which impairs mental health."

Psychiatrists and others have long noted the inherent sex-role stereotyping at the very root of Freudian as well as most other theories of psychology. Thus, psychiatrists trained in these philosophies who are asked to give professional opinions as to the "mental health" of a woman who acts differently from their model of a "healthy woman," will often diagnose personality traits such as aggression, anger or assertiveness as indicators of mental illness in women. The same traits, of course, would be considered normal or even desirable in men.

Expressly basing the civil commitment of women to mental institutions on the professional opinions of persons whose whole training has encouraged sex-biased and sex-based thinking, may, according to a very recent article, violate the equal protection clause and therefore the Equal Rights Amendment.

Possible solutions: No clear solution exists to this problem. It is one which is inherent in the philosophical training of the professionals who define "mental illness" and treat the "mentally ill." The only solution suggested by the authors who first described this situation and whose work is cited in reference no. 1 below is militant awareness of it by all attorneys who represent women in civil commitment hearings. Only through such awareness, they feel, can questions be asked and attitudes probed in an effort to uncover the sex bias of many professional psychiatrists and psychologists.

The civil commitment statutes and their obeisance to sex-based psychiatric theory are mentioned here chiefly because of the importance of the problem and the very little public discussion it has received to date.

References

1. Roth and Lerner, "Sex-based Discrimination in the Mental Institutionalization of Women," 62 Calif. L. Rev. 789, 789-801 (1974).

2. For general descriptions of problems in civil commitment, see:

a. Note, "Mental Illness and Commitment," 39 Mo. L. Rev. 602 (1974); and

b. Note, "Commitment and Release Standards and Procedures: Uniform Treatment for the Mentally Ill," 41 U. Chi. L. Rev. 825 (1974).

Treatment in State Mental Institutions

Performance of Lobotomies

Legal problem: Three times as many women as men receive lobotomies in all mental institutions, governmental as well as private, in the United States. Such startling statistics imply strongly that the operation, which reduces aggression and renders the patient docile and submissive, is being performed on women due to a sex-role stereotype of the "correct" way in which women should behave. State mental hospitals will, of course, be subject to the requirements of the Equal Rights Amendment; sex-based decisions on the advisibility of performing this operation should be challenged in court or treated in a uniform code dealing with the operation of state mental institutions.

82

Possible solutions: To prevent sex-based decisions as
to when lobotomies are medically indicated, a board comprised
of both medical professionals and lay persons from a variety
of fields might be established to approve the performance of
any lobotomy in a state hospital. A second possibility might
be to require by statute that: (1) a court approve in
advance any lobotomy performed in a state hospital; and (2) an
attorney be appointed to represent the patient upon whom the
operation is to be performed.

The operation is such a serious and irreversible one that
some means of supervising it seems necessary. While the
suggestions advanced here might not be the final or best
answers, the question deserves thoughtful and serious study.
The practices of every state mental institution should be
specifically investigated and the problem addressed in a
statute which regulates the performance of the operation in
some effective manner.

Reference

Roth and Lerner, "Sex-based Discrimination in the Mental
Institutionalization of Women," 62 Calif. L. Rev. 789, 805-806
(1974).

Punishment for Sexual Behavior

Legal problem: The application of traditional sex-role
stereotypes and the sexual double standard can be found in such
diverse fields as punishment of women in state mental hospitals,
as well as in the more familiar arenas of custody proceedings
for children and commitment of juvenile girls to reformatories.
Women in state mental hospitals are routinely punished severely
for sexual behavior while the male inmates who are their
partners often receive no punishment whatsoever. The males'
sexual desires are regarded as "normal," while the females are
typically described as "sexually acting out"; their sexual
behavior is thought to require treatment. The Equal Rights
Amendment would render unconstitutional any treatment or
punishment of women by state mental hospitals for sexual or
other behavior not punished or treated when engaged in by men.

Possible solutions: Because it seems likely that there are
many sex-role stereotypes which have important effects in the
treatment of women and men committed to state mental institutions,
a detailed study of the ways in which such stereotypes affect
inmates and the means of correcting them is imperative.
Investigation and description of all sex-discriminatory

practices in state mental institutions is well beyond the
scope of this summary treatment, but the importance of the
problem and the need for further study is noted.

Reference

Roth and Lerner, "Sex-based Discrimination in the Mental
Institutionalization of Women," 62 Calif. L. Rev. 789, 801-
806 (1974).

Standards for Release from State Mental Institutions

Legal problem: As in the commitment and treatment of
women in mental institutions, standards for release from
those institutions are permeated with the sex biases of
traditional Freudian psychoanalytic theory. Studies have
shown that the women released from mental institutions after
the shortest period of commitment are those with families and
little education who have spent their lives as housewives.
Professional women and those with better educations are less
likely candidates for early release, presumably because they
do not conform as readily to the stereotype of the "normal"
woman. Another recent study shows that women who demonstrate
low ego strength and high anxiety patterns on personality
tests are released earlier than women with high ego strength
and low anxiety traits, again, presumably, because the former
group corresponds to the "normal," "feminine" personality,
while the latter are considered abnormally aggressive. State
mental institutions which demonstrably differentiate in their
standards for release of male and female patients will be in
violation of the Equal Rights Amendment.

Possible solutions: Again, no ready solution for this
problem is evident except the vigilance of attorneys who
represent women committed to mental institutions. As in the
entire field of "mental illness" in women, the problem stems
from the basic Freudian perception of the factors and
personality traits which constitute a "healthy" woman. Until
psychiatry drastically changes its fundamental theories
relating to sex roles, the problem for the many women who
come in contact with mental institutions is an extremely
serious one.

References

1. Roth and Lerner, "Sex-based Discrimination in the
Mental Institutionalization of Women," 62 Calif. L. Rev. 789,
806 (1974).

84

2. Note, "Commitment and Release Standards and Procedures: Uniform Treatment for the Mentally Ill," 41 U.Chi. L. Rev. 825 (1974).

3. The Center for the Study of Legal Authority and Mental Patient Status, Post Office Box 822, Berkeley, Calif., may be contacted for more information on the specific subject of sex-discriminatory treatment of men and women in state mental institutions.

4. There has been very little written specifically concerning sex discrimination in the commitment and treatment of women in mental institutions. However, in recent years a fairly large number of articles have documented the need to ensure that due process and equal protection rights are not violated either in commitment procedures or during institutionalization. In addition, there has been an increasing movement directed towards guaranteeing patients the right to treatment. For a sample of the large literature on the constitutional rights of mental patients, see:

a. Moya, "Behavior Modification: Legal Limitations on Methods and Goals," 50 Notre Dame Law 230 (1974);

b. "Conference in Mental Health and the Law," 23 Cath. U. L. Rev. 643 (1974);

c. "Symposium: Mental Disability and the Law," 62 Calif. L. Rev. 397 (1974);

d. Peele, Chedoff and Taub, "Involuntary Hospitalization and Treatability: Observations from the District of Columbia Experience," 23 Cath. U. L. Rev. 744 (1974);

e. Rothman, "Decarcerating Prisons and Patients," 1 Civ. Lib. Rev. 8 (1973);

f. Pyfer, "Deprivation of Liberty and the Right to Treatment," 7 Cl. Rev. 519 (1974);

g. Note, "Developments in the Law: Civil Commitment of the Mentally Ill," 87 Harv. L. Rev. 1190 (1974);

h. Note, "Mental Illness: A Suspect Classification?," 83 Yale L. J. 1237 (1974); and

i. "Symposium: Mental Illness, the Law and Civil Liberties," 13 Santa Clara Law 367 (1973).

SEX-DISCRIMINATORY ASPECTS OF STATE LAWS
RELATING TO SEXUAL ASSAULT

Traditional Definition of Rape as "Penetration of the Vagina by the Penis"

Legal problem: The statutes of some states expressly define the crime of rape as "penetration of the vagina by the penis." In other states, the crime is more broadly defined as "penetration of the vagina"; but judicial decisions have construed such statutes to include penetration only by the penis. Under such definitions, penetration of the vagina by an instrument, or by a man's or woman's hands, either of which can be as psychologically harmful as forcible penetration by a penis, are excluded from the definition of rape and can be prosecuted only under a general assault statute.

Sterility of the victim is no defense to the crime of rape and the possibility that pregnancy may result is not an element of the crime of forcible rape. Some authors have concluded, therefore, that courts may hold after passage of the Equal Rights Amendment that a definition of forcible rape which excluded penetration of the vagina by something other than a penis was irrational. Because women are capable of assaults with instruments upon other women, it is possible that laws which include only penetration of the vagina by a penis in the definition of the crime of rape will be invalid under an Equal Rights Amendment.

Possible solution: The entire body of criminal law dealing with forcible rape and sexual assault needs thorough review. This problem, like others dealt with here, is one which would be treated in any general revision. The recently enacted sexual assault statutes in Michigan and New Mexico provide examples of ways in which legislatures can revise traditional rape laws, both to correct problems which arise under an Equal Rights Amendment and to improve the fairness of the laws to defendants and victims.

For a discussion of major improvements needed in the traditional law of rape as it is still found in most states, see generally the section on reforms in this chapter below.

References

1. The authors who suggest that a definition of rape which included only penetration of the vagina by the penis might be unconstitutional after passage of the ERA are Brown,

Emerson, Falk and Freedman, in "The Equal Rights Amendment: A Constitutional Basis for Equal Rights for Women," 80 Yale L. J. 871, 905 n. 205 (1971).

2. For Michigan's criminal sexual conduct statute, see Secs. 750.520(a)-750.520(1), MCLA effective April 1, 1975.

3. For New Mexico's Sexual Crimes Act passed by the 1975 New Mexico Legislature, see Laws 1975, Chap. 109, effective July 1, 1975.

Differing Punishments for Crimes of Forcible Rape of a Woman and Forcible Sodomy Performed on a Man

Legal problem: In the law of many states, rape is defined exclusively as the penetration of the vagina of a woman. Rape is usually a first-degree felony, punishable in some states by death, in others by life imprisonment or by ten to fifty years in the penitentiary. Forcible sodomy, on the other hand, which includes penetration of the anus of a man by a penis, is usually a third-degree felony, punishable by two to ten years in the penitentiary. Will the Equal Rights Amendment render these differences in the punishment for forcible rape and forcible sodomy as traditionally defined, unconstitutional?

Possible solutions: The authors of the Yale article on the Equal Rights Amendment argue that courts could uphold traditional rape statutes which punish only the penetration of a vagina on the grounds that such statutes are meant to give special protection to women's vaginas, a "unique physical characteristic" of women, and not to other parts of the anatomy, whether a man's or woman's. Thus, they argue that traditional distinctions in punishment for rape and forcible sodomy can be justified under the "unique physical characteristics" qualification of the Amendment.

The authors cited in reference no. 2, however, believe that the argument that a "unique physical characteristic" validates traditional rape laws can be sustained only because of the possibility of a woman's becoming pregnant. Given the statistically remote chances of pregnancy from a single act of intercourse and the fact that sterility of the victim is no defense to rape, the difference between these statutes cannot be justified. In effect, these laws discriminate against victims of forcible sodomy, a crime against the person which is as traumatic as rape, by not punishing forcible sodomy as severely as rape is punished.

While this conflict in views cannot be resolved here, it might be noted that the trend in recent legislation is toward equalizing the punishment for all similar sexual assaults, regardless of the sexes of the actor and the victim. See for example, the Michigan and New Mexico statutes on sexual assault cited below. If this trend is followed in the revisions of state criminal codes which the Equal Rights Amendment will necessitate, the question raised here will become moot. If the question is not resolved by legislative equalization of the punishments imposed for these crimes, it will undoubtedly be the subject of litigation after passage of the Amendment.

It should be carefully noted, however, that to argue that the Amendment will require forcible rape and forcible sodomy to be punished equally is not to say that all rape laws will be invalidated by the Amendment: it is only a recognition that in this area, as in many others, the Amendment will require thoughtful revision of existing statutes.

References

1. See Brown, Emerson, Falk and Freedman, "The Equal Rights Amendment: A Constitutional Basis for Equal Rights for Women," 80 Yale L. J. 871, 955-961 (1971), for an exposition of their view that the vagina is a "unique physical characteristic" which would justify statutes defining rape as a crime which can only be perpetrated on women.

2. B. Babcock, A. Freedman, E. Norton and S. Ross, in Sex Discrimination and the Law 872 (1975) take issue with the authors of the Yale article on this point.

Statutory Rape of Minor Females and Seduction of Minor Males

Legal problem: Under the law in many states, intercourse with a female under a certain age, sixteen or often eighteen, is punished as "statutory" rape. The law conclusively presumes that minor girls under the established age limit are incapable of giving meaningful consent to intercourse, regardless of their actual consent. Statutory rape is generally punished as a second or third degree felony.

In some states, "seduction" of a minor male by an older woman is either not punished at all, or is punished very lightly. The fact that the male involved may be under sixteen or eighteen either does not, in legal theory, hinder his ability to give meaningful consent to intercourse; or, if it does, his lack of consent is not viewed as creating a serious criminal offense. Quite obviously, such laws are based on the sexual double standard, and will be patently unconstitutional after passage of the Equal Rights Amendment.

These statutes usually have a further defect; they assume that only males have sexual contact with young females, and that only females "seduce" young males. As homosexuality has become more discussed in our society, that assumption has been belied. Thus, such statutes will also be defective under the Equal Rights Amendment because they define the crimes involved in terms of the sex of the actors and victims.

Possible solutions: Again, this subject should be treated in a general revision of sexual assault laws after passage of the Equal Rights Amendment. Four general trends are apparent in those states which have already revised their criminal laws dealing with consensual sexual conduct.

First, these states have made intercourse or other sexual contact with either males or females under an established statutory age, which is the same for both sexes, a criminal act. These statutes have an underlying philosophy which is consonant with the requirements of the Equal Rights Amendment-- that either males or females under a given age are legally incapable of consenting to intercourse or other sexual contact.

Second, these statutes generally punish only intercourse or sexual contact with a child under the statutory age when performed by: (1) a person a given number of years older than the minor; or (2) a person in a position of authority who coerces the child into consenting to the act. In this manner, consensual sexual acts between minors of the same or similar ages, when neither is in a position of authority over the other, have been removed from the purview of criminal law.[5]

---

5. Complaints of statutory rape under present laws are often made by a girl's parents in order to punish her and a boyfriend for their sexual activity. It is only in rare instances that District Attorneys actually prosecute such cases. Therefore, removing this type of activity from the reach of statutory rape statutes will have no appreciable effect on criminal law as it is actually enforced by prosecutors.

However, as stated in the text, where an older person, or one who has authority over a child or youth, engages in sexual activity with him or her, such conduct remains criminal conduct under the recent codes and will be prosecuted. It is this type of case which District Attorneys actually do prosecute under present law.

Third, the age limits which apply to the seduction of minors have been lowered in recognition of the generally increased level of sexual activity in our society. The New Mexico statute, for instance, punishes certain sexual contact with a child under thirteen. For youths between thirteen and sixteen, sexual acts are punished only if the actor-defendant is in a position of authority over the child and used that authority to coerce the youth into consenting to the act. Any person sixteen or older may legally consent to sexual acts; if such consent is given, the act is not the subject of the criminal law.

Finally, because harmful sexual contact with children under a statutorily-established age can be performed by members of the same sex as the child, as well as by members of the opposite sex, these recent revisions punish any sexual contact with children under the statutory age, without regard to the sex of the actor or the child.

These approaches to the problem of the criminal law's treatment of sexual contact with children satisfy the Equal Rights Amendment and, at the same time, provide needed improvement in the law itself. This area, then, offers one more example of the way in which the Equal Rights Amendment can serve as an important and effective instrument for meaningful law reform.

References

1. The New Mexico Sexual Crimes Act, Laws 1975, Chap. 109, Secs. 1(D), 2(A)(1), 2(B)(1) and 4, effective July 1, 1975.

2. For Michigan's approach to seduction of children, see MCLA Secs. 750.520(a) and (b); and 750.520d(a) et seq., effective April 1, 1975.

3. The Model Penal Code, drafted by the American Law Institute, establishes ten years of age as the age of consent for intercourse, which is much lower than that in most states today. See B. Babcock, A. Freedman, E. Norton and S. Ross, Sex Discrimination and the Law 822 (1975).

Major Reforms Which Are Desirable in the Traditional Law of Rape

Beyond the specific areas discussed above which may or will violate the Equal Rights Amendment, critics of the traditional law of rape have agreed upon several major reforms which should be widely implemented. These reforms would offer needed protection to rape victims and make rape convictions easier to obtain. Hopefully the result would be a decrease in the rising incidence of that crime. Each of the areas in which change has been suggested is set forth briefly below.

The Corroboration Requirement

Legal problem: Due to the nature of the act of rape, performed out of the sight and hearing of witnesses, and the fear that women will falsify rape charges unless stringent proof requirements are placed upon the prosecution, many states have, by statute or judicial decision, required "corroboration," or proof in addition to the victim's testimony, of the essential elements of a charge of rape. The elements usually required to be corroborated by circumstantial evidence or by testimony from someone other than the victim are: (1) the identity of the defendant; (2) the fact of penetration; and (3) the use of force to accomplish the act of penetration.

Because forcible rape is, by definition in most states, a crime committed only against women, the corroboration requirement is in effect sex-discriminatory. Rather than leaving the question of credibility of the victim to the jury, it assumes that: (1) the victim may be, or is, lying; and (2) a jury will convict unless it is prevented from doing so by a judicial rule which requires outside proof of the victim's testimony. Where strictly applied, the corroboration requirement has discouraged prosecutors from prosecuting many rape cases and has prevented convictions in many cases actually brought to trial. In New York State, where absurdly strict corroboration requirements were judicially imposed until legislation reversed those rules, only eighteen rape convictions were obtained in a recent year, despite thousands of complaints.

Possible solutions: Some have noted that the harshness of the corroboration requirement is mitigated by the relaxation of the rule against hearsay evidence which usually accompanies it. Thus, police officers are allowed to testify to what the victim said when she reported the rape, and this testimony, although hearsay, will be allowed to corroborate the victim's testimony at trial. Others, however, believe that relaxation of the hearsay rule alone is not enough to warrant retention of the corroboration requirement, citing both the experience in New York State and the literally hundreds of rape convictions in other states which have been reversed on appeal because of a lack of sufficient corroboration of the victim's testimony.

The most advanced view advocates abolition of the corroboration requirement as a special rule which applies only to rape cases. Were this approach taken, convictions for rape, just like any other criminal conviction, could be overturned on appeal, or jury verdicts set aside by judges, where a reviewing court believed that the evidence presented at trial did not support the verdict.

Others believe that the major problem with the corroboration requirement lies in its application to all rapes, without regard to whether the victim and the defendant had known each other before or to the circumstances of the act itself. These authors, cited in reference no. 1 below, have suggested that if the corroboration requirement is retained at all, it should be strictly limited to situations in which the victim and defendant had been acquainted previously. They would also require that a statute detail the types of evidence which will satisfy the requirement.

Given the rising numbers of rapes and increased concern over the seriousness of the crime, the corroboration requirement deserves serious study and revision by state legislatures.

References

1. B. Babcock, A. Freedman, E. Norton and S. Ross, Sex Discrimination and the Law 843-863 (1975).

2. Note, "The Rape Corroboration Requirement: Repeal Not Reform," 81 Yale L. J. 1365 (1972).

3. Hiby, "The Trial of a Rape Case: An Advocate's Analysis of Corroboration, Consent and Character," 11 Am. Crim. L. Rev. 309, 310-321 (1973).

4. Note, "Corroborating Charges of Rape," 67 Col. L. Rev. 1137 (1967).

5. New Mexico Laws 1975, Ch. 109, Sec. 6, effective July 1, 1975.

6. MCLA Sec. 750.520(h).

Penalty Imposed for Rape

Legal problem: In 1970, sixteen jurisdictions in the United States allowed a sentencing court in its discretion to impose the death penalty for persons convicted of rape. As a result of the Supreme Court's decision in Furman v. Georgia,

408 U.S. 238 (1972), concerning the constitutionality of the death penalty, many of the statutes in those states now impose a mandatory death penalty in rape cases. The constitutionalty of imposing death for any crime will shortly be decided by the U.S. Supreme Court under the eighth amendment's prohibition of cruel and unusual punishment; see also the articles cited in reference no. 1 below for arguments concerning the constitutionality of the death penalty in rape cases.

Even if the death penalty is declared unconstitutional, rape will still be punished in most states as severely as first or second degree murder. Thus, in the majority of U.S. jurisdictions, a person convicted of rape, virtually certain to be a man under present statutes, may receive a sentence of either life imprisonment or ten to fifty years in the penitentiary. Some have argued that imposition of such a severe penalty on one sex alone may violate the Equal Rights Amendment. Even if it does not, most informed observers believe that these harsh penalties have actually hindered the prosecution of rape cases by making juries less willing to convict except under the most extreme and aggravated circumstances. In any general revision of rape laws pursuant to an Equal Rights Amendment, the question of the penalties imposed for rape and other forcible sexual assaults deserves serious reconsideration.

Possible solutions: Many believe that the penalty for rape must be lowered to the penalties imposed for other physical assaults. Such a step might actually increase convictions for rape, with a possible concomitant decrease in the crime itself.

In Michigan's recent revision of its rape statute, the punishment uniformly imposed for all sexual assaults is two to ten years in the state penitentiary. Where the circumstances of the crime involved violence or the use of a deadly weapon, a prosecutor may charge the defendant with these offenses as well, thereby possibly increasing the sentence to be imposed. Such an approach seems eminently more sensible than imposition of a uniform ten to fifty year penalty for all rapes. Further, most commentators believe that when juries realize that convictions for rape do not automatically mean imposition of the severe penalties imposed in the past, they will convict in less serious circumstances than they are presently willing to do.

In any event, it is generally recognized that the very harsh punishment for rape does not always fit the particular crime committed and may therefore hinder convictions. For these reasons, most believe that more convictions for rape will be obtained if penalties are lowered.

References

1. For law review articles concerning the constitutionality of the death penalty in rape cases, see:

    a. Note, "Constitutionality of the Death Penalty for
Non-aggravated Rape," 1972 Wash. U. L. Q. 170 (1972);

    b. Note, "Eighth Amendment Prohibition Against
Cruel and Unusual Punishment Forbids Execution When the Victim's
Life was Neither Taken nor Endangered," 40 U. Cinn. L. Rev.
396 (1971); and

    c. Note, "Capital Punishment for Rapes Constitutes
Cruel and Unusual Punishment When No Life is Taken or
Endangered," 56 Minn. L. Rev. 95 (1971).

2. For a discussion of rape penalties and an argument
that they be lowered, see B. Babcock, A. Freedman, E. Norton
and S. Ross, Sex Discrimination and the Law 869-75 (1975).

3. For Michigan's penalty section in its new sexual
assault statute, see MCLA Secs. 750.520(b)-520(g), effective
April 1, 1975.

Use of the Victim's Prior Sexual History at Trial

Legal problem: One of the elements which the prosecution
must prove in a rape case is the threat of the use of force by
the defendant to accomplish intercourse. To rebut, the
defense often attempts to prove that the victim consented and
that force was therefore neither necessary nor used to
accomplish the act. Because of the general suspicion with
which rape charges have traditionally been viewed, a rule of
evidence developed which is now uniformly applied throughout
the United States. That rule allows the defense to present
evidence concerning the victim's acts of intercourse with men
other than the defendant, or concerning her general reputation
in the community with regard to her sexual conduct, or both.
Such evidence, some think, is relevant to the question of
whether the victim in fact consented to the act which she
alleges to have been forcible rape. This infamous rule of
evidence serves as an extremely effective deterrent to victims'
complaints of rape: cross-examination in public about every
aspect of one's sexual life is not an appealing prospect to
anyone. Thus, it is generally agreed that in order to increase
convictions for rape, some revision of this evidentiary rule
is urgently needed.

94

Possible solutions: Logically, testimony about a victim's prior acts of intercourse with persons other than the defendant should be excluded under present rules of evidence. Consent to intercourse with one person does not raise an inference that the victim would therefore consent to intercourse with any person, regardless of whether she had seen him before or not. Thus, it could be argued that all evidence of sexual activity with persons other than the defendant should be excluded because it is logically irrelevant and does not tend to show consent to the act charged. However, motions to exclude evidence are rarely prepared by prosecutor's offices, and it is not likely that this solution--although already at hand in the law--will be widely applied. Another problem, of course, is that judges who are accustomed to admitting such testimony in rape cases would have to re-think the grounds for admission, a practice which might take years of appellate court decisions to induce.

The route to reform suggested by most, then, is statutory revision. Because specific acts of intercourse with the defendant prior to the alleged rape may be relevant and admissible, what has been suggested, and adopted in California, Florida, Iowa, Michigan and New Mexico is a procedure for in camera examination by a trial judge prior to admitting any evidence of the victim's prior sexual conduct to the jury. Under this procedure, if the defense wishes to introduce evidence of the victim's prior sexual conduct, then the defense attorney, prosecutor and judge must confer in judge's chambers. The defense will state the nature of the evidence to be introduced and why it is relevant to the issue of consent and the prosecution will make counter-arguments. The judge will then issue a written order ruling on the admissibility of the proposed evidence. If the defense is allowed to introduce it, only evidence which is specifically approved in the court's order may be put in evidence.

This in camera examination procedure is an attempt to recognize the legitimate needs of defendants accused of rape while preserving the victim's right to privacy. Because this procedure strikes a fair balance between the interests of both sides, it deserves wide-spread study and adoption in any general revision of rape statutes after passage of the ERA.

References

1. Note, "Forcible and Statutory Rape: Exploration of the Consent Standard," 62 Yale L. J. 55 (1952).

2. Landau, "Rape: The Victim as Defendant," 10 Trial 19 (1974).

3. Note, "Evidence--Admissibility--In a Trial for Rape, Prosecutrix May Not Be Cross-Examined as to Specific Acts of Prior Sexual Conduct with Men Other than Defendant, Whether the Purpose of Such Cross-Examination Is to Establish Her Consent or to Impeach Her Credibility as a Witness," 8 Ga. L. Rev. 973 (1974).

4. Note, "The Victim in a Forcible Rape Case: A Feminist View," 11 Am. Crim. L. Rev. 335 (1973).

5. For a general review of case law, evidentiary standards, and suggestions for reform, including a reprint of an ACLU Memorandum concerning the in camera examination procedure, see B. Babcock, A. Freedman, E. Norton and S. Ross, Sex Discrimination and the Law 829-843 (1975).

6. See California Evidence Code, Sec. 782, 1975 Supp. (West 1973), for California's in camera examination procedure.

7. Florida's in camera examination procedure is found in Fla. Stat., 1974 Supp., Sec. 794.022.

8. Iowa adopted an in camera examination procedure without making any other substantial changes in its rape statutes. See Code of Iowa 1975 (Vol. 2), Sec. 782.4.

9. Michigan's in camera examination procedure is contained in MCLA Sec. 750.520(j), effective April 1, 1975.

10. New Mexico's recent adoption of in camera examination is contained in Laws 1975, Chap. 109, Sec. 7, effective July 1, 1975.

Impossibility of Rape Between Married Persons

Legal problem: In most U.S. jurisdictions, a wife cannot complain of being raped by her husband. The theories underlying this rule seem to be both that sexual intercourse is a privilege of marriage and that allowing such complaints would encourage wives to swear out false complaints of rape by their husbands.

In a recent decision, the highest court in Israel held that that country's Equal Rights Amendment rendered unconstitutional a similar rule. The Court said that the marriage contract could not change the right of any person to choose not to consent to sexual intercourse, and that prohibiting such complaints by law unconstitutionally discriminated against married women.

While it is not clear that the Equal Rights Amendment in the United States would receive a similar interpretation, it has been suggested that if the present law in effect in most of the United States were abolished, prosecutors would take the fact of marriage into account before deciding to bring such a case, and that the marriage of the victim and the defendant would receive full consideration by any jury which sat on such a case. Thus, many believe that prohibition of such actions by a rule of law works an unwarranted injustice in many cases.

Possible solutions: Husbands and wives are allowed to swear out complaints against each other for other forms of physical abuse--beating, striking and the like. Since prosecutors and juries have been able to screen out the fraudulent cases in those areas, it is not immediately apparent why the fact that a sexual assault, rather than some other form of physical assault, is involved should justify the total exclusion of such complaints from the criminal process. In any general revision of the rape statutes, the reasons for, and wisdom of, retaining the traditional immunity of husbands from charges of rape of their wives should be reviewed.

References

1. For a citation to the Israel court decision under its Equal Rights Amendment, see "The ERA: A Symposium," 3 Human Rts. L. Rev. 125 at 137 (1973).

2. The Model Penal Code, in final Proposed Official Draft form in 1962, exempts husbands and wives from the definition of rape, thus maintaining the traditional rule. See Model Penal Code Sec. 213.4 (Proposed Official Draft, 1962).

3. The recently enacted New Mexico Sexual Crimes Act does not include in the definition of "spouse" a couple who are living apart or either a husband or wife who has filed for separate maintenance or divorce. See Laws 1975, Ch. 109, Sec. 1(E), effective July 1, 1975. Thus, New Mexico has in effect repealed the husband's traditional immunity from his wife's complaint of rape in these instances.

4. The Michigan criminal sexual conduct statute is identical in effect to that recently enacted in New Mexico. See MCLA Sec. 750.520(1), effective April 1, 1975.

Judge's Instruction to Jury in Rape Cases

Legal problem: Since at least 1680 in England, it has

been customary for judges in rape cases to give the following
instruction to the jury before it retires to consider the
evidence and come to a verdict:

> A charge such as that made against the
> defendant in this case is one which is easily made
> and once made, difficult to defend against, even if
> the person accused is innocent. <u>Therefore, the law
> requires that you examine the testimony of the
> female person named in the Information with
> caution.</u> (emphasis added)

This instruction provides yet another example of the
suspicion with which the criminal law views complaints of rape
and rape victims. However, given the demonstrated reluctance
of juries to convict in many rape cases, perpetuation of this
charge, now approaching its 300th birthday, seems unwarranted.
It is possible to argue that because most rape complainants
are women, such a jury charge is a rule "neutral on its face,
but discriminatory in impact," which will arguably be
unconstitutional under the Equal Rights Amendment.

Possible solutions: Although it is impossible to
discover exactly what effect the charge has on juries, any
general revision of rape statutes should specifically prohibit
this special instruction.

References

1. The quotation of the charge cited herein was taken
from B. Babcock, A. Freedman, E. Norton and S. Ross, <u>Sex
Discrimination and the Law</u> 853 (1975).

2. For a massive study of juries' reactions to rape
cases and their reluctance to convict in many circumstances,
see H. Kalven and H. Zeisel, <u>The American Jury</u> 249 <u>et seq.</u>
(1966). The study indicates that in reaching verdicts juries
take into account such factors as "assumption of risk" by the
victim; the victim's seeming encouragement of the defendant
(such as drinking with him and then going out with him); and
the amount of prior sexual experience of the victim. Where
such factors are present, juries are much less likely to
convict than where they are not. Thus, it seems clear that
juries consider the circumstances in which a rape took place
very carefully, and thereby effectively--perhaps too effectively under present laws--screen out questionable complaints of
rape.

General References to Articles Concerning Revision of Sexual Assault Statutes

In addition to the references and statutes cited in the discussions of specific problems above, the following works may be useful.

1. Note, "Sex Offenses and the Penal Code Revision in Michigan," 14 Wayne St. L. Rev. 934 (1968).

2. Note, "Rape and Rape Laws: Sexism in Society and Law," 61 Calif. L. Rev. 919 (1973).

3. Chappell, Geis and Fogarty, "Forcible Rape: A Bibliography," 65 J. Crim. L. 248 (1974).

4. Penland, "History of Rape Laws," Smith, "Rape Prosecutions," and Aitken, "Cultural Context of Rape," in 60 Women Law J. 176 (1972).

5. Derr, "Criminal Justice: A Crime Against Women," 9 Trial 24 (1973).

6. Note, "The Resistance Standard in Rape Legislation," 18 Stan. L. Rev. 680 (1966).

7. For Washington's 1974 revision of its rape statutes, see R.C.W.A. Sec. 9.79.010 (1974).

8. Florida has adopted a "sexual battery" provision, which may be found in Fla. Stat., 1974 Supp., Sec. 794.011.

SEX-DISCRIMINATORY ASPECTS OF STATE STATUTES AND CITY ORDINANCES RELATING TO PROSTITUTION

Introduction

There is a growing movement in the United States to "decriminalize" prostitution. Much of the legal attack has centered on the sex-discriminatory aspects of present statutes and ordinances regulating prostitution. The following three sections will discuss areas in which present prostitution laws will or may be unconstitutional after passage of the Equal Rights Amendment and will suggest means by which such statutes could be constitutionally drafted or enforced.

The decision on the basic question, however--whether prostitution should be the subject of any criminal law--is well beyond the scope of this Commentary. For purposes here, it has been assumed that most jurisdictions will choose to retain some form of regulation of prostitution after passage of the Equal Rights Amendment.

Beyond the question of whether prostitution should be a criminal offense at all, it should be noted that this area of criminal law is unusual in that many local ordinances, as well as statutes of state-wide application, govern prostitution. Thus, municipal ordinances relating to the use of rooming houses, massage parlors, escort agencies and lessors of rooms in apartments or hotels are often the vehicles used to enforce prohibitions against prostitution. To ensure that local ordinances are constitutional and to avoid much duplication of effort, a model prostitution ordinance should be drafted which conforms to the Equal Rights Amendment and can be easily adopted by municipalities across the United States.

The remainder of this part discusses the substantive areas in which amendment of present prostitution laws should be considered.

References

1. For a complete discussion of all possible constitutional attacks on prostitution statutes available under present law, see Rosenbleet and Pariente, "Prostitution of the Criminal Law," 11 Am. Crim. L. Rev. 373 (1973).

2. For an exposition of the view that prostitution should not be the subject of the criminal law in any manner, see Note, "The Principle of Harm and Its Application to Laws Criminalizing Prostitution," 51 Denver L. J. 235 (1974).

3. Roby, "Politics and Prostitution," 9 Criminology 425 (1972).

4. Note, "Criminal Code--Bill of Rights--Whether Offense of Vagrancy by Common Prostitute Constitutes Discrimination by Sex," 6 U.B.C. L. Rev. 442 (1971).

5. S. Ross, in The Rights of Women 176-179 (1973), argues strongly that as long as male patrons are not criminally punished for sexual activity, female prostitutes should not be subject to the criminal laws.

Statutes Which Punish Only Prostitution by Females

Legal problem: Although the majority of jurisdictions in the United States punish male and female prostitutes equally, some statutes punish only prostitution performed by females. Male prostitution can be reached under general sodomy statutes in these jurisdictions. However, female prostitution is usually subject to a higher penalty than is imposed under sodomy statutes. Also, female prostitutes may be charged under both prostitution statutes and fornication statutes. Therefore, there is little doubt that statutes which punish only female prostitutes will be unconstitutional after passage of an Equal Rights Amendment.

Possible solution: Prostitution statutes which apply only to female prostitutes should be extended to cover both male and female prostitutes. Many state statutes, as well as the Model Penal Code, are already written in sex-neutral terms, and provide ready models for those states in which revision is needed.

References

1. See Rosenbleet and Pariente, "Prostitution of the Criminal Law," 11 Am. Crim. L. Rev. 373, 422 et seq., (1973) for a table listing citations to the prostitution statutes of every state, with notations as to the precise coverage of each statute; whether it includes both male and female prostitutes; whether patrons are punished; and the penalties provided.

2. Brown, Emerson, Falk and Freedman, "The Equal Rights Amendment: A Constitutional Basis for Equal Rights for Women," 80 Yale L. J. 871, 962-963 (1971).

3. The Model Penal Code, Sec. 251.2 (Proposed Official Draft, 1962) provides an example of a sex-neutral prostitution statute.

Unequal Enforcement of Prostitution Statutes Which Punish Male and Female Prostitutes Equally

Legal problem: Although most state statutes regulating prostitution are "neutral on their face"--that is, they punish prostitutes of either sex equally--most are enforced almost exclusively against female prostitutes. State or city

enforcement of prostitution statutes or ordinances constitutes
the state action which the Equal Rights Amendment will reach.
Official discrimination in the enforcement of neutral laws
will unquestionably violate the Amendment.

Possible solutions: The Superior Court of the District
of Columbia held in United States v. Moses (1972), cited in
reference no. 1 below, that enforcement of a neutral prostitution statute in the District of Columbia only against female
prostitutes violated both due process and equal protection.
In an excellent opinion, the court held that the statute, so
enforced, was unconstitutional.

This precedent provides ready support for defense
attorneys who may argue convincingly that sex-neutral prostitution statutes which are enforced primarily or exclusively
against female prostitutes are unconstitutional, both today,
under the equal protection and due process clauses, and under
the Equal Rights Amendment after its passage.

To avoid this result, police departments must make every
effort to enforce neutral statutes equally against prostitutes
of both sexes. This does not mean that as many male prostitutes
must be arrested as female prostitutes. It does mean, however,
that the approximate ratio of the percentages of arrests and
prosecutions for prostitutes of both sexes must be similar.

References

1. U.S. v. Moses, 41 U.S.L.W. 2298 (D.C. Super. Ct.
November 3, 1972), cited in K. Davidson, R. Ginsburg and H. Kay,
Sex-based Discrimination 908 (1974). The opinion is well worth
reading for those interested in this subject.

2. Derr, "Criminal Justice: A Crime Against Women?,"
9 Trial 24 (1973).

Statutes Which Do Not Punish Patrons or Punish Them Less
Severely than Prostitutes

Legal problem: As the table of state statutes contained
in the work cited in reference no. 1 below demonstrates, very
few state statutes provide any punishment at all for patrons
of prostitutes. Of those which do punish patrons, the common
pattern is for the punishment to be much less severe than the
same statute provides for prostitutes themselves. Further,
these statutes are much less commonly enforced.

Because the majority of prostitutes in the United States are women and the majority of patrons of prostitutes are men, state statutes which punish only prostitutes and not their patrons are "neutral on their face, but discriminatory in impact" because they bear much more heavily on one sex than upon the other. The authors of the Yale article on the Equal Rights Amendment believe that such laws will probably be unconstitutional after passage of the Equal Rights Amendment.

The counter-argument is found in the analogy of prostitute-patron statutes to laws in other areas which only punish the seller of illegal goods or service or punish the seller much more heavily than the buyer of such goods or services. Examples of such statutes are narcotics and gambling laws.

Possible solutions: Regardless of the outcome of court tests under the Equal Rights Amendment, the trend of recent legislation has been to penalize patrons equally with prostitutes. If states and municipalities are serious about deterring prostitution, punishment of patrons by statute, and equal enforcement of such statutes, is a much more effective way to achieve that goal than punishment of prostitutes alone.

References

1. Rosenbleet and Pariente, "Prostitution of the Criminal Law," 11 Am. Crim. L. Rev. 373, 422 et seq. (1973), sets forth citations to the prostitution statutes of every state, with a note as to whether patrons are penalized and if so, what penalties are provided for them.

2. Brown, Emerson, Falk and Freedman, "The Equal Rights Amendment: A Constitutional Basis for Equal Rights for Women," 80 Yale L. J. 871, 963-964 (1971).

3. K. Davidson, R. Ginsburg and H. Kay, Sex-based Discrimination 910 (1974).

4. B. Babcock, A. Freedman, E. Norton and S. Ross, in Sex Discrimination and the Law 905 (1974), note that New York's 1967 prostitution statute, which punishes patrons equally with prostitutes, is very unevenly enforced. Of all prostitution-related arrests, less than one percent are of patrons. Such unequal enforcement of equal laws will violate the Amendment. See the discussion of unequal enforcement of male-female prostitution laws above and the references contained there.

Miscellaneous Laws Relating to Prostitution Which Will Be Unconstitutional after Passage of the ERA.

Statutes governing pimping and pandering are often limited in their terms to males, because it has been customary in the past for males to perform those roles. Statutes so limited will unquestionably be unconstitutional under an Equal Rights Amendment, and should be re-drafted in sex-neutral terms.

Another form of prostitution statute commonly written to apply only to women are "solicitation" statutes, which prohibit women from "soliciting" men to have sexual intercourse for hire. These statutes also, of course, must be drafted in sex-neutral terms after passage of the ERA.

Methods of Dealing with Prostitution

Prostitution has been criminalized for many years with little noticeable deterrent effect. It seems likely, therefore, that if the problem is to be dealt with effectively, society will have to come up with other means of discouraging the practice.

Harassment Arrests

Police in many cities today routinely arrest and book women whom they believe to be prostitutes without ever formally charging them or bringing them to trial. In many cases, arrests are made under city ordinances against loitering. While such arrests represent local police departments' attempts to deal with and discourage prostitution, they are patently illegal and should be discontinued.

Reference

See B. Babcock, A. Freedman, E. Norton and S. Ross, Sex Discrimination and the Law 880-882 (1975) for a description of harassment arrests.

"Halfway Houses" for Prostitutes

In an attempt to devise a constructive means of dealing with prostitution, one author has suggested that sentences for prostitution be raised from ten or fifteen days to ninety days in a "halfway house" which will attempt to rehabilitate the prostitute and change her mode of living, rather than simply incarcerate her temporarily. While such an approach may not seem ideal, it is at least an attempt to deal constructively with the problem of prostitution. As such, it deserves further attention.

Reference

See Lindsay, "Prostitution--Delinquency's Time Bomb," 16 Crime and Delinq. 151, 153-156 (1970), reproduced in part in B. Babcock, A. Freedman, E. Norton and S. Ross, Sex Discrimination and the Law 900 (1975) where this suggestion is made.

MISCELLANEOUS CRIMINAL STATUTES WHICH WILL
VIOLATE THE EQUAL RIGHTS AMENDMENT

Laws Relating to Sexual Behavior

Legal problem: Many criminal laws of infrequent application punish sexual behavior. Because these laws are not found in every state, the list included here is intended only to illustrate the types of uncommon but sex-discriminatory statutes which must either be repealed or extended to both sexes after passage of the Equal Rights Amendment.

Seduction

This crime, in the few states where it is still found, prohibits a male upon the promise of marriage from having intercourse with a chaste female. The mores of modern society dictate repeal of seduction statutes.

Retribution

In a very few states, statutory or case law expressly allows a husband to murder his wife's lover if he finds them in the act of intercourse. Obviously, repeal, rather than extension of such a privilege to both sexes, is indicated here.

Obscenity

In some states, males who use obscenity in the presence of females are liable for criminal punishment. In light of the United States Supreme Court's problems with defining "obscenity" in other contexts and the infrequent application of such statutes, repeal seems the wiser course here also.

Destruction of a Woman's Reputation

In a very few states, males can be criminally punished for making false statements which harm a woman's reputation for chastity or moral sexual behavior. In view of any person's civil remedy for slander, repeal would seem to be the proper course here too.

Abduction

Some thirty-one states have statutes which prohibit the forcible "taking" of a female for marriage or prostitution. Such statutes are apparently based on the "White Slave" theory of the Mann Act. They, too, should probably be repealed, since general kidnapping statutes in effect in every state already punish such acts.

Sodomy

In states where sodomy statutes apply only to males, they will be unconstitutional after passage of the Equal Rights Amendment. Such statutes are unusual, however; most sodomy statutes are drafted in sex-neutral terms.

Adultery

In those states in which adultery is defined only as "intercourse with another man's wife," the statutes must either be repealed or extended to both sexes.

106

References

1. For a complete listing of the states in which the first five types of statutes listed here are found, see Note, "Sex Discrimination in the Criminal Law: The Effect of the Equal Rights Amendment," 11 Am. Crim. L. Rev. 469 et seq. (1973).

2. For a discussion of the unconstitutionality of sodomy and adultery statutes which apply to only one sex, see Brown, Emerson, Falk and Freedman, "The Equal Rights Amendment: A Constitutional Basis for Equal Rights for Women," 80 Yale L. J. 871, 961 (1971).

Laws Relating to Criminal Conduct by Husbands and Wives Jointly

Conspiracy

Under the common law doctrine which views husband and wife legally as one person, an astute defense attorney for a husband and wife accused of conspiracy once convinced an American court to accept the theory that husbands and wives could not be convicted of conspiracy where they had acted jointly. One state, Hawaii, has expressly written this rule into its criminal code.

Although the doctrine applies by its terms equally to husbands and wives, it is based on a concept which the spirit, if not the letter, of the Equal Rights Amendment rejects. Each person should be responsible for his or her own criminal acts, regardless of the identity of any other person with whom the crime was committed.

Doctrine of "Presumed Coercion"

In a few states, by statute or judicial decision, a wife who commits a crime may raise the defense of "presumed coercion" where her husband was involved in the same crime. The doctrine "presumes" that married women are under the control of their husbands and are thus not responsible for criminal acts they commit.

Obviously, the Equal Rights Amendment will invalidate this common law doctrine in the few places where it persists.

References

1. Note, "Sex Discrimination in the Criminal Law: The Effect of the Equal Rights Amendment," 11 <u>Am. Crim. L. Rev.</u> 469, 489-491 (1973).

2. Note, "Coverture in Criminal Law: Ancient 'Defender' of Married Women," 6 <u>U.C.D. L. Rev.</u> 83 (1973).

Chapter Three

EDUCATION

Table of Contents

110

INTRODUCTION

The passage of the Equal Rights Amendment will affect every aspect of our lives. Perhaps the most far-reaching, long-term effects will be its changes in the area of education. Second only to one's family and immediate community, the classroom provides training in necessary skills and lays the basis for our attitudes towards ourselves and others. To date, these attitudes have included sex-based stereotypes; the limited training and skills available to girls and women at every level of education has relegated them to a second-class status in this society. Education is not a cure-all, as the history of racial integration has shown; but it is a critical component of any serious effort to overturn the sex-discriminatory pillars upon which our social, political and economic institutions have been built.[1]

Because public schools are agencies of state government, there is no question that the Equal Rights Amendment will apply to them. An issue not so easily resolved and which will probably be the subject of litigation once the ERA is passed concerns the application of the Amendment to private educational institutions. The next section discusses the dimensions of this problem. The general consensus to date is that the ERA will probably not be enforced against them. Some commentators believe, however, that other indirect pressures, such as the loss of government financial assistance, may force even private schools into substantial compliance with the Amendment.

Title IX, a 1972 educational amendment to the federal Civil Rights Act, prohibits sex discrimination in educational programs and activities which receive financial assistance from the federal government. Title IX provides, in pertinent part:

> No person in the United States shall, on the basis of sex, be excluded from participation in, be denied the benefits of, or be subjected to discrimination under any program or activity receiving Federal financial assistance.[2]

---

1. See Note, "Teaching Woman Her Place: The Role of Public Education in the Development of Sex Roles," 24 Hastings L. J. 1191 (1973).

2. 20 U.S.C. Secs. 1681 et seq. For discussion of Title IX, see "Title IX of the 1972 Education Amendments: Preventing Sex Discrimination in Public Schools," 53 Tex. L. Rev. 103 (1974).

Title IX covers most of the public institutions to which the Equal Rights Amendment will apply and many private institutions as well; however, the Act does contain several important exceptions from its coverage of admissions policies of single-sex schools. These exceptions are discussed in the section on admissions policies below.

The regulations which put the broad prohibitions of Title IX into practice are noted throughout this chapter in order to indicate the kinds of solutions which have already been undertaken in this area. It should be recognized, however, that the regulations proposed for Title IX are often much less stringent than the requirements which the Equal Rights Amendment will impose on public schools.[3]

All facets of public schools' operations will be affected by the Equal Rights Amendment. Some of the major activities considered here include athletics, curriculum, admissions, employment, extra-curricular activities and facilities.

The concluding discussion in this chapter pertains to educational policies and programs which are not legally required by the Amendment, but which would help to implement its underlying philosophy of genuine equality of the sexes. In a sense, these might be designated as affirmative action proposals. Suggestions in this area include, among others: day-care centers at all colleges and universities; the exclusion of textbooks which contain sex-role stereotyping; and part-time teaching jobs for all teachers, male or female, who bear major responsibility for rearing children.

EDUCATIONAL INSTITUTIONS TO WHICH THE EQUAL RIGHTS AMENDMENT WILL APPLY

Legal problem: It is well settled that the Equal Rights Amendment, like the fourteenth amendment, will apply to all state and federal agencies. Thus, public schools of every kind will be covered by and subject to the requirements of the Amendment. Specific questions in various areas of education which will arise under the Amendment are the subjects of the bulk of this Commentary.

It has also been acknowledged that the Amendment will apply to those private educational institutions whose activities are found by the courts to come within the concept of state

---

3. These regulations are found in 39 Fed. Reg. 22232-22240 and 25667 (1974), as amended in 40 Fed. Reg. 24128-24145 (1975).

action. What is not yet clear is precisely which private institutions the state action doctrine will encompass under the Equal Rights Amendment.[4]

Many of the nation's most prestigious schools are private, sex-segregated institutions or, if not segregated, they have sex-restricted admissions policies. While there are prestigious schools which discriminate in favor of women, on the whole it is women who suffer because of sex discrimination by private educational institutions. Therefore, the failure to apply the Equal Rights Amendment to such institutions will have an important impact on women's educational opportunities in the United States.

There is presently a wide divergence of views on the desirability of maintaining sex-segregated educational institutions. The Carnegie Commission is the most famous of those who oppose the sexual integration of all educational institutions in the country. They believe that women benefit from the opportunity to attend schools in which there are only women; they argue that women feel freer to compete and develop academically in an environment without male competitors.[5] Other leading commentators, however, believe that sex-segregated, private educational institutions are part and parcel of an entire social system which discriminates against women in various ways. They argue that such institutions are "likely to be a witting or unwitting device for preserving tacit assumptions of male superiority--assumptions for which women must eventually pay."[6]

The difference of opinion on this subject, however, is not likely to deter those who believe that private educational institutions which now discriminate on the basis of sex in their admissions policies should sexually integrate. Thus, after the effective date of the Amendment, litigation attempting to place these institutions under the Equal Rights Amendment is virtually certain to ensue.

---

4. See chapter on the Equal Rights Amendment and the Constitution, above, for an explanation of the state action concept under the fourteenth amendment and the Equal Rights Amendment.

5. See the Report of the Carnegie Commission on Higher Education, Opportunities for Women in Higher Education: Their Current Participation, Prospects for the Future, and Recommendations for Action (1973).

6. C. Jencks and D. Reisman, The Academic Revolution 297-298 (1968).

What are the possible results of such litigation?

Possible solutions: At the outset, it is not known whether
case law developed under the fourteenth amendment will automatically apply to determine the contours of the state action doctrine
for purposes of the Equal Rights Amendment. The fourteenth
amendment cases to date, however, have uniformly held that the
receipt of substantial government funds and tax exemptions does
not so significantly involve the state in the activities of these
private institutions as to subject them to the requirements which
the fourteenth amendment imposes on state institutions. A
series of restrictive state cases under the fourteenth amendment
began with the decision in Powe v. Miles, 294 F. Supp. 1269
(W.D.N.Y. 1966) modified, 407 F. 2d 73 (2d Cir. 1968), which
has carried great weight in subsequent litigation. As a result,
no private educational institution, no matter how large or what
amount of federal or state funding it receives, has yet been held
to the requirements of the fourteenth amendment. See reference
no. 1, below, for the major cases in which the courts have
refused to find state action in this area.

If these precedents are followed under an Equal Rights
Amendment, it seems very likely the courts will refuse to hold
that private educational institutions, regardless of the amount
of funding received, are involved in state action so as to
subject those institutions to the requirements of the Equal Rights
Amendment.

In the article cited at reference no. 6 below, Professor
Gallagher suggests another possible approach which would have the
effect of imposing the Equal Rights Amendment on private, sex-
discriminatory educational institutions, but would avoid the
difficulties of case-by-case litigation under the state action
doctrine. Analogizing to a line of fourteenth amendment cases,
she argues that while such institutions will not constitute
state action for purposes of the Equal Rights Amendment, the
Amendment may very well render them ineligible for government
subsidies, tax exempt status or financial assistance for their
students. In the fourteenth amendment cases, cited in reference
no. 7 below, lower courts have held that while private institutions may choose to discriminate on the basis of race, the state
and federal governments may not aid their racial discrimination
by giving them grants, tax exemptions or other financial aids.
Gallagher argues that if these fourteenth amendment cases are
applied under the Equal Rights Amendment, the threat of the loss
of important government subsidies—in the form of outright
grants, tax exemptions and student loans—will cause these
private institutions to choose a policy of sexual integration.

Thus, although the traditional state action cases in the field of education may not render private, sex-discriminatory educational institutions subject to the Equal Rights Amendment, it is possible that the line of cases withholding government support from racially discriminatory institutions may in the end lead to the same practical result--the sexual integration of all major educational institutions in the United States.

One further possibility for ending sex discrimination by private educational institutions would be for Congress to expand the prohibitions of Title IX. As enacted in 1972, the Act prohibited sex discrimination in educational programs and activities which receive federal funds. Expressly exempted from the Act's coverage, however, are the admissions policies of several major types of institutions. Thus, for example, Title IX does not affect the sex-discriminatory admissions policies of private undergraduate institutions. Because serious consideration was given by Congress in 1972 to include these institutions in the coverage of Title IX, however, and because of the lessening resistance to integration by sex of leading private schools, it is possible that within a relatively short time, Title IX could be expanded to include these institutions.

It should be noted that presently the power to enforce Title IX is solely reserved to federal agencies; no private suits to enforce the Act may be brought. Thus, while expansion of the coverage of Title IX would be desirable, thought should also be given to improving the Act's enforcement mechanisms and remedies.

Under the Gallagher approach described above, any private litigant who had been injured by sex discrimination practiced by a private institution receiving government funds could sue to enjoin the government from continuing to support such sex discrimination with subsidies. Thus, the passage of the Equal Rights Amendment will immensely enlarge the class of persons who may, under the Gallagher approach, challenge sex discrimination by private institutions receiving government subsidies.

References

1. The cases which have held that large private universities are not sufficiently involved with the state to constitute state action and are therefore not subject to the requirements of the fourteenth amendment include: Guillory v. Administrators of Tulane University, 203 F. Supp. 855 (E. D. La.), vacated, 207 F. Supp., 554 aff'd 306 Ff. 2d 489 (5th Cir., 1962); Green v. Howard University, 271 F. Supp. 609 (D.D.C. 1967), remanded, 412 F. 2d 1129 (D.C. Cir.1969); Grossner v. Trustees of Columbia University, 287 F. Supp. 535 (S.D.N.Y. 1968).

2. B. Babcock, A. Freedman, E. Norton and S. Ross, <u>Sex Discrimination and the Law</u> 997-1020 (1975).

3. For a discussion of the state action concept as it applies to private educational institutions and the Equal Rights Amendment, <u>see</u> Brown, Emerson, Falk and Freedman, "The Equal Rights Amendment: A Constitutional Basis for Equal Rights for Women," 80 <u>Yale L. J.</u> 871, 905-907 (1971).

4. For a discussion of the state action concept as it might arguably apply to private education institutions, <u>see</u> O'Neil, "Private Universities and Public Law," 18 <u>Buf. L. Rev.</u> 155 (1970).

5. Hendrickson, "State Action and Private Higher Education," 2 <u>J. L. and Educ.</u> 53 (1973).

6. Gallagher, "Desegregation: The Effect of the Proposed Equal Rights Amendment on Single-Sex Colleges," 18 <u>St. Louis U. L. J.</u> 41 (1973).

7. To date, a number of lower court cases have supported Gallagher's theory that the Equal Rights Amendment may render private institutions which discriminate on the basis of sex ineligible for various kinds of government subsidies. Regarding government grants, <u>see</u> Gautreaux v. Romney, 448 F. 2d 731 (7th Cir. 1971); for tax exemption, <u>see</u> Green v. Kennedy, 309 F. Supp. 1127 (D.D.C.) (three-judge court, per curiam), <u>appeal dismissed</u> 398 U.S. 956 (1970); Green v. Connally, 330 F. Supp. 1150 (D.D.C.) (three-judge court), <u>aff'd sub nom</u>; Coit v. Green, 404 U.S. 997 (1971); McGlotten v. Connally, 338 F. Supp. 448 (D.D.C. 1972) (three-judge court); Falkenstein v. Department of Revenue, 350 F. Supp. 887 (D. Ore. 1972) (three-judge court), <u>stay denied sub nom</u>; Oregon Elks v. Falkenstein, 409 U.S. 1032 (Douglas, J., dissenting), <u>appeal dismissed</u>, 409 U.S. 1099 (1973); Bob Jones University v. Connally, 341 F. Supp. 277 (D.S.C. 1971) <u>rev'd</u> 472 F. 2d 903 (4th Cir. 1973), <u>petition for cert. filed</u>, No. 72-1470, U.S., April 30, 1973; Crenshaw County Private School Foundation v. Connally, 343 F. Supp. 495 (M.D. Ala. 1972); Pitts v. Department of Revenue, 333 F. Supp. 662 (E.D. Wis. 1971) (three-judge court); and for student assistance, <u>see</u> Norwood v. Harrison, 340 F. Supp. 1003 (N.D. Miss. 1972), 413 U.S. 455 (1973).

8. <u>See</u> Murray, "Economic and Educational Inequality Based on Sex: An Overview," 5 <u>Val. L. Rev.</u> 237 (1971), for a summary of the congressional hearings concerning sex discrimination in education conducted prior to the passage of Title IX.

9. Buek and Orleans, "Sex Discrimination--A Bar to a Democratic Education: Overview of Title IX of the Education Amendments of 1972," 6 <u>Conn. L. Rev.</u> 1 (1973).

ADMISSIONS POLICIES

Single-Sex Schools

Legal problem: Many public educational institutions are currently completely sex-segregated; their admission policies are expressly exempted from the prohibition on sex discrimination in educational programs which receive federal funding.[7] Because of this exemption, many single-sex public institutions will exist on the effective date of the Equal Rights Amendment.

Will the Amendment require all schools subject to it to sexually integrate?

Possible solution: Cases litigated under the fourteenth amendment make it clear that even today, states may not maintain sex-segregated public schools, at any level, if those schools enjoy a "prestige" factor,[8] or offer courses of study not available at any other institution in the state.[9]

In fact, as several authors in this field have noted, in our society single-sex schools are almost never exactly, and in every respect, "equal." If attorneys are astute in litigation, they will search for and build records established around the multitude of differences which almost always exist between different single-sex schools.[10]

---

7. 20 U.S.C. Sec. 1681 (a) (5).

8. Kirstein v. Rector and Visitors of the University of Virginia, 309 F. Supp. 184 (1970).

9. See Kirstein, supra: see contra, concerning admissions to Texas A&M, which offered courses in floriculture not available at other schools in Texas, dicta in Heaton v. Bristol, 317 S.E. 3d 86 (Tex. Civ. App. 1958), cert. denied 359 U.S. 230 (1959), and Allred v. Heaton, 336 S.W. 3d 251 Tex. Civ. App. (1961), cert. denied 364 U.S. 517 (1961). See also, Williams v. McNair, 316 F. Supp. 134, aff'd mem. 401 U.S. 951 (1971), holding that South Carolina could operate an all women's college where the male plaintiffs did not allege or prove that there were advantages denied them by virtue of their exclusion from the school. However, both the Texas cases and Williams v. McNair were decided under a minimum scrutiny standard of review under the equal protection clause which would not be that used under the ERA. See chapter on the Equal Rights Amendment and the Constitution for a discussion of the standard of review which will be applied under the Amendment.

10. See S. Ross, The Rights of Women 119-122 (1973) for a description of how such records may be built.

118

However, even in the rare cases of genuinely separate **and** equal sex-segregated schools, it would seem that, if the Equal Rights Amendment is interpreted in education as the fourteenth amendment was in Brown v. Board of Education, 347 U.S. 483 (1954), single-sex schools would not be permissible. Such a conclusion is the desirable result because it would prevent use of the separate-but-equal doctrine to sustain the many separate but unequal sex-segregated schools.

Further, such an interpretation of the Equal Rights Amendment would parallel the history of the fourteenth amendment in the area of racial discrimination in education. Although there are differences between the two, sexual and racial discrimination in education have very similar effects on the class of people discriminated against. With a few exceptions in both fields, black and women's colleges are generally less prestigious than and inferior to integrated institutions or all-white or all-male institutions. Those who graduate from all but the most outstanding racially or sexually-segregated institutions are handicapped through life by inferior educations and fewer opportunities. Thus, to ensure the full enforcement of the guarantees of the Amendment, it should be interpreted to require the physical integration of all single-sex schools operated by entities subject to the ERA.

References

1. For a discussion of the place of the separate-but-equal doctrine under an Equal Rights Amendment, and an exposition of the view that the doctrine should be rejected in interpreting the Amendment, see Brown, Emerson, Falk and Freedman, "The Equal Rights Amendment: A Constitutional Basis for Equal Rights for Women," 80 Yale L. J. 871, 902 (1971). See also the chapter on The Equal Rights Amendment and the Constitution, above, for a brief discussion of the separate-but-equal doctrine.

2. For the view that single-sex colleges should be maintained, see Moody, "The Constitution and the One-Sex College," 20 Cleve. St. L. Rev. 465 (1971). The author believes that the racial analogy is inapplicable where sex is the basis of discrimination.

3. For views that the constitution already prohibits single-sex state schools, see Shaman, "College Admission Policies Based on Sex and the Equal Protection Clause," 20 Buf. L. Rev. 609 (1971); and Comment, "Sex Discrimination in College Admissions: The Quest for Equal Educational Opportunities," 56 Ia. L. Rev. 209 (1970).

4. See, for a general discussion of the constitutionality
of single-sex schools under present constitutional provisions,
K. Davidson, R. Ginsburg and H. Kay, Sex-based Discrimination
813-840 (1974). The authors also discuss the federally-funded
Upward Bound program for educationally disadvantaged young
people. In many localities, this program is operated on a
sex-restricted basis. If the Equal Rights Amendment is
interpreted as suggested here, sex-segregated Upward Bound
programs would also be unconstitutional.

5. Comment, "Sex Discrimination in Higher Education:
Constitutional Equality for Women," 10 J. Family Law 327 (1970).

6. Sandler, "Sex Discrimination, Educational Institutions
and the Law: A New Issue on Campus," 2 J. L. and Educ. 613
(1974).

Rate of Integration of Single-Sex Schools

Legal problem: On the day the Equal Rights Amendment
takes effect, two years after it is ratified, there will be
hundreds, if not thousands, of single-sex schools in existence
to which the Amendment applies. Obviously, such schools
cannot integrate in one week or one month, or perhaps even one
school year. What, then, are the constitutional standards
governing the rate of sex-integration with which such schools
must comply?

Possible solutions: In the historic case of Brown v.
Board of Education, 347 U.S. 483 (1954), the United States
Supreme Court declared that all public schools in the United
States must racially integrate "with all deliberate speed."
Sadly, that nice phrase proved less than effective. Thus, some
carefully considered statutory standards which guide the speed
of integration in single-sex public schools seem advisable to
avoid prolonged litigation of this question.

A three-judge federal court held in Kirstein v. Rector
and Visitors of University of Virginia, 309 F. Supp. 184
(1970), that a plan submitted by the Board of Visitors of the
University of Virginia which called for admission of women to
that school on an equal basis with men within three years
satisfied constitutional requirements. Title IX, on the other
hand, provides seven years within which any single-sex
institution may voluntarily convert to a completely sex-equal
admissions policy.[11]

It would seem, then, that a "reasonable" time for public
schools to complete the process of integration should take at
the longest seven years. However, the period of time which is

11. 20 U.S. C. 1681 (a) (2).

120

"reasonable" in the case of any given school may vary greatly
from that which is reasonable for others. Factors such as
the amount and design of dormitory space; teaching staff;
availability of other facilities in the state; whether such
other facilities are integrated or not; the demand anticipated
for places at the school by members of the opposite sex; and
any number of other factors might deserve consideration in a
statute drafted to fit the needs of a particular institution,
while still accommodating the constitutional requirements of
the Equal Rights Amendment. Thus, the question is one which
every state with single-sex institutions should resolve by
statute in order both to avoid the need for lawsuits to force
integration and to take into account all factors relevant to
individual schools.

Reference

See, in addition to the Kirstein and Brown cases cited in
the text, White v. Crook, 251 F. Supp. 402, n. 16 (M.D. Ala.
1966); and Reynolds v. Sims, 377 U.S. 533 (1964), dealing with
the question of what is a "reasonable time" within which to
effectuate constitutionally required change.

Standards of Admission to Sex-integrated Schools

Legal problem: The Ninth Circuit Court of Appeals
recently held that the Lowell High School in San Francisco, a
prestigious dual-sex high school, could not constitutionally
admit exactly equal numbers of men and women students. By doing
so, the admissions standards established for each sex were
necessarily different and not sex-neutral. It is possible that
some state school systems which now operate single-sex schools
will, rather than establishing sex-neutral admissions standards,
integrate by admitting exactly equal numbers of women and men
students.

Possible solution: To avoid litigation over a principle
which was established even before passage of the Equal Rights
Amendment, a simple statute which requires that state educational institutions apply sex-neutral admissions standards
should be drafted and enacted in every state.

In the case of vocational or trade schools which are now
single-sex institutions, it is possible that admission standards
based on size, weight or strength will be formulated. Because
such standards bear more heavily on women than on men, they
should be strictly scrutinized after passage of the Equal
Rights Amendment to see that they are in fact necessarily

related to the educational program which the school follows and are not merely a facade for the maintenance of a largely one-sex school.

The regulations to Title IX also require that institutions covered by the Act not discriminate on the basis of sex in admissions. Practices which the regulations define as sex discrimination in admissions include ranking applicants based on sex; applying numerical limitations on the number or proportions of each sex to be admitted; or in any other way treating applicants differently on the basis of sex.[12] These practices would also violate the Equal Rights Amendment.

The regulations further prohibit the use of any test or criterion which adversely affects one sex unless either the test is shown to validly predict success in that program or alternative tests or criteria which do not have such a disproportionately adverse effect are unavailable.[13] This constitutes, in effect, a prohibition of classifications which are "neutral on their face, but discriminatory in impact" unless a positive showing of a relationship to the program which the test is used for can be made by the school. This regulation would appear to satisfy the Equal Rights Amendment, since it imposes strict scrutiny upon admissions tests which bear more heavily on one sex.

References

1. The recent Ninth Circuit decision is Berkelman v. San Francisco Unified School District, 501 F. 2d 1264 (1974). See, for a description of the situation in Lowell High School, which generated the case, and an analysis of constitutional provisions, Note, "Academic High Schools: The Need for Equal Protection for Girls," 8 U. San Francisco L. Rev. 639 (1974).

2. Johnston and Knapp, "Sex Discrimination by Law: A Study in Judicial Perspective," 46 N.Y.U. L. Rev. 675 (1971).

3. Comment, "Sex Discrimination in College Admissions: The Quest for Equal Educational Opportunities," 56 Ia. L. Rev. 209 (1970).

4. Shaman, "College Admission Policies Based on Sex and The Equal Protection Clause," 20 Buf. L. Rev. 609 (1971).

---

12. Title IX Regulations, Sec. 86.21, 39 Fed. Reg. 22234 (1974), as amended in 40 Fed. Reg. 24130-24131, 24140 (1975).

13. Title IX Regulations, id.

Veterans' Preferences

Legal problem: In many states, veterans are given
preference by statute in admissions to state schools. Because
the participation of women in the armed forces has been very
limited to date, such statutes constitute rules which are
"neutral on their face, but discriminatory in impact" and
probably will be unconstitutional under the Equal Rights
Amendment.

Possible solutions: Two solutions are possible here.
First, of course, veterans' preferences could be eliminated
altogether. However, it seems unlikely that legislatures will
choose that course unless none other is available. A second
alternative which might be consonant with the Amendment would
be to extend veterans' preferences to any veteran and his or
her spouse. In this way, many women would be included in the
scope of the preference granted, which would lessen the
discriminatory impact of preferences given to veterans alone.

ATHLETIC PROGRAMS

Athletic Teams

Legal problem: The question of athletic programs for men
and women in public schools is one of the most difficult and
hotly debated in the entire area of equal rights and education.
This brief summary cannot resolve these matters, but it will
set forth the problems and some suggested solutions. The issue
is most certainly one which should be treated in a carefully
considered statute rather than left to litigation after the
effective date of the Amendment.

One problem encountered today in public schools across
the country is that women's teams simply do not exist in many
sports. Where that is the case, and the sport is a "non-
contact" sport, recent case law has held that women must be
admitted to men's teams if they can qualify for those teams.
Rules of state interscholastic associations forbidding women
from competing on men's teams have been struck down where no
women's teams existed in the same sport. See, Brenden v.
Independent School District, 477 F. 2D 1292 (8th Cir. 1973);
and Reed v. Nebraska School Activities Association, 341 F.
Supp. 258 (D. Neb. 1972). Thus, it is clear that both under
present law and the Equal Rights Amendment, where no women's
team exists in a particular sport, women must be allowed to
compete equally with men for places on a single, school-
sponsored integrated team.

A second and more difficult question which has arisen under present law is whether the operation of separate teams for men and women in different sports is constitutional. Applying the minimum scrutiny test under the fourteenth amendment, two federal district courts have ruled that the practice is constitutional. See, Bucha v. Illinois High School Association, 351 F. Supp. 69 (N.D. Ill. 1972); and Ritacco v. Norwin School District, 361 F. Supp. 930 (W.D. Pa. 1973).

The questions which have engendered such hot debate are: (1) whether the separate men's and women's teams approved in Bucha and Ritacco provide the best means of giving the greatest number of women a chance to gain athletic experience and competence; and (2) whether separate men's and women's teams, selected solely by sex, will be unconstitutional under the Equal Rights Amendment.

As to (1), Brenda Feigen Fasteau has argued that given present circumstances, the separate-but-equal principle in athletics is the only one which will give the greatest number of women a chance to participate in athletic programs, although it admittedly penalizes very talented women athletes by forcing them to compete against less skilled women rather than against men. Simply to adopt two sex-neutral teams, a "first-string" and a "second-string," she argues would result in two mostly male teams, the practical effect of which would be to exclude all but the most talented women athletes from athletic experience.

The difficulty with Ms. Fasteau's approach, of course, is that it cuts against every other proposed application of the Equal Rights Amendment. In all other areas, it has uniformly been suggested that the Amendment should be interpreted to mean that sex, in and of itself, cannot be the factor used by the state to make choices. Rather, sex-neutral standards, such as athletic ability, must be adopted. Those who meet the standards may participate in whatever athletic competition is provided by the school. To go against the principle in the area of athletics, Ms. Fasteau's opponents say, however beneficent her motive, is to open a door to weakening the principle most basic to the Amendment. These, very simply stated, are the issues at the heart of the controversy over public school athletics and the Equal Rights Amendment.

Possible solutions: Three principal solutions to this problem has been suggested.

1. Regardless of the Amendment's application in other areas, an exception should be made in athletics, which would allow separate men's and women's teams to be established. As noted briefly above, this is Ms. Fasteau's suggestion, and it is based on her belief that it will accomplish the greatest

good for the greatest number of women, although it would harm the few truly outstanding women athletes by denying them the sharper competition men could provide. Further, it is concededly at odds with interpretations of the Amendment in other areas of the law.

If separate men's and women's teams are the choice ultimately made in any particular state, however, care should be taken to provide specifically that both the rules and rewards for the two teams must be identical. In Bucha, described above, the Court noted incidentally that the women's teams did not have the same perquisites as the men's. To avoid this possibility, states should establish by statute that as to such matters as equipment, overnight trips, scholarships, facilities, budget, coaching staff, and number of trips provided, parity for each sex must be achieved.

The proposed regulations to Title IX essentially adopt the approach outlined here.[14] The regulations also allow for possible affirmative action efforts. It should be noted that such affirmative action along specified standards had been required by the proposed regulations to Title IX. The final regulations, however, leave such efforts to the discretion of the institution involved. Also, in this context, the proposed regulations had called for an annual determination of student interest on which the institution would base its athletic offerings. The final regulations only require that an institution take the interests of both sexes into account in determining what sports to offer. However, the institution must provide "equal athletic opportunity for . . . both sexes" in a manner which "effectively accommodate(s) the interests and abilities . . . of both sexes."

It is very possible that the Equal Rights Amendment will render the approach taken in the regulations unconstitutional. Any state which makes this legislative choice should be aware that it will most likely result in litigation challenging such a practice under the Amendment.

2. Sex-neutral teams should be established with the qualifications for each established only by athletic ability. As noted above, this approach, while completely consistent with the Amendment's interpretation in other areas, is subject to the criticism that its practical effect will be simply to establish two or more predominantly male teams. Thus, this approach may be challenged as a rule which is "neutral on its

---

14. Title IX Regulations, Sec. 86.38, 39 Fed. Reg. 22236 (1974), as amended Sec. 86.41, 40 Fed Reg. 24134-24135, 24142-24143 (1975) and Sec. 86.3(b) and (c), 40 Fed. Reg. 24138 (1975).

face, but discriminatory in impact," since it will in effect deny women a chance to participate in state-sponsored athletic programs.

If enough teams were fielded in every sport to satisfy the demand by men for athletic experience, it is also possible that the quality of women's teams would be so low that they would be harmed by their loss of the "prestige" factor and a consequent lack of interest in them.

3. Sex-neutral qualifications such as height and weight limits, with rules permitting individuals to compete above their levels if they are skillful enough to do so should be established. This suggestion, while similar to no. 2 in its approach, would use size rather than athletic ability as the sex-neutral factor to be taken into account to determine membership on a team. By also permitting individuals to compete with members of a team larger in physical size, it would allow the exceptional athlete of either sex to compete with others of like ability regardless of size.

Thus, depending on exactly where the height and weight limits were drawn, this approach might establish two teams, each of which was largely men or largely women, but which would allow all persons on the physically smaller team to compete with those on the larger team if they were sufficiently skilled to do so. The authors of this suggestion, B. Babcock, A. Freedman, E. Norton and S. Ross, in Sex Discrimination and the Law 1030 (1975) go further and state that:

> The resulting sport program would be scrutinized to ensure that the neutral rules on which a system was based did not fall more heavily on women than on men. Thus, a school would have to spend its sports money in such a way as to ensure that both men and women participated in equivalent numbers and with roughly equal facilities and expenditures per capita, while allowing students to participate on the basis of their individual characteristics and preferences rather than sex-based average.

Athletic programs are too complex and involve too many factors and too many sports to be dealt with on a case-by-case basis over years of litigation. Failure to draft a comprehensive statute which attempts to resolve the problems outlined here will only harm women students for many years ahead--harm which will be both unconstitutional after passage of the Equal Rights Amendment and completely avoidable if thoughful legislative action is taken in advance.

References

1. _See_ Fasteau, "Giving Women a Sporting Chance," _Ms. Magazine_, July 1973, 58, excerpted in B. Babcock, A. Freedman, E. Norton and S. Ross, _Sex Discrimination and the Law_ 1028 (1975).

2. Concerning _Brenden_, _supra_, _see_ Comment, "Constitutional Law--Equal Protection--Sex Discrimination in High School Athletics Unreasonable," 19 _N.Y.U. L. F._ 166 (1973).

3. Concerning _Bucha_, _supra_, _see_ Comment, "Constitutional Law--Sex Discrimination--The Female High School Athlete," 50 _Chi-Kent L. Rev._ 169 (1973).

4. _See_ Comment, "Sex Discrimination in Interscholastic High School Athletics," 25 _Syracuse L. Rev._ 535, 556 (1974), for a much more complete exposition than is set out in this summary review of the different possibilities for approaching the problem of men's and women's athletics; the author concedes that several of the suggested approaches probably will be unconstitutional under an Equal Rights Amendment.

5. Note, "The Case for Equality in Athletics," 22 _Cleve. St. L. Rev._ 570 (1973).

6. Note, "Equality in Athletics: The Cheerleader v. the Athlete," 19 _S.D. L. Rev._ 428 (1974).

7. Comment, "Constitutional Law--Equal Protection--Sex Discrimination in High School Athletics Unreasonable," 19 _N.Y.U. L. F._ 166 (1973).

Participation of Women in "Contact Sports"

Legal problem: No reported case to date has held that women are entitled to play on men's teams where the sport involved is a "contact" sport, even though women's teams in such sports have not existed. _See Magill v. Avonworth Baseball Conference_, 364 F. Supp. 1212 (W.D. Pa. 1973), which denied girls the right to participate in Little League baseball, partly on the ground that the sport was a "contact" sport; _see also_ reference no. 1, below. The Equal Rights Amendment will require that women be allowed to play on school teams in "contact" sports, which include football, baseball, basketball and hockey.

Possible solution: There is no basis under an Equal Rights Amendment for distinguishing between "contact" and "non-contact" sports insofar as an individual's right to participate on a team is concerned. In this regard, it is interesting to note that the proposed regulations for Title IX also did not make such a distinction. However, the final regulations exempt boxing, wrestling, rugby, ice hockey, football, basketball and other sports the purpose or major activity of which involves bodily contact. Generally, if there is only one team for a particular sport, Title IX requires that members of the excluded sex be allowed to try out for that team; however, the final regulations exempt so-called "contact sports" from this requirement.[15]

The Amendment will require that sex-neutral standards, such as size, strength and stamina, be applied to determine eligibility for membership on a team in a particular sport. Further, of course, the Amendment will require that the sex-neutral standards be necessarily related to the physical requirements actually relevant to participation in a particular sport. Thus, for example, physical standards for participation on a baseball team constitutionally should be lower than those required to participate on a football team.

An alternative to extremely high physical standards, where the sport involved has traditionally been a physically dangerous one, is to impose safety rules which would allow smaller persons to participate safely in that particular sport. Not to do so, when failure to impose such rules results in all or almost all participants in the sport being men, might be violative of the Amendment. Such rule changes constitute "less drastic means" than keeping all women out of a particular sport. The "less drastic means" analysis is used to strictly scrutinize a rule "neutral on its face, but discriminatory in impact." Maintenance of physically demanding rules in particular sports which operated to preclude women from participation in them would constitute such a rule because it bears more heavily on women than upon men.

References

1. For a description of the cases litigated through July, 1974 involving "contact" sports and women's participation in them, see Comment, "Sex Discrimination in Interscholastic High School Athletics," 25 Syracuse L. Ref. 535, 545 (1974).

---

15. Title IX Regulations, Sec. 86.38, 39 Fed. Reg. 22236 (1974), as amended Sec. 86.41(b), 40 Fed. Reg. 24142-24143 (1975).

128

2.   See B. Babcock, A. Freedman, E. Norton and S. Ross, Sex Discrimination and the Law 1032 (1975), for the suggestion that a "less drastic means" than setting very high physical standards for participation in rough sports would be to change the rules of those sports.

Integration of Athletic Departments and Facilities

Legal problem: Closely related to the problem of men's and women's teams is the question of whether separate men's and women's athletic departments and facilities may be maintained after passage of an Equal Rights Amendment. Under current practice, of course, most public schools staff separate departments, with separate department heads and separate physical facilities for men's and women's physical education. It is difficult to see how this may be continued constitutionally after passage of the Equal Rights Amendment.

Possible solution: The only solution consonant with the Amendment will be to integrate men's and women's athletic departments and facilities after the effective date of the Amendment.

Because of possible problems with immediate integration, such as the need to re-build or remodel facilities to accommodate both sexes, some amount of time may be necessary to effectuate complete integration. As in the case of integrating presently single-sex schools, statutes or regulations should be drafted to cover this problem so that it is not left to litigation and so that the problems of individual schools may be taken into account. To accomplish this, a commission might be established to oversee the transition in all schools in a particular state. Such a comission could be empowered to accomplish the transition by issuing regulations, rather than treating the details of it by statute. Title IX regulations require that athletic departments at the elementary school level comply with Title IX within one year from the effective date of the regulations; secondary and post-secondary schools are allowed three years.[16]

It should be noted that while gymnasiums and other school facilities must be integrated under the terms of the Amendment, a legitimate right of privacy issue exists with respect to separate locker and change rooms for each sex in such facilities, which the Amendment will allow. See the section on physical facilities, below, for a discussion of the right of privacy qualification to the Equal Rights Amendment as it applies to school facilities.

---

16. Title IX Regulations, Sec. 86.41(d), 40 Fed. Reg. 24143 (1975).

Reference

For a discussion of what constitutes a "reasonable" time for complying with constitutionally-required change, see the section on admissions policies, above, and references thereto.

Equalization of Athletic Budgets

Legal problem: It is a well-known fact that the public budgets for men's and women's athletics are greatly at variance in the United States today. The Equal Rights Amendment will require roughly equal expenditures of state and public funds for men's and women's athletics.

Possible solution: Once more, the problem in this area is to give schools a reasonable time within which to comply with the Amendment, while also ensuring that steps are being taken in the direction of compliance. The legitimate problems which schools will encounter here stem from the grossly disproportionate nature of current athletic expenditures. In order to make women's and men's athletic budgets roughly equal, many more women coaches will have to be trained and hired, much more equipment purchased and many more classes developed and scheduled into the curriculum, to mention only a few of the needed changes.

Again, the problem of compliance with the Amendment in a "reasonable" time should not be left to the discretion of various school officials in every school district in every state. The matter should be handled by statute, or through the establishment of a state-wide commission to oversee the equalization of budgets in schools throughout a particular state to ensure that it is handled both orderly and speedily.

Title IX's regulations do not require "equal aggregate expenditures" for athletics for members of each sex. However, the regulations would require teams to be provided with necessary equipment and supplies without regard to sex.[17] Perhaps this allowance for unequal athletic budgets is based on the recognition that there may be more limited interest in some sports by members of one sex. Also, the regulations' recognition that affirmative efforts may be taken to equalize athletic opportunities for both sexes, mentioned above, may also engender differences in athletic budgets.

---

17. Title IX Regulations, Sec. 86.38(f), 39 Fed. Reg. 22236 (1974), as amended Sec. 86.41(c), 40 Fed. Reg. 24135 and 24143 (1975).

However, while these differences may exist in athletic programs for young men and women because of a history of discrimination, it would seem that in the elementary schools the opportunity to avoid the effects of sex-discriminatory programming exists. If discrimination in physical education were eliminated from the elementary school context, then the need for differential budgets in later years would eventually be eliminated.

References

1. See discussion of the rate of integration of single-sex schools, above, for a consideration of the "reasonable" time problems and constitutional requirements in this area.

2. See B. Babcock, A. Freedman, E. Norton and S. Ross, Sex Discrimination and the Law 1031 (1975) for a table comparing men's and women's athletic budgets in public and private schools. The amounts are shockingly disproportionate and give some idea of the immensity of the present disparity.

ACADEMIC COURSES: SINGLE-SEX COURSE OFFERINGS

Legal problem: Admission to many courses in public schools today is restricted by sex. The most common of these are shop and home economics, physical education, ROTC training, vocational education in certain subjects, sex education, and, recently, courses in women's studies. The Equal Rights Amendment will require that all public schools and other schools subject to the Amendment open all courses to all students without regard to sex.

Possible solution: Because restricting course enrollment by sex is so common today, many local school officials and administrators will probably continue the practice even after the effective date of the Amendment if specific directions are not placed either in a statute covering the public schools or in a regulation of state-wide application.

However, enrollment in courses legitimately may be restricted, not on the basis of sex, but on the basis of sex-neutral standards intrinsically related to course requirements. Each area of possible controversy is discussed below with permissible and impermissible requirements for enrollment set forth.

Shop and Home Economics

Although admission to these courses today is often
restricted by sex, it is difficult to see how any sex-based
restriction whatsoever could be placed on enrollment under
the Equal Rights Amendment. There are no size or strength
requirements which could justifiably be imposed for taking
shop as it is taught in most schools, and certainly none for
home economics. However, more subtle forms of enrollment
restrictions, which could operate in fact as sex-based
restrictions, should be guarded against. These include:

1. Requirements of a prerequisite to take certain
advanced courses, where the prerequisite was restricted as to
sex before the effective date of the Amendment. A similar
issue has arisen in Title VII litigation, and the EEOC and
courts have uniformly held that requiring work experience which
could be gained prior to the passage of Title VII only by men
constitutes prohibited sex discrimination against women. The
possible issue which may arise concerning course prerequisites
should be resolved the same way.

2. Limiting classes to 50% men and 50% women, or placing
any other form of sex-related enrollment restriction on the
course. Courses should be offered strictly on a first-come,
first-served basis, with no quotas whatsoever imposed on
enrollment. Where courses are offered to whomever is first to
sign up, the method for allowing persons to sign should not,
of course, be related to sex in any manner.

Physical Education

Here, depending on the particular sport involved or
activities planned in the class, size, strength or stamina
requirements could justifiably be imposed by a school for
enrollment in a particular class. However, as was suggested
with regard to size and stamina requirements for membership
on athletic teams above, such requirements must be strictly
scrutinized to see that they do not fall more heavily on
women than on men. Without strict scrutiny, the effect could
be to have all physical education classes conducted in those
sports which require great physical strength.

Further, where a "less drastic means" of changing rules
to make particular sports less dangerous is available, that
alternative should be considered in order to open physical
education classes in the widest possible variety of sports to
women.

It should be noted, however, that if elementary and junior high schools were required to have identical physical education classes and taught the same physical skills to all students, regardless of sex, then in the future physical strength discrepancies between young men and women would not exist in the higher grades. The current discrepancies in physical strength and athletic skills between men and women are, of course, a result of past discrimination and are difficult to overcome; the critical period for developing such skills is between the ages of 11 and 18.

In no event, of course, will the Amendment allow any physical education class to be restricted on the ground of sex alone.

ROTC Training

The Amendment will allow no restrictions whatsoever to be placed on enrollment for ROTC training. One possible evasion, neutral on its face, would be to limit enrollment of each sex to the number of that sex currently serving as officers for whichever branch of the Armed Forces a particular unit is training students. To adopt this approach, of course, would have the effect of "freezing" the number of women who come up through ROTC programs in any particular branch of the service. It would definitely be unconstitutional under the Equal Rights Amendment.

Vocational Education

Many vocational education courses are presently sex-restricted, which, of course, will be unconstitutional under the ERA. Again, depending on the particular vocation being taught, it is conceivable that certain size or strength requirements could be placed on enrollment in certain courses. Once again, however, any such requirement will have to be strictly scrutinized to see that it bears a necessary relationship to the requirements of participation in the actual course. Also, where such requirements are justified, enough courses would have to be available which do not impose such requirements in order to satisfy the needs of women students.

Women's Studies

In the women's studies courses recently developed at the college level and which are now being given in some high schools, many of the students enrolled in the courses, as well as their teachers, prefer that they be restricted to women students only. It is difficult to see how such courses could be constitutionally restricted to one sex alone after passage of the Equal Rights Amendment.

It might be argued that doing so is in effect a form of "compensatory aid" to make up for past discrimination by the state. However, under the absolute approach to the Amendment's interpretation, no such programs will be allowable. See the chapter on the Equal Rights Amendment and the Constitution, above, for a fuller discussion of the "compensatory aid" question under the ERA.

Special Courses for Pregnant Students in Pre-natal Health Care, Delivery and Child Care

Legal problem: Given that schools may not expel unwed pregnant students, a problem discussed in the section on student conduct below, may they positively encourage them to stay in school by offering special courses, open only to them, in such subjects as pre-natal health, delivery and child care?

Possible solutions: The Equal Rights Amendment should be interpreted to allow schools to offer courses which are open only to pregnant students in order to encourage them to stay in school. This case is the precise opposite from that posed concerning the expulsion of such students. There, no state interest is served by not allowing them to attend school. Here, there is a definite state interest in educating as many persons as possible. If offering special courses of particular interest to one group of students will keep them in school, the Equal Rights Amendment should not be read as prohibiting that result. See the section on "unique physical characteristics" in the chapter on the Equal Rights Amendment and the Constitution, above, for an analysis of the six factors applicable to a state practice based on a "unique physical characteristic" such as pregnancy. Under those factors, the result posited here seems correct because it benefits pregnant students. On the other hand, of course, schools may open such courses to any student who is interested in the subject.

Sex Education

It is common practice today to separate young men and women in junior high and high schools for sex education classes. Such a practice will be unconstitutional after passage of the Equal Rights Amendment.

Some may argue that the right of privacy includes the
right to be educated as to sex only in the presence of the
members of one's own sex. However, the right of privacy
qualification should not be extended to any area of education;
it must be limited to personal bodily functions and disrobing.
Were it extended to other areas, it could undercut a large
portion of the Amendment's coverage under the guise of
establishing a right of privacy.

The regulations to Title IX would allow separate sex
education classes for boys and girls.[18] This regulation
would almost certainly be unconstitutional under the Equal
Rights Amendment.

The proper scope and interpretation of the right of
privacy is discussed below in the section on physical
facilities.

Conclusion

Because of the variety of issues and possible subterfuges
which could arise regarding admission to particular classes
commonly offered in public schools, and the vast difficulties
of solving such problems one school at a time and one state at
a time, these types of problems must be given thoughtful
consideration and the solutions to them incorporated in a code
of statewide effect, whether statutory or regulatory. This
would avoid years of litigation during which many women and
men would be denied their constitutional right to take any
courses offered by public schools without restrictions based
on sex. Legislative action of some sort is essential in this
area.

References

1. See K. Davidson, R. Ginsburg and H. Kay, Sex-based
Discrimination 847 and 868 (1974), discussing the right of
privacy qualification to the Amendment as it applies to classes
in physical education and sex education and the sex-integration
of vocational education courses.

---

18. For this regulation and others regarding course
offerings, see Title IX Regulations, Sec. 86.34, 39 Fed. Reg.
22235 and 25667 (1974), as amended 40 Fed. Reg. 24132-24133
and 24141 (1975).

2. See Brown, Emerson, Falk and Freedman, "The Equal Rights Amendment: A Constitutional Basis for Equal Rights for Women," 80 Yale L. J. 871, 903-905 (1971), regarding the "compensatory aid" problems in the interpretation of the Amendment; and, 895, regarding special courses for pregnant students.

3. Shelton and Berndt, "Sex Discrimination in Vocational Education--Title IX and Other Remedies," 62 Calif. L. Rev. 1121 (1968).

EXTRA-CURRICULAR SINGLE-SEX CLUBS AND ORGANIZATIONS

The Application of the Equal Rights Amendment

Legal problem: Unofficially or officially attached to all public schools are private organizations of students formed to serve educational, recreational or other purposes for their members. Such groups are often not sponsored in any manner by the schools themselves, but are permitted to exist and, some-times, to make use of school facilities. The problem of such groups' use of public facilities is discussed in the next section.

These groups include Key Clubs and other organizations sponsored for young men or women by groups such as the Kiwanis; the Little League; 4-H Clubs; and sororities and fraternities. Will the Equal Rights Amendment require that they permit both men and women to join on an equal basis?

Possible solutions: As noted above, the Equal Rights Amendment will apply only to state and federal government, and those private entities which are held to constitute state action. However, the Supreme Court cases defining the state action concept under the fourteenth amendment are vague and difficult to apply. What those cases will probably require under the ERA is to look to the nature of the support a school offers each particular group. Such support might be in the form of a charter; funding; exclusive use of school facilities for the group's activities; provision of faculty advisors paid from public funds; and any other number of actions which might in some way aid the functioning of the private organization. However, because the state action tests must be applied to each particular group as it operates at a particular school, it is impossible to give certain answers in advance as to which groups might or might not constitute state action and therefore be subject to the requirements of the Equal Rights Amendment.

It should be noted that in determining the state action question in this context, the first amendment rights to free association of the group members themselves will be considered, as well as the nature and extent of the state's involvement. Because freedom of association has traditionally been a highly valued constitutional right, the amount of state involvement would probably have to be quite extensive before a court would hold that a private, sex-restricted group constituted state action under the Equal Rights Amendment and must therefore admit members without regard to sex. In all likelihood, then, groups, such as Key Clubs will probably not be subject to the Amendment, and will be allowed to remain as sex-restricted organizations, just as the Kiwanis themselves probably will be.

As to Little League, one court has held that the Little League organization in New Jersey was not state action, Magill v. Avonworth Baseball Conference, 364 F. Supp. 1212 (W.D. Pa. 1973). It is possible, however, that this question could be re-litigated and state action found, depending on the precise source and amounts of funding of a particular Little League; the nature and extent of its use of public school facilities; and whether that use effectively kept other groups from using such facilities. See Gilmore v. City of Montgomery, 417 U.S. 163 (1974) and the discussion of the use of state facilities by sex-segregated groups, below.

The same types of questions would have to be litigated to determine whether 4-H Clubs and sororities and fraternities, in the particular fact situations in which they operate at individual schools constitute state action and must therefore admit members of both sexes equally.

It is almost impossible to generalize in this area, because the cases decided by the Supreme Court turn on very particular fact situations; but, it may safely be said that where no state funding is received; school facilities are not used at all or are not extensively used; and the school is not involved in the actual activities of organizations, sex-restricted, private organizations will probably not be held to conform to the Equal Rights Amendment.

Under the Regulations of Title IX, it appears that a sex-restricted organization operated at an educational institution covered by Title IX would also be affected if that organization received or benefited from federal financial assistance.[19]

---

19. Title IX Regulations, Sec. 86.6(c), 39 Fed. Reg. 22233 (1974), as amended 40 Fed. Reg. 24138 (1975).

References

1.   The state action doctrine is explained at length in the first chapter, The Equal Rights Amendment and the Constitution, above.

2.   Major state action cases decided by the United States Supreme Court under the fourteenth amendment include: Shelley v. Kraemer, 334 U.S. 1 (1948); Burton v. Wilmington Parking Authority, 365 U.S. 715 (1961); Rietman v. Mulkey, 387 U.S. 369 (1967); Gilmore v. City of Montgomery, 417 U.S. 163 (1972). Literally volumes of scholarly commentary have been written on the state action doctrine. Most of that commentary has concluded that very few, if any, reliable predictive factors can be gathered from the case law. Thus, in litigating a state action question, the current approach is to attempt to find all possible ways in which the state is in any way involved, no matter how seemingly insignificant, in the activities or functions of any group which is claimed to be subject to constitutional requirements.

What has been implicitly recognized in some of the cases is that the first amendment right to free association carries great weight. When that interest conflicts with other constitutional requirements, the standard of participation by the state rises accordingly. See, concerning the first amendment right to free association, Moose Lodge v. Irvis, 407 U.S. 163 (1972); and Gilmore v. City of Montgomery, 417 U.S. 163 (1974).

The Right of Sex-restricted Private Groups to Use School or State Facilities

Legal problem: This question has arisen under the fourteenth amendment, where the right of racially restricted groups to use state facilities was litigated. A constitutional issue arises because, although the state itself will be barred by the Equal Rights Amendment from discriminating on the basis of sex, the Amendment would be a nullity if private, sex-restricted groups were allowed exclusive or primary use of facilities which the state owns. Thus, while no clear-cut answer is available, the question may be simply stated: to what extent, if any, may sex-restricted groups make use of state facilities for meetings, games, or other private activities?

Possible solutions: In the 1974 case of Gilmore v. City of Montgomery, 417 U.S. 163, the United States Supreme Court was faced with the question of whether the City of Montgomery, Alabama, could allow racially restricted all-white groups to use city facilities. The Court found only one easy answer: exclusive use of city facilities by such groups was unconstitutional. Thus, from this holding, it would appear that if a nominally private sex-restricted Little League team schedules a school's baseball diamond for use five nights out of seven for four months of practice and games--thus effectively precluding use by other teams--the Little League in this situation would constitute state action and would either have to discontinue using school facilities or admit girls on an equal basis with boys.

The problem of use of school facilities becomes more difficult, however, with the much more common occurrence--the occasional use of school facilities by sex-restricted groups. As to this question, the Gilmore court remanded to the lower court for a determination as to: (1) what other facilities were available; (2) the extent of the use by segregated groups; (3) whether, because facilities were scarce, a "rationing" system was in effect under which segregated groups gained a disproportionate share of public facilities. Thus, again, the outcome of the question is difficult to predict in advance under state action principles.

More help may be gained from the regulations promulgated under Title IX, which deal specifically with the problem of the use of covered school facilities by sex-segregated groups.[20] The principles developed there would prohibit use of state facilities by all sex-segregated groups except sororities and fraternities. It is possible that those principles might be applied under the Equal Rights Amendment.

Reference

See K. Davidson, R. Ginsburg and H. Kay, Sex-based Discrimination 840 (1974), concerning Title IX and the use of school facilities by sex-segregated groups.

---

20. Title IX Regulations, id.

PHYSICAL FACILITIES IN PUBLIC SCHOOLS

Introduction: The Right to Privacy Qualification

Since the publication of the Yale article on the Equal Rights Amendment in 1971, it has been widely accepted that the separate-but-equal doctrine has no place in interpreting the Equal Rights Amendment. Rather, the constitutional principle which has come to be accepted as a qualification of the principle of absolute equal rights in the right of privacy.

That right is one of recent constitutional origin, but one which the Court has repeatedly used in the last ten years. It first appeared in Griswold v. Connecticut, 381 U.S. 479 (1965), which held that the state could not intrude upon the privacy of the marriage relationship by prohibiting married couples' use of contraceptives. The Court again relied on the right in Eisenstadt v. Baird, 405 U.S. 438 (1972), and in the abortion cases, Roe v. Wade, 410 U.S. 113 (1973) and Doe V. Bolton, 410 U.S. 179 (1973); the Court declared that it was a woman's right to privacy which protected her decision, absolute in the first trimester of pregnancy, as to whether to bear a child or have an abortion.

Thus, the Roe and Doe decisions demonstrate that the right of privacy, although young as constitutional rights go, is one upon which the current Court has been willing to rely heavily. That recent reliance lends further credence to the earlier Yale analysis of the role of the right of privacy in interpreting the Equal Rights Amendment.

School Dormitories

Legal problem: Both tradition and the preference of many persons of both sexes support the current practice of maintaining single-sex dormitories in public schools. Critics of the Equal Rights Amendment have often claimed that it would force integration of the sexes in private living quarters, bathrooms and the like. The question, then, is whether state schools may constitutionally maintain separate living facilities for men and women under the ERA.

Possible solutions: As long as separate facilities offered for men and women are identical in quality and convenience, it seems absolutely clear that states not only may, but must, maintain separate living facilities for the sexes. The right of privacy discussed above has thus far been related to matters concerning the body, such as contraception and abortion; and, to the personal right to make decisions which intimately affect the body without state coercion. Thus,

<u>Griswold</u>, <u>Roe</u> and <u>Doe</u> offer clear support for the principle that the state may not coerce persons to live with members of the opposite sex if they do not choose to do so.

The Regulations to Title IX allow separate housing for each sex, but require that such housing be proportionate in quantity to the numbers of students of each sex applying for it and that it be comparable in cost and quality and subject to the same rules and regulations. A discussion of sex-discriminatory school rules is found in the section on student conduct, below. Title IX's Regulations also apply to off-campus housing.[21]

References

1. Concerning the right of privacy and the Equal Rights Amendment, <u>see</u> Brown, Emerson, Falk and Freedmen, "The Equal Rights Amendment: A Constitutional Basis for Equal Rights for Women," 80 <u>Yale L. J.</u> 871, 900 (1971).

2. A more detailed discussion of the right of privacy is found in the first chapter, The Equal Rights Amendment and the Constitution, above.

Locker and Change Rooms in School Gymnasiums

Legal problem: Opponents of the ERA have claimed that it would require the elimination of separate restrooms and change rooms in state institutions, which, if true, would mean that locker rooms and change rooms in school gymnasiums would also have to be sex-integrated.

Possible solutions: Again, it is clear that if the right of privacy extends to school dormitories, it will certainly extend to school locker and change rooms. There seems little question that opponents of the Amendment have seized on what they perceive to be an emotion-charged issue. Title IX's Regulations also allow for such separate facilities as long as the facilities are comparable.[22]

---

21. Title IX Regulations, Sec. 86.32, 39 Fed. Reg. 22235 (1974), as amended 40 Fed. Reg. 24131 and 24141 (1975).

22. Title IX Regulations, Sec. 86.33, 39 Fed. Reg. 22235 (1974), as amended 40 Fed. Reg. 24141 (1975).

Reference

Concerning the impact of changing social customs and mores on the right to privacy, and the interpretation of the right in light of current social practices, see Brown, Emerson, Falk and Freedman, "The Equal Rights Amendment: A Constitutional Basis for Equal Rights for Women," Yale L. J. 871, 902 (1971).

STUDENT   CONDUCT

Sex-Discriminatory School Rules

Legal problem: Many state schools now enforce different rules for men and women students. The most common among these are requirements that women live in school dormitories, while men are free to choose where they will live; the hours and regulations in such dormitories; and, in junior high and high schools, rules concerning the length of men's hair. The Equal Rights Amendment will invalidate all sex-discriminatory school rules or regulations.

Possible solutions: Again, to avoid needless litigation over points which are so well settled under the Amendment, and are recognized by the regulations of Title IX, enactment of a prohibition against differing rules for men and women students in some generally applicable education code seems desirable.

While it is obvious that the questions of dormitory living and hours cannot possibly be sustained under an Equal Rights Amendment, some explanation may be needed as to hair length. Simply stated, hair length, in both men and women, is a matter of personal preference. If the "absolute" approach advocated in the Yale article were applied to the ERA by the Supreme Court, hair length could not be regulated in only one sex. However, even under the more lenient strict scrutiny approach to the Amendment,[23] if a school wanted to regulate hair length at all, it would have to find some compelling reason to regulate the length of men students' hair. It is extremely doubtful that a school could make such a showing.

---

23. For a discussion of the "strict scrutiny" versus "absolute" approach to possible standards of review under the Amendment, see the first chapter, The Equal Rights Amendment and the Constitution, above.

Some of the hair length cases which have been litigated under Title VII illustrate the point. There, an employer may make rules as to hair length if: (1) they are generally applicable to both male and female employees; and (2) they are closely related to job requirements. One male employee won a case against an employer because the employer had fired the male with long hair who worked in a kitchen, while allowing women employees to wear hair nets. Thus, because any safety requirements of shop courses or the like could be satisfied by providing students with hats or hair nets, it seems unlikely that a school could justify regulating hair length under the Equal Rights Amendment.

References

1. For an article concerning Title VII and hair length, in which the author states that hair length regulations are not, in his opinion, sex-discriminatory, see "Sex Discrimination and Hair Length Regulations under Title VII of the Civil Rights Act of 1964--the Long and Short of It," 25 Lab. L. J. 336 (1974).

2. Title IX Regulations, Sec. 86.32, 39 Fed. Reg. 22235 (1974), as amended, 40 Fed. Reg. 24131 and 24141 (1975) require that school rules not discriminate on the basis of sex.

3. Note, "Long Hair and the Equal Protection Clause: King v. Saddleback Junior College District," 1 UCLA-Alaska L. Rev. 134 (1974).

4. Note, "Long-Haired Student: A Constitutionally Protected Right of Personal Taste," 8 Idaho L. Rev. 194 (1971).

5. Note, "Public School Hair Regulations: Are They Constitutional?," 16 St. Louis U. L. J. 112 (1971).

6. "Education: Sports, Sex Tracking, in loco parentis, Dress Codes," 2 Women's Rights L. Rep. 41 (1972).

7. Brown, "Hair, the Constitution and the Public Schools," 1 J. L. and Educ. 371 (1972).

8. Note, "Karr v. Schmidt (460 F. 2d. 609): The Continuing Saga of Long Hair," 27 S.W. L. J. 390 (1973).

Expulsion of Pregnant Unwed Students

Legal problem: One author has noted that of 200,000 pregnant teenagers, only one-third are enrolled in high school. Thus, the tragedy of unwanted teenage pregnancies is compounded by the high rate at which these young women quit school. Under current policies in many school districts, school rules require pregnant students to quit; but such rules have been successfully challenged even without the Equal Rights Amendment. See Ordway v. Hargraves, 323 F. Supp. 115 (D. Mass. 1971); Perry v. Grenada Munic Separate School District, 300 F. Supp. 748 (N.D. Miss. 1972) and Shull v. Columbus Munic. Separate District, 338 F. Supp. 1376 (N.D.Miss. 1972). Moreover, expulsion of a student from school on the sole ground of her unmarried pregnancy will unquestionably violate the Equal Rights Amendment.

Possible solutions: In order to avoid the need to litigate a point which is rapidly becoming settled law even without the Amendment, any uniform education code should specifically prohibit expulsion of students on the sole ground of pregnancy, whether the student is married or unmarried.

While school officials might argue that pregnancy falls within the "unique physical characteristic" exception to the Equal Rights Amendment, it should be understood that that exception is available only where some valid state objective is served by a law which relates to only one sex. While pregnancy is unique to women, the condition of pregnancy has no relationship whatsoever to the ability to attend schools and receive an education; nor has the pregnancy of students ever been shown to be a significantly disruptive factor in the operation of public schools or harmful to other students' morals.

Thus, while pregnancy is undoubtedly a "unique physical characteristic," it bears no logical relationship to the state regulation, expulsion from school. Because of that lack of relationship, use of the "unique physical characteristics" exception is not justified here. Expulsion of students from public schools for this reason would clearly violate the Equal Rights Amendment. For a full discussion of this issue and analysis of the six factors to be considered where the state seeks to justify a rule which affects only one sex on the ground that it deals with a "unique physical characteristic," see the first chapter, The Equal Rights Amendment and the Constitution, above.

The Regulations of Title IX specifically provide that educational institutions are prohibited from considering pregnancy, childbirth, miscarriage, abortion or recovery therefrom as a basis for either the admission or exclusion of any student from an educational program. Such disabilities are to be dealt with like any other temporary disability or physical condition. The regulations do allow for different degrees of participation in a program or activity if the student who is pregnant voluntarily requests it. A pregnant student is permitted to take a leave of absence for a reasonable period of time. The regulations require that she be reinstated to her original status upon her return.[24]

References

1. K. Davidson, R. Ginsburg and H. Kay, _Sex-based Discrimination_ 863-868 (1974).

2. Concerning the "unique physical characteristics" exception to the Amendment and its proper interpretation, see Brown, Emerson, Falk and Freedman, "The Equal Rights Amendment: A Constitutional Basis for Equal Rights for Women," 80 _Yale L. J._ 871, 893-897 (1971).

3. Note, "Marriage, Pregnancy and the Right to Go to School," 50 _Tex. L. Rev._ 1196 (1972).

4. Note, "Marriage vs. Education: A Constitutional Conflict," 44 _Miss. L. J._ 248 (1973).

5. Perle and Browning, "Student Classifications and Equal Protection: Marriage and Sex," 3 _J. L. and Educ._ 100 (1974).

FACULTY

Sex Discrimination in Employment

Title VII of the 1964 Civil Rights Act already prohibits discrimination in employment on the basis of race, color, religion, sex and national origin; Title VII has applied to all schools since 1972.[25] Therefore, as far as a woman's right to

---

24. Title IX Regulations, Sec. 86.21(c) and 86.37, 39 Fed. Reg. 22234, 22235 and 22236 respectively (1974), as amended 40 Fed. Reg. 24130, 24140 and 24142 (1975).

25. Title VII is discussed extensively in the chapter on Labor Laws, below.

be free from sex discrimination in her employment in the public schools is concerned, the Equal Rights Amendment will have no substantive effect--that is, it will not create a new right.

However, the Amendment may very well create a new remedy for faculty members who believe they have been discriminated against on the basis of sex. This remedy will be independent of, and in addition to, any remedy they have under Title VII. Under the case law regarding racial discrimination in employment, a woman could sue in federal court for damages if she has been discriminated against by the public schools because of her sex. Essentially, this remedy would be the result of applying 42 U.S.C. Sec. 1983, a post-Civil War civil rights statute which gives a cause of action for damages suffered if a state deprives any person of rights guaranteed by the Constitution. Because the Equal Rights Amendment will create a new constitutional right--the right not to be treated differently by states on account of sex--action for damages may be brought under 42 U.S. C. Sec. 1983 if a person believes that such discrimination has occurred.

The advantages of this new remedy are two-fold. First, it would allow a woman to sue for damages, back pay, reinstatement and injunctive relief. See Johnson v. Cincinnati, 450 F. 2d 796 (6th Cir. 1971); and Sanders v. Dobbs House, Inc., 431 F. 2d 1097 (5th Cir. 1970), cert. denied, 401 U.S. 948 (1971).

Second, and more important, it would provide much more time within which to file a suit than the Title VII statute of limitations now permits. Under Title VII, an individual must file a claim with the agency charged with enforcing Title VII, the Equal Employment Opportunity Commission (EEOC), within 180 days of the occurrence of the discrimination if there is no state agency which handles such a claim. If there is a state agency, a claim must be filed with that agency first and then 60 days thereafter with the EEOC. If the EEOC takes no action on the claim within 180 days, the complainant must bring a civil action within 90 days after receiving EEOC authorization to sue (commonly called a "right to sue" letter).

Under 42 U.S.C. Sec. 1983, however, there is no statute of limitations and the courts will apply the appropriate state statute of limitation. For example, in Green v. McDonnell Douglas Corp., 463 F. 2d 337 (8th Cir. 1972), a Missouri court applied a 5-year Missouri statute of limitations which applied to contracts in an employment discrimination case.

Furthermore, a suit brought under 42 U.S.C. Sec. 1983 can be pursued concurrently with a Title VII action. See Young v. International Telephone and Telegraph Co., 438 F. 2d 757 (3rd Cir. 1971); and Gilliam v. Omaha, 459 F. 2d 63 (8th Cir. 1972). Also, if an individual has already filed with the EEOC and the EEOC is in the process of conciliating the claim, one can sue under a 42 U.S.C. Sec. 1983 claim. Title VII does not deprive the federal district courts of jurisdiction over an action brought under the civil rights statutes. See Johnson v. Cincinnati, cited above.

Title IX of the Education Amendments of 1972 specifically prohibits sex discrimination in full or part-time employment in educational programs and activities which are covered by that Act. The areas of this prohibition, as described in the regulations to Title IX, include: recruitment and advertising; hiring, promotions, tenure, layoffs, right of return and transfers; rate of pay; job assignment classifications and seniority; collective bargaining agreements; fringe benefits; granting and return from leaves of absence, pregnancy leave or leave for persons of either sex to care for children; and any other term, condition or privilege of employment.[26]

Reference

For a full discussion of the legal relationship between Title VII and 42 U.S.C. Secs. 1981, 1983, and 1985 (3), see K. Davidson, R. Ginsburg and H. Kay, Sex-based Discrimination, 799-804 (1974).

---

26. Title IX's Regulations do, however, include a provision which allows disctinctions based on sex if the consideration of sex "is essential to successful operation of the employment function concerned." See Title IX Regulations, Secs. 86.41-86.51, 39 Fed. Reg. 22236-22238 (1974), as amended Secs. 86.51-86.61, 40 Fed. Reg. 24135-24136 and 24143-24144 (1975). A similar limitation contained in Title VII is known as the "bona-fide occupational qualification" or "BFOQ." If the "BFOQ" concept under Title VII and the analogous provision in the Title IX Regulations are strictly limited to "unique physical characteristics," they will be constitutional under the Equal Rights Amendment. Examples of such "BFOQ's" are wet nurses and sperm donors. Broader definitions would, however, fall under the Amendment. See the first chapter, The Equal Rights Amendment and the Constitution, above, for a discussion of the "unique physical characteristics" test.

See Brown, Emerson, Falk and Freedman, "The Equal Rights Amendment: A Constitutional Basis for Equal Rights for Women," 80 Yale L. J. 871, 926-927 (1971) for a discussion of the BFOQ exception to Title VII and its constitutionality under the Equal Rights Amendment.

Pregnancy and Employment in the Public Schools

Legal problem: While Title VII of the 1964 Civil Rights
Act has applied to all state institutions since 1972, and thus
prohibits sex discrimination in employment in the public
schools in every state, the law is often difficult to enforce
due to the tremendous backlog of complaints on file with the
EEOC, and the need to hire private counsel to prosecute
private complaints. Thus, although the following suggestions
are already law under Title VII, since they will also be
required under an ERA, compliance would be greatly improved
if they were written into a statewide education code rather
than left solely to private enforcement under Title VII or
42 U.S.C. Sec. 1983.

Possible solutions: The following provisions should be
included in any general education code: (1) public schools
cannot refuse to hire teachers or teachers' aides because of
pregnancy; (2) pregnancy must be treated like any other
temporary disability as regards sick leave pay, time off,
and right to return to the job;[27] (3) male teachers should
receive leave for childrearing for the same length of time
that female teachers may take such leave without risk to their
jobs or employment benefits. The regulations to Title IX
regarding employment by educational institutions conform to
the suggestions contained here.[28]

---

27. The due process clause of the fourteenth amendment
prohibits school boards from enforcing mandatory maternity
leaves which do not take into account individual health and
ability. See Cleveland Board of Education v. LaFleur and
Cohen v. Chesterfield County School Board, 414 U.S. 632 (1974).
See also the section on restrictive labor laws applying to
women only in the chapter on Labor Laws, for a discussion of
mandatory maternity leaves, the due process clause and
Title VII.

28. Title IX Regulations, Sec. 86.41(b) (6) and 86.47,
39 Fed. Reg. 22236 and 22237 (1974), as amended Secs. 86.51(b)
(6) and 86.57, 40 Fed. Reg. 24135, 24143-24144 (1975).

148

References

1.   The question of leave for fathers to rear children has been raised under Title VII, although it may not be definitively answered.   A motion to dismiss was denied in Danielson v. Board of Education, 4 F.E.P. Cases 885 (S.D.N.Y. 1972).

2.   Note, "Constitutional Law--Mandatory Maternity Leave Termination and Return Provisions of School Boards Violate the Due Process Clause of the Fourteenth Amendment," Drake L. Rev. 23:690 (1974).

3.   Note, "Mandatory Maternity Leave for Teachers--Now a Thing of the Past?," 3 Capital U. L. Rev. 323 (1974).

4.   Binder, "Pregnancy, Maternity Leave and Title VII," 1 Ohio North L. Rev. 31 (1973).

5.   Cary, "Pregnancy Without Penalty," 1 Civ. Lib. Rev. 31 (1973).

6.   Note, "Current Trends in Pregnancy Benefits--1972 EEOC Guidelines Interpreted," 24 De Paul L. Rev. 127 (1974).

7.   Note, "Effect of Title VII and the Proposed Equal Rights Amendment on Mandatory Maternity Leaves for Teachers," 12 J. Family L. 447 (1973).

8.   Note, "Problem for the School Systems: Are Mandatory Maternity Leave Rules Enforceable?," 27 Sw. L. J. 542 (1973).

9.   Ruben and Willis, "Discrimination Against Women in Employment in Higher Education," 20 Clev. St. L. R. 472 (1971).

10.   Bartlett, "Pregnancy and the Constitution: the Uniqueness Trap," 62 Calif. L. Rev. 1532 (1974).

11.   Picker, "Sex Discrimination in Public Education and Local Government Employment," 5 Urban Law 307 (1973).

STATE ADMINISTRATION OF SEX-RESTRICTED PRIVATE SCHOLARSHIPS

Legal problem: In a famous series of decisions concerning the will of Stephen Girard, the problem of state administration of a racially restricted private trust was addressed by the U.S. Supreme Court and by the Court of Appeals of the Third Circuit.   In the first case, Pennsylvania v. Board of Trusts, 353 U.S. 230 (1957), the Supreme Court held the administration of a "whites only" private trust by a Board composed of city officials and others to be discrimination by the state and therefore prohibited by the fourteenth amendment; the Court found Girard College to be an agency of the state.

Subsequently, Pennsylvania state courts substituted private persons as trustees. The Supreme Court denied certiorari; in re Girard College Trusteeship, 391 Pa. 434, 138 A. 2d 844, cert. denied, 357 U.S. 570 (1958). The Third Circuit, however, held that the substitution of the trustees was unconstitutional state action. See Brown v. Pennsylvania, 392 F. 2d 120 (1968), cert. denied, 391 U.S. 921 (1968).[29]

That litigation under the fourteenth amendment raises an analogous issue under an Equal Rights amendment: may state schools accept and administer privately-established scholarships which are restricted by their terms to benefit only one sex?

Possible solutions: The Equal Rights Amendment should be interpreted as prohibiting the administration of all private sex-restricted scholarships by state institutions. While it is clear that this is the result with regard to men, analogous to whites in the Girard College litigation, it might be argued that where the beneficiaries of such discrimination are women, allowing discrimination in their favor will help to compensate for past discrimination against them. However, for the reasons set forth at length in the Yale article[30] and elsewhere in this Commentary,[31] "benign" discrimination has no place in the interpretation of the Equal Rights Amendment. The regulations of Title IX also prohibit the administration of sex-restricted scholarships by institutions to which the Act applies.[32]

------

29. It is interesting to note that the Girard Trust was sexually, as well as racially, discriminatory; it set up a school for white, male orphans. The sex discrimination point was never raised in the litigation.

30. Brown, Emerson, Falk and Freedman, "The Equal Rights Amendment: A Constitutional Basis for Equal Rights for Women," 80 Yale L. J. 871, 892 and 903 (1971).

31. See the section on compensatory aid in the chapter on The Equal Rights Amendment and the Constitution, above.

32. Title IX Regulations, Sec. 86.35, 39 Fed. Reg. 22236 (1974), as amended Secs. 86.37 and 86.38, 40 Fed. Reg. 24131 and 24142 (1975). The regulations also prohibit providing students with different types or amounts of financial assistance based on the sex of the applicant regardless of the source of the funds.

Thus, any private sex-restricted scholarships now administered by state schools will have to be distributed to both sexes without regard to the sex-specific terms of the scholarship, or returned to the donor if only that result will correspond with the intent of the gift. Because this is a matter which state officials might honestly but easily overlook after the effective date of the Amendment, it is suggested that a state statute or regulation be enacted to resolve the matter.

References

1. Concerning the lengthy Girard College litigation, see Clark, "Charitable Trusts, The Fourteenth Amendment and the Will of Stephen Girard," 66 Yale L. J. 979 (1957).

2. Concerning this subject generally, see Comment, "Sex-Restricted Scholarships and the Charitable Trust," 50 Ia. L. Rev. 1000 (1974).

SUGGESTIONS FOR AFFIRMATIVE ACTION IN EDUCATION

The following brief suggestions are only a few of those which could be made for programs not legally required in public schools by the Equal Rights Amendment but which, if instituted, would implement the spirit of the Amendment throughout society.

Day Care Centers for Children of Students, Staff and Faculty at Colleges and Universities

Many students in university settings have small children; it is most often women's educations which are hampered by the need to care for them. To make it easier for women students to complete their educations, an adequate number of child care centers should be established around all public campuses to meet the needs of all persons connected with such institutions. Such centers would relieve women of some of the burdens of child care, and thus encourage more women to work and teach full-time, thereby developing their own careers.

Reference

B. Babcock, A. Freedman, E. Norton and S. Ross, Sex Discrimination and the Law 804-816 (1975).

Before and After School Programs at Public Grade Schools for the Children of Working Parents

Millions of young children's mothers and fathers work out of necessity; these children are left unattended in the majority of instances. To further both the careers of women and the development of children, public schools should offer stimulating before and after school programs for all children who attend a particular school.

Admissions Policies of State Institutions Should Take into Account the Current Sex Role of Women in American Society

Many undergraduate and graduate institutions evaluate applications upon what are essentially sex-based criteria, because they reward roles most often played by men in society while ignoring those most often played by women. For instance, in evaluating applicants, all schools give credit for extra-curricular sports activities or leadership positions in student governments, but few would think the experience of being a mother or a secretary worthy of much note. Such criteria in effect discriminate against women because of the roles which society still expects women to play.

Secondly, schools must change their policies concerning part-time attendance to make it easier for women, who still bear the primary burden of child care, to attend school and also carry out their home responsibilities. Insisting, for instance, that all law school students finish in three years discourages many women from attending law school at all. Given the present state of the society, women with children to care for are placed under an unfair burden when asked to complete school in the same length of time which it takes an unmarried man, or a married man whose wife assumes most or all household responsibilities.

Finally, transfers between schools should be made a great deal easier in recognition of the fact that women customarily move when their husbands' jobs require it. If all schools in the country made transfers more readily available, women would not have to make the untenable choice of quitting their education or leaving their families.

Teachers and Counselors in All State Schools Should Be Required
to Take Periodic Courses in the Equal Rights Amendment and the
Role of Women in American Society

It is a fact that many of our nation's young people are
being educated and counseled by persons who are either ignorant
of, or hostile to, the aims of the Equal Rights Amendment and
the women's movement. States should require, as a condition
of teachers' and counselors' certifications, that they take
periodic "sensitivity" courses to educate them to the need for
the Amendment and the genuine problems women face in society.

All State Schools, from Kindergarten to Graduate Level,
Should Establish Part-time Teaching Jobs for Teachers with
Primary Responsibility for Rearing Children

Such a program would encourage women to develop their
careers, while recognizing that women are still those primarily
responsible for child care in the United States. Any such
program should be open, of course, to those men who are the
childrearers in their families.

State Universities Should Repeal or Revise Anti-nepotism
Rules

A major effect of the anti-nepotism rules now in effect
in many, if not most, state colleges and universities is to
keep women professionals from pursuing their careers. This is
so because many women with Ph.D.s are married to men with Ph.D.s--
and it is still most often the man's job that will determine
where the couple lives. Thus, if the husband is on a faculty
which has an anti-nepotism rule in force, and there is no other
university or college in the community, the effect of the rule
is to deprive the wife of a chance to develop her own career.

State Universities Should Revise Their Policies Concerning
Hiring of Their Own Graduates

Many women who obtain Master's Degrees of Ph.D.s are
married; most often, their husbands are settled into a career
which is considered more important than the wife's. Thus,
the place where a couple lived while the wife was attending
school is also most likely to be their life-long residence.
If the university there will not hire its own graduates, the

wife is effectively denied a chance to pursue the career she could otherwise have. The very common rule many institutions have against hiring their own graduates, then, often works against the career aspirations of women.

Textbooks

Sexism in textbooks is now well-recognized, although the problem is far from being solved. School systems and state boards of education should do everything possible to see that the textbooks used in schools, from first grade on, are as free as possible from sex-role stereotyping.

Reference

Note, "Sex Discrimination--The Textbook Case," 62 Calif. L. Rev. 1312 (1974).

Consideration of Compulsory Shop and Home Economics Courses for Students of Both Sexes

Sweden has adopted a program which requires both boys and girls to study both home economics and shop in an attempt to avoid the sex-role pitfalls of the present generation. Such compulsory requirements for students of both sexes might be considered by schools in this country as a helpful move in the direction of ameliorating the present division of labor between women and men.

Chapter Four

FAMILY LAWS

Table of Contents

INTRODUCTION

The potential effect of the Equal Rights Amendment on family law in the United States has generated more misunderstanding than any other area to be affected. Opponents of the Amendment have said repeatedly that it will require all wives to immediately take paying jobs in order to fulfill the equalized duty of support which the Amendment will necessitate. Opponents have even said that because all wives will have to work outside the home, the Amendment will <u>require</u> the establishment of day-care centers for young children on a massive scale.

Such fears are totally unfounded. The fact is that in some states an equalized duty of support has existed by statute for over 70 years;[1] in no state has such a statute meant that all wives had to take paying jobs outside the home. Further, eleven states have adopted Equal Rights Amendments to their state constitutions and under them have equalized the duty of support: in none of these states has the state Equal Rights Amendment meant that all wives are today under a legal duty to work for compensation outside the home.

In fact, as the authors of the influential Yale article on the Equal Rights Amendment argue--and as was stated clearly in the Congressional debate on the Amendment--the duty of support can be rendered <u>in</u> the home by performing services, or <u>outside</u> the home by earning money with which to pay for a family's needs. Thus, to suggest, as opponents of the Amendment do, that labor performed for the family in the home will not legally be construed as "support" of the family after passage of the Equal Rights Amendment belies its history.

The suggestion becomes totally unrealistic when the economic effects of such an interpretation are considered. Under the construction offered by opponents of the Amendment, literally millions upon millions of women, almost all of whom would surely be unemployed, would be put into the labor market immediately. Unemployment rolls would swell beyond imagination; every state unemployment compensation program would be bankrupt in a matter of weeks. To say that the Equal Rights Amendment will be construed by the courts to <u>require</u> that result, as a matter of law, strains credulity.

---

1. <u>See</u> for example, N.M. Stat. Ann. Sec. 57-2-1 (1953), enacted in 1907 by the New Mexico Territorial Legislature which provides: "Husband and wife contract toward each other obligations of mutual respect, fidelity and support."

Thus, the history of state Equal Rights Amendments and their interpretations; the interpretation of equalized duties of support where they have existed by statute for many years; the clear intent of Congress in this regard in passing the ERA; and the wrenching economic chaos which such a construction of the Amendment would bring make this interpretation of the Amendment's effect on family law utterly unrealistic.

If the Amendment will not legally require all women to immediately take paying jobs and day care centers to be established to tend their children, what will it do in the area of family law? This Commentary seeks to answer that question in a straightforward manner.

First, the Amendment will require that states carefully re-examine the marital property laws which determine the ownership of the earnings and property of both spouses acquired by either of them during marriage. This extremely important aspect of the Amendment's effect is discussed below in the chapter on Marital Property Laws.

Second, the Amendment should generate imaginative solutions to problems many women in American society now face almost alone. Those problems are illustrated by stark and undeniable statistics: (1) the divorce rate has doubled between 1963 and 1973;[2] (2) in the twelve-month period ending in February 1975, there were 2,215,000 marriages and 981,000 divorces;[3] (3) many of those broken marriages have produced children who are minors and must be cared for by one or the other parent; (4) mothers are given custody of children in 95% of child custody cases, but in 85% of those cases, the father has expressly consented to the mother's custody;[4] although child support is ordered in almost every case, in 42% of those cases the husband, almost always the party ordered to make payments, defaults on the court-ordered payments during the first year. By the tenth year, fully 79% of ex-husbands are in total noncompliance;[5] (6) faced with this

---

2. Monthly Vital Statistics Report, Provisional Statistics, Annual Summary for the United States, 1973. (HRA) 74-1120, Vol. 22 (13), June 27, 1974, p. 9.

3. Monthly Vital Statistics Report, Provisional Statistics, (HRA) 75-1120, Vol. 24 (2), April 24, 1975, pp. 1-3.

4. Nagel and Weitzman, "Women as Litigants," 23 Hastings L. J. 171, 189n. 47, citing W. Goode, After Divorce 311, 313 (1956).

5. Weitzman, "Legal Regulation of Marriage: Tradition and Change," 62 Calif. L. Rev. 1169 (1974).

158

situation, many, if not most, divorced mothers, often with little higher education or professional training, enter a labor market in which the average wage of a working woman is 57% that of a working man.[6]

These statistics reveal, quite simply, a national tragedy. Those who oppose the Amendment may not be aware that millions upon millions of women in the United States are shouldering the entire economic burden, as well as the overwhelming physical and psychological burdens, of raising children from a former marriage with little or no help from their ex-husbands. In this critically important area, then, the Amendment should and will offer great improvement in the lives of many women if sincere efforts are made to fashion new solutions to problems which are largely unrecognized today.

THE MARRIAGE CONTRACT: RIGHTS AND DUTIES

Rights and Duties in Marriage: Governed by Private Contract or State Law?

Legal problem: Marriage today is a legally binding contract, the terms of which are established by the law of the state in which a couple resides. In most states, each marriage partner is deemed to have agreed to certain conditions--the husband to support his wife, the wife to render services to her husband; the ownership of property acquired during the marriage, as determined by the state's property laws; and other, often sex-discriminatory, terms of marriage which are discussed further below.

Although a couple may privately agree to adhere to different duties than those imposed by the state, their private agreement is completely unenforceable in a court of law. Thus, there is no sanction whatsoever available today to enforce private marriage contracts as to marriage duties. The state-imposed contract is enforceable, but only upon the parties' divorce--not during the marriage itself.

The parties may, however, agree to different terms of property ownership than state law would otherwise provide. Unlike agreements concerning personal duties, private agreements as to marital property and its ownership are legally enforceable.

---

6. Statistical Abstract of the United States 340 (1974) (1973 data).

How should the present concepts of the rights and duties assumed upon marriage be reformed after passage of the Equal Rights Amendment?

Possible solution: There are two views currently put forward as to the legal rights and duties which accrue upon marriage. One is that the parties to any marriage should be free to contract between themselves as to the duties and rights of each of the partners, including responsibility for housekeeping, childbearing and rearing, work outside the home, property ownership and other incidents. For an exposition of this view, see Weitzman, "Legal Regulation of Marriage: Tradition and Change," 62 Calif. L. Rev. 1169 (1974).

An alternate proposal is that the rights and duties assumed upon marriage should continue to be those imposed by the state, as altered and equalized by laws passed after ratification of the Equal Rights Amendment. Proponents of this view believe that under current social customs, many women, in an attempt to please their future husbands, will bargain away rights which they would have under an equal, but state-imposed, marriage contract. For a brief explanation of this position, see B. Babcock, A. Freedman, E. Norton and S. Ross, Sex Discrimination and the Law 564 (1975).

While this basic question will certainly have to be discussed in any revision of the presently state-imposed and sex-discriminatory rights and duties incident to marriage, it cannot be resolved here.

The possibility of allowing both alternatives simultaneously might be considered, however. A statute might provide that the equalized state-imposed duties would prevail and govern the marriage unless the parties themselves supplanted them, either before or at any time during marriage, with a private agreement which imposed different or additional duties.[7] If private

---

7. In providing for "no-fault" divorce, many states have, as a result, taken a long step toward removing many of the state-imposed duties of marriage. The traditional grounds for divorce, which were often sex-discriminatory, had the effect of imposing marriage duties, in that grounds existed for divorce where such duties were broken. By substituting a single ground of "irreconcilable differences" for divorce, the new statutes essentially allow the parties themselves to decide when and why the marriage has failed, rather than forcing them to adhere to a state-imposed definition of the failure of a marriage, as the older statutes did.

marriage contracts are sanctioned by state law, either solely or where they supplant the terms of a state-imposed contract, some mechanism will have to be devised to provide for the court enforcement of such private contracts, since they are now legally unenforceable.[8]

References

1. Weitzman, "Legal Regulation of Marriage: Tradition and Change," 62 Calif. L. Rev. 1169 (1974).

2. B. Babcock, A. Freedman, E. Norton and S. Ross, Sex Discrimination and the Law 564, 631-658 (1975).

3. Fleischmann, "Marriage by Contract: Defining the Terms of Relationship," 8 Family L. Q. 27 (1974).

4. Comment, "Marital Contracts Which May Be Put Asunder," 13 J. Family L. 23 (1973).

5. Note, "Interspousal Contracts: The Potential for Validation in Massachusetts," 9 Suffolk U. L. Rev. 185 (1974).

6. Comment, "Family Law--Volid v. Volid, Reconsideration of the Role of the Antenuptial Agreement in Illinois," 4 Loyola U. L. J. (Chicago) 497 (1973).

7. Note, "Unander v. Unander: Recognition of the Alimony Provision in Antenuptial Contracts," 10 Willamette L. J. 117 (1973).

8. Note, "Public Policy, the Courts, and Antenuptial Agreements Specifying Alimony," 23 U. Fla. L. Rev. 113 (1970).

9. Comment, "Marital Property: A New Look at Old Inequities," 39 Albany L. Rev. 52, 73-79 (1974).

10. Comment, "The Modern Theory and Practice of Antenuptial Agreements," 5 John Marshall J. 179 (1971).

---

8. It should be noted, however, that under traditional principles of contract law, contracts for services will not be "specifically enforced" by courts. Under this principle, only damages may be awarded where a party to a contract calling for services to be performed defaults on that contract; a court will not order the party to perform the service itself.

Marital Property Laws

In the absence of a contract between the spouses regarding their property rights, the law of the state in which they are domiciled will determine the ownership of the property and earnings of each during marriage.

These marital property laws are of such great importance and full-scale reform is so essential that they are explained and discussed at length in a separate chapter of this Commentary. However, because some understanding of the two systems of marital property law in operation in the United States today is necessary to understand support rights and duties during marriage and property division on divorce, a brief explanation of each is set forth here.

The two systems of marital property law in the United States are very different, both in theory and operation. Community property, descended from Spanish and French law, is the marital property law of Arizona, California, Idaho, Louisiana, Nevada, New Mexico, Texas and Washington. In those states, each spouse has a legal one-half ownership interest in the earnings of the other spouse acquired after marriage and in all proceeds of those earnings. In five of the community property states--all except Louisiana, Nevada and Texas--the husband and wife have equal powers to manage and control the community property; to create debts which bind the community; and to obtain credit based on the community's creditworthiness without regard to which spouse's income forms the community property. Under the community property system, all property brought to the marriage by either of the spouses, or inherited or given to one of them during marriage, remains that spouse's separate property in which the other has no right, title or interest.

The remainder of the fifty states and the District of Columbia comprise the forty-three separate property jurisdictions in the United States. Under that law, derived from the common law of England, each spouse owns as his or her "separate" property whatever he or she earns, just as each did as a single person. Obviously, under present employment conditions, the husband will earn more than the wife, or may be the only wage earner in the family. All his income, under the theory of the separate property jurisdictions, is his alone, subject only to a duty to support the wife and any children. Upon divorce, the wife may or may not receive a share of the property accumulated by the husband during marriage; the questions of property division on divorce and suggested reforms are discussed at length below.

The separate property systems do recognize a community of interest in property acquired by either spouse during marriage

162

in the provisions, found in forty of the forty-three jurisdictions, for a "forced share" interest of a surviving spouse in property of the deceased, regardless of the deceased spouse's personal wishes. This aspect of the separate property systems is discussed in greater detail in the chapter on Marital Property Laws.

With this brief overview of the underlying theories of the community and separate property systems, we turn to a discussion of family laws in the United States.

References

In addition to the references in the chapter on Marital Property Laws, see:

1. Wenig, "Sex, Property and Probate," 9 Real Prop. Probate & Trust J. 642 (1974).

2. Younger, "Women's Property Rights Are Unfair," 111 Trusts & Estates 942 (1972).

3. Glendon, "Matrimonial Property: A Comparative Study of Law and Social Change," 49 Tul. L. Rev. 21 (1974).

4. Gabler, "The Impact of the ERA on Domestic Relations Law: Specific Focus on California," 8 Family L. Q. 51 (1974).

5. Lay, "The Role of the Matrimonial Domicile in Marital Property Rights," 5 Family L. Q. 61 (1970).

The Duty of Child and Spousal Support

Legal problem: At common law and in many states by statute today, the state-imposed duties of marriage differ according to the sex of the spouse. The husband is given the primary duty of supporting the wife and children. The wife is primarily obligated to render household and wifely services, with liability imposed to support the husband and any children only if the husband cannot or will not fulfill his support duties. Such laws, whether made by statute or court decision, will be unconstitutional under the Equal Rights Amendment.

Possible solution: In those states which have recently revised their statutes in conformance with state Equal Rights Amendments, the duty to support has been extended by statute to both spouses equally, with no mention made of any duty on either spouse's part to render services.

As interpreted by the authors of the Yale article, such statutes mean only that support can be contributed in a variety of ways. Therefore, a wife who performs unpaid labor in the home will be contributing the required support to the other spouse. If both work outside the home for compensation, and have equal earning capacities, neither will be liable for the other's support.[9]

Given the reluctance of the courts to interfere in an ongoing marriage, allocation of responsibility for earning income and caring for the home and children will continue to be largely a private decision of husband and wife. However, men as well as women suffer from the traditional assumption that only husbands are responsible for support and only wives are responsible for domestic duties.

In two recent cases, the United States Supreme Court held statutes based on those assumptions, and which therefore denied dependent husbands and widowers government benefits which were routinely available to dependent wives and widows, to be in violation of the fourteenth amendment equal protection clause. See Frontiero v. Richardson, 411 U.S. 677 (1973) and Weinberger v. Wiesenfeld, 95 S. Ct. 1225 (1975).

The duty to support, when extended to both spouses equally under an ERA, is troublesome not in its statement but in its application in an ongoing marriage. Under present law, the duty to support is totally unenforceable in a civil action except upon divorce or separation. For a brief discussion of the problem of enforcement of support duties during marriage, see the section immediately following.

Although civil orders concerning the duty to support cannot be obtained during a marriage, there are criminal penalties for the nonsupport of children or a spouse during marriage. As with the civil duty to support, these criminal penalties are typically placed upon a man who fails to support his wife or children, but only upon a mother who fails to support her children.

There is much doubt as to both the effectiveness and the fairness of criminal nonsupport laws. Many believe that sound policy dictates their repeal. In lieu of that, the ERA will

---

9. It might be noted that one effect of extending the duty of support to both sexes will be to make the wife's property liable under the present law for "necessaries" furnished to any member of the family.

require that criminal nonsupport laws, just as the civil duty of support, be imposed equally on wives as well as husbands. The Model Penal Code's section 230.5 (Proposed Official Draft 1962) is an example of a sex-neutral criminal nonsupport statute.

However, the most important aspect of the duty of support which must be considered in any thorough revision of state laws pertaining to marriage and the family is the economic dependency which both present support laws and a simply "equalized" support statute force upon a person who performs uncompensated domestic labor for many years.

Under present law in the separate property states, the uncompensated homemaker, usually the wife, has no legal right to credit during marriage except with her husband's consent; has no legal ownership of property which her husband earns, except if he chooses to give it to her; and accrues no Social Security or pension rights of her own. In other words, simple extension of the duty to support to both spouses after passage of the Equal Rights Amendment, will leave the status and economic opportunities of unsalaried women largely unaffected, unless there is thorough consideration and statutory treatment of the practical problems created by the lack of compensation for household labor in our society.

One answer to this problem might be widespread adoption of the community property system, with the revisions suggested below in the chapter on Marital Property Laws to improve the system. Another partial solution would be enactment of a massive change in the federal Social Security system to give workers in the home a share in the Social Security system in their own right.

While thorough discussion of possible solutions to this problem is beyond the scope of this Commentary, it must be recognized that a meaningful answer to the economic problems of married women who work without salaries is far more complex and challenging than simply extending the "duty to support" in a sex-neutral fashion. It is, in fact, one of the central problems to which the spirit, if not the letter, of the Amendment is addressed. It cannot be ignored in any serious attempt to deal with the situation of married women in American society.

References

1. K. Davidson, R. Ginsburg and H. Kay, Sex-based Discrimination 139-149 (1974).

2. Brown, Emerson, Falk and Freedman, "The Equal Rights Amendment; A Constitutional Basis for Equal Rights for Women," 80 Yale L. J. 871, 944-946 (1971).

3. Report of the Citizen's Advisory Council on the Status of Women, Women in 1971, Appendix C, "The Equal Rights Amendment and Alimony and Child Support Laws," 38 (1972).

4. For a view that legal provisions should be made to give homemaking the status and perquisites of a full-time career for those who choose it, see Report of the Marriage and Family Committee of the National Organization for Women, Suggested Guidelines in Studying and Comments on the Uniform Marriage and Divorce Act (April 11, 1971).

5. Sayre, "Property Rights of Husband and Wife," Selected Essays on Family Law 503 (A.A.L.S. 1950).

6. Sayre, "A Reconsideration of the Husband's Duty to Support and the Wife's Duty to Render Services," 29 Va. L. Rev. 857 (1943).

7. See also the Uniform Civil Liability for Support Act, which imposes differing duties of support on husband and wife and will need revision under the ERA. 9 Uniform Laws Annotated (1973).

8. Model Penal Code, Sec. 230.5 (Proposed Official Draft 1962).

9. Weitzman, "Legal Regulation of Marriage: Tradition and Change," 62 Calif. L. Rev. 1169, 1180-1197 (1974).

10. S. Ross, The Rights of Women 267-273 (1973).

11. Comment, "The Effect of the Equal Rights Amendment on Kentucky's Domestic Relations Law," 12 J. Family L. 151 (1972-73).

12. Krauskopf and Thomas, "Partnership Marriage: The Solution to an Ineffective and Inequitable Law of Support," 35 Ohio St. L. J. 558 (1974).

The Problem of Civil Enforcement of Support Rights in the Ongoing Family

Legal problem: Under present law, courts universally refuse to "interfere" in a marriage relationship to enforce the husband's duty, imposed by the state upon marriage, to support his wife and children. For the most notorious example of such a refusal, see McGuire v. McGuire, 157 Neb. 226, 59 N.W. 2d 336 (S. Ct. Neb. 1953), where the Nebraska Supreme Court refused to order a husband with substantial assets to install indoor plumbing.

With passage of the Equal Rights Amendment, what is now the husband's duty of support will be extended equally to both spouses. However, the problem of effective enforcement of that duty of support will remain. Thus, while children and the spouse who performs the duty of support by doing uncompensated domestic work will have the legal right to monetary support from the compensated spouse, the enforcement of that right will be impossible unless current law is substantially changed.

Possible solutions: One solution which seems obvious would be to require by statute that courts enter support orders during an ongoing marriage. The problem, of course, is that most economically dependent spouses lack access to expensive legal help and would take such action only in the most dire circumstances.

A second problem is that after passage of the ERA, while a wage-earning spouse might be ordered to pay money, the uncompensated spouse who carries out support duties by doing household labor could not, under well-established principles of contract law, be ordered to perform services in return for monetary support. Thus, the most obvious solution is not the most helpful.

A second possible solution is outlined below in the chapter on Marital Property Laws, where the interplay between the community property system, as amended to give each spouse equal management powers, and the Equal Credit Opportunity Act, passed by Congress in 1974 and effective on October 28, 1975, is described. After the effective date of that Act, in the five community property states with completely equal management systems, wives who perform uncompensated domestic work in the home will enjoy precisely the same access to credit which their husbands have. Of course, if the community (the two spouses together) is not creditworthy, the right to support cannot be effectuated by the wife's use of the community's credit. In such instances, the right of support would be difficult to enforce under any law: households without credit are often households without adequate income or assets from which a spouse and children can be supported.

While the problem of enforcement of support rights during marriage is widely recognized, it has yet to be commented upon extensively. However, any meaningful revision of state laws must take the problem into account. Widespread enactment of the community property system, with equal management rights in both spouses, at least would give middle and upper-class wives a practical and simple means of enforcing support rights in an ongoing marriage through the use of credit.

Yet another alternative would be to give wives in separate property states the right to obtain credit for any item they wished to purchase, whether or not that item constituted a "necessary" or a "family expense." See the chapter on Marital Property Laws for an explanation of those doctrines and a discussion of desirable revisions in them.

References

1. B. Babcock, A. Freedman, E. Norton and S. Ross, Sex Discrimination and the Law 623-630 (1975).

2. "The ERA: A Symposium," 3 Human Rights L. Rev. 125, 143 (1973).

3. K. Davidson, R. Ginsburg and H. Kay, Sex-based Discrimination 139-149 (1974).

4. H. Clark, The Law of Domestic Relations, ch. 6 (1968).

Legal Rights and Duties in Putative and Common-Law Marriages

Legal problem: Many jurisdictions in the United States do not recognize the validity of putative marriages, or those entered into in good faith by the party claiming rights under the ceremony. Many other states do not recognize the validity of common-law marriages (in which no ceremony has been performed, but the parties have agreed to live as husband and wife and have held themselves out as such).

A legal marriage confers rights and duties, as well as property ownership and benefits. In a society in which the majority of married women are not employed outside the home for compensation, a rule of state law which denies the validity of putative or common-law marriages will deny the wives in such marriages important benefits, including rights to property accrued by the "husband" during the marriage. Such a rule possibly violates the Equal Rights Amendment because it is "neutral on its face, but discriminatory in impact."

Possible solution: To ensure the property and other rights of women in putative and common-law marriages, sections 209, 210 and 211 (alternative A) of the Uniform Marriage and Divorce Act, which recognize the validity of such marriages, should be adopted in all states. Failure to make such laws part of the statutory law of a jurisdiction will mean prolonged litigation when the question does arise; and in the interim, the women in such marriages will be denied property and other rights.

References

1. Uniform Marriage and Divorce Act, 9 Uniform Laws Annotated, 209, 210 and 211 (alternative A) (West 1973).

2. Comment, "In Re-Marriage of Cary (109 Cal. Rptr. 862); Equitable Rights Granted to the Meretricious Spouse," 9 U. San Fran. L. Rev. 186 (1974).

3. Miller, "The Return of the Common Law Marriage to California," 8 J. Beverly Hills B. Ass'n. 19 (1974).

4. Note, "Competitive Rights of the Legal and Putative Wives," 1 Loyola U. L. Rev. (L.A.) 99 (1968).

5. Valeri, "Informal Marriages and Other Curative Devices," 17 How. L. J. 558 (1972).

6. Luther and Luther, "Support and Property Rights of the Putative Spouse," 24 Hastings L. J. 311 (1973).

7. Note, "In Re Cary: A Judicial Recognition of Illicit Cohabitation," 25 Hastings L. J. 1226 (1974).

SEX-DISCRIMINATORY ASPECTS OF THE LEGAL EFFECTS OF MARRIAGE

Rights of Consortium

Legal problem: Today, under the law in thirty-one jurisdictions, a husband has the right to sue for his own loss if his wife suffers a permanent injury which results in depriving the husband of the wife's services, affection and sexual relations. In the law, this action is called "loss of consortium." The husband's right to sue is independent of his wife's cause of action against the person who injured her. On the other hand, in those same jurisdictions, if a husband receives a permanent injury, his wife has no such independent cause of action for her loss. Such a rule of tort law will be unconstitutional after passage of the Equal Rights Amendment.

Possible solution: While the rationale for refusing to extend the right to sue for loss of consortium to wives was based on the theory that it would permit the spouses jointly a "double recovery," such a theory has now been expressly rejected in twenty states. Thus, although it is theoretically possible that this inequality could be corrected by denying husbands their right to sue for loss of consortium, such a result seems unlikely in view of the recent trend toward allowing wives to sue on this cause of action. Thus, the probable effect of the Amendment in this area will be to give wives an independent cause of action for loss of consortium in all fifty states.

References

1. Brown, Emerson, Falk and Freedman, "The Equal Rights Amendment: A Constitutional Basis for Equal Rights for Women," 80 Yale L. J. 871, 943 (1971).

2. Gabler, "The Impact of the ERA: Specific Focus on California," 8 Family L. Q. 51, 70 (1974).

3. For a comment on the case holding that an action for loss of consortium had to be brought with the spouse's suit or was lost altogether, see Comment, "Husband and Wife: Collateral Estoppel in the Consortium Action," 27 Okla. L. Rev. 267 (1974). (This result could be prohibited by statute.)

4. Comment, "Torts--Recovery for Negligently Inflicting Loss of Consortium Recognized for Both Spouses," 8 Univ. Suffolk L. Rev. 1334 (1974).

5. Note, "Equal Protection: The Wife's Action for Loss of Consortium," 54 Ia. L. Rev. 510 (1968).

6. Spero, "Wife's Action for Loss of Consortium," 17 Clev. Mar. L. Rev. 462 (1968).

7. Hume, "Liability to Wife for Loss of Consortium: An Update," 24 Federation Ins. Counsel Q. 36 (1974).

8. Comment, "Wife's Right to Recover for the Loss of Consortium," 2 Cumber.-Sam. L. Rev. 189 (1971).

9. Note, "Domestic Relations--Wife Has Right of Action Against Tortfeasor for Loss of Consortium," 2 Cumber.-Sam L. Rev. 464 (1971).

10. Note, "Husband and Wife--Loss of Consortium," 6 Suffolk U. L. Rev. 158 (1971).

11. Note, "Torts--The Action for Loss of Consortium in New Mexico," 2 N.M. L. Rev. 107 (1972).

12. Weisman, "Wife's Action for Loss of Consortium," 20 Clev. St. L. Rev. 315 (1971).

Wife's Name and Domicile After Marriage

Names of Married Women

Legal problem: Although only Hawaii explicitly requires by statute that a wife assume her husband's name upon marriage, other states have statutes, such as voter registration laws, driver's license laws, laws which exclude married women from the class of those who may legally change their names, and laws which provide that a wife may resume her maiden name upon divorce, which implicitly assume that upon marriage a woman either may or must take her husband's surname. Under an Equal Rights Amendment, statutes which either expressly or implicitly require that a wife take her husband's name will be unconstitutional.

Possible solutions: If the Amendment takes effect with no state statute enacted on the subject of married women's names, the Amendment and the common law would allow married persons to use any name which any other person may legally adopt. The common law rule (based on custom and court decisions rather than on statutes) as to names in general is that a person may use any name so long as it is not adopted for fraudulent purposes. Although the U.S. Supreme Court recently affirmed a decision that the common law of Alabama required a woman to take her husband's surname, the Equal Rights Amendment would reverse the common law rule and the Supreme Court's affirmation of it.[10]

However, in the interest of identification of married couples and their children, it is possible that even after passage of an Equal Rights Amendment, a state could statutorily require that married persons use the same surname, which could be any legal name upon which they both agreed--the surname of either of them, some combination thereof or an entirely different name.

Finally, a statute could be enacted which simply affirmed the right of married persons to retain their birth names or to use any other legal names they choose. Such a statute seems the most desirable of the possible solutions, in order to avoid the litigation which would occur if no statute were enacted. It would also avoid the element of coercion which present custom would impose upon many women if the state required married persons to assume one name.

---

10. See Forbush v. Wallace, 401 U.S. 970 (1972), mem. aff'g 341 F. Supp. 217 (M.D. Ala. 1971), discussed above in the first chapter, The Equal Rights Amendment and the Constitution.

Subordinate problem: Names used on state tax returns. Many state tax processing systems are not now programmed to allow the use of two different names by persons filing a joint return. This is because under federal and state income tax statutes only married persons are entitled to file joint tax returns. In the past, tax authorities have assumed that where the names on a joint return were different, the parties were not married. To avoid litigation and confusion on this point, a simple statute should be drafted directing state tax agencies to allow the use of different names for persons filing joint returns.

References

1. Unlike Forbush v. Wallace, cited in n. 10 above, the cases of State ex rel. Krupa v. Green, 114 Ohio App. 497, 177 N.E. 2d 616 (1961), and Stuart v. Board of Supervisors of Elections, 226 Md. 440, 295 A. 2d 223 (1972) hold that the common law of those states does not require a woman to adopt her husband's surname.

2. Brown, Emerson, Falk and Freedman, "The Equal Rights Amendment: A Constitutional Basis for Equal Rights for Women," 80 Yale L. J. 871, 940 (1971).

3. Lamber, "Married Women's Surname: Is Custom Law?," 1973 Wash. L. Q. 779 (1973).

4. Comment, "Right of Women to Use Their Maiden Names," 38 Alb. L. Rev. 105 (1973).

5. Note, "Woman's Right to Her Name," 21 U.C.L.A. L. Rev. 665 (1973).

6. Weitzman, "Legal Regulation of Marriage: Tradition and Change," Calif. L. Rev. 1169, 1173-1175 (1974).

7. K. Davidson, R. Ginsburg and H. Kay, Sex-based Discrimination 123-127 (1974).

8. L. Kanowitz, Women and the Law 41-43 (1969).

9. S. Ross, The Rights of Women 239-255 (1973).

10. Carlson, "Surnames of Married Women and Legitimate Children," 17 N.Y.U. L. F. 552 (1971).

11. Hughes, "And Then There Were Two," 23 Hastings L. J. 233 (1971).

12. "Pre-Marriage Name Change, Resumption and Re-registration Statutes," 74 Colum. L. Rev. 1508 (1974).

13. Daum, "The Right of Married Women to Asset Their Own Surnames," 8 U. Mich. J. L. Rev. 63 (1974).

14. Note, "The Right of Married Woman to Use Her Birth-given Surname for Voter Registration," 32 Md. L. Rev. 409 (1973).

15. Bysiewics and MacDonnell, "Married Women's Surnames," Conn. L. Rev. 598 (1973).

16. Carlsson, "Surnames of Married Women and Legitimate Children" 17 N.Y.U. L. F. 552 (1971).

17. MacDougall, "Married Women's Common Law Right to Their Own Surnames," 1 Women's Rights L. Rep. No. 3, 2 (Fall/Winter 1972-73).

Domicile of Married Women

Legal problem: Under the current law in the majority of states, the legal domicile of a married woman is that of her husband. One result of present domiciliary rules is that a woman student who has been a resident paying resident tuition at a state university will be classified as a nonresident, subject to higher out-of-state tuition fees when she marries a nonresident male student. See Clarke v. Redeker, 259 F. Supp. 117 (S.D. Iowa 1966). Other rights and duties which attach according to the place of a person's legal domicile are the rights to vote and to receive welfare assistance; the duty to pay taxes and serve on local juries; and the ability of local courts to hear certain kinds of cases or suits brought by or pertaining to an individual domiciled there. As to all of these, a married woman is legally domiciled in the state of her husband's legal domicile, regardless of where she may actually reside.

Any rule of law which establishes domicile by reference to an individual's sex will, of course, be unconstitutional after passage of the Equal Rights Amendment.

Possible solution: The Amendment will probably be implemented in this area by passage of statutes which positively allow married persons to establish separate domiciles or by simply repealing present statutes which establish a married woman's domicile as that of her husband. If married persons establish separate domiciles, they will become liable to different states for different duties and be eligible for different benefits which accrue according to domicile.

References

1. L. Kanowitz, Women and the Law 46 (1966).

2. Brown, Emerson, Falk and Freedman, "The Equal Rights for Women," 80 Yale L. J. 871, 941 (1971).

3. K. Davidson, R. Ginsburg and H. Kay, Sex-based Discrimination 127-130 (1974).

4. Annot., "Validity, under Federal Constitution, of State Residency Requirements Relevant to Changing Tuition and Other Fees by Colleges and Universities--Federal Cases," 37 L. Ed. 2d 1056, 1069 (1974).

5. Weitzman, "Legal Regulation of Marriage: Tradition and Change," 62 Calif. L. Rev. 1169, 1175-1177 (1974).

6. Cavers, "Habitual Residence: A Useful Concept?," Am. U. L. Rev. 475 (1972).

Children's Names and Domiciles

Names of Children

Legal problem: If married persons are allowed by state law to use different names after the effective date of the Amendment, a question may arise as to what names would be taken by children born to parents with different names.

Possible solution: The only legislative choice consistent with allowing the parents individually to choose the name or names each of them will use is to also allow them to determine the name or names their children will have. The most a statute could require is that a child's last name be the same as that of one or both parents.

Courts have been extremely reluctant to permit a divorced woman with the legal custody of a child to change her child's surname either to her maiden name or to the name of a step-father if the mother has remarried. In this area, too, the Equal Rights Amendment would give the mother as much right to control the child's name as the father, but the Amendment provides the courts with no guidance for resolving any conflicts between parents. Perhaps the person having legal custody of the child should be given the statutory right to make decisions concerning the child's name, just as a legal guardian has the right to make other decisions concerning the child's maintenance or education.

174

Reference

        H. Clark, Cases and Problems on Domestic Relations
728-729 (2d ed. 1974).

        Domicile of Children

        Legal problem: Current law in all states, reflected in
the Restatement Second, Conflict of Laws, makes the legal
domicile of a child born to married parents that of the father
and the legal domicile of a child born to unmarried parents
that of the mother. Such laws, whether made by statute or
court decision, will violate the Equal Rights Amendment.

        Possible solution: In the case of adults, domicile is
determined by the combination of physical presence and intent
to remain in a given place. However, presumably because courts
have believed that children were incapable of forming the
requisite intent to be domiciled in a place, the current law
establishes rules as to the domicile of "unemancipated" children
which apply regardless of a child's intent.

        "Emancipation" usually means economic independence from
one's parents. Thus, very few persons under the age of majority
are in today's society emancipated. However, many such persons
may in fact have residences which would be their legal domiciles
if the usual rules of "physical presence-plus-intent" were applied
to them instead of arbitrary rules.

        Perhaps a statutory age below which a child was presumed
incapable of forming the requisite intent to establish a
domicile would be a better approach than emancipation. Under
a statutory age approach, if a child were over a given age, the
normal rules which apply to adults would apply to determine the
domicile of the child on the theory that the child was capable
of forming an intent with respect to domicile. If the child
were under the statutory age, arbitrary rules would determine
domicile without regard to intent. The simplest rule would be
that the domicile of a child is where the child actually resides
for the major part of the year.

References

        1. Restatement Second, Conflict of Laws, Sec. 11, 16, 18
and 22 (1971).

2. Brown, Emerson, Falk and Freedman, "The Equal Rights Amendment: A Constitutional Basis for Equal Rights for Women," 80 Yale L. J. 871, 941 (1971).

3. H. Clark, The Law of Domestic Relations 151-152, 241-242 (1968).

THE LEGAL RIGHT TO MARRY

Age at Which Men and Women May Marry

Legal problem: Many state statutes provide that women may marry without parental consent at age 18, while men may marry without such consent only at age 21. Such statutes commonly further provide that women may marry with parental consent at 16, men at 18. Although the recent Supreme Court decision cited in reference no. 4 below has probably already rendered such statutes unconstitutional, the Equal Rights Amendment will certainly have that effect.

Possible solution: In states where the same minimum age for marriage for both sexes has already been established by statute, the trend has been to lower the age for men to that which had prevailed for women. In light of current sexual and social mores, such a pattern seems likely to continue. Conversely, of course, the age at which women may marry could be raised to that at which men may marry, or some intermediate age could be chosen.

References

1. Brown, Emerson, Falk and Freedman, "The Equal Rights Amendment: A Constitutional Basis for Equal Rights for Women," 80 Yale L. J. 871, 938-939 (1971).

2. K. Davidson, R. Ginsburg and H. Kay, Sex-based Discrimination 119-123 (1974).

3. Note, "The Uniform Marriage and Divorce Act--Marital Age Provisions," 57 Minn. L. Rev. 179 (1972).

4. In Stanton v. Stanton, 43 U.S. L. W. 4449 (April 15, 1975), the United States Supreme Court reversed a decision of the Utah Supreme Court and held that a statute establishing different ages of majority for men and women in Utah was unconstitutional. In light of this recent case, it is probable that statutes which establish different ages for marriage are today unconstitutional under the fourteenth amendment equal protection clause.

Homosexual Marriages

Legal problem: In all jurisdictions, marriage by persons of the same sex is either expressly or implicitly prohibited. A student note writer in the Yale Law Journal, as well as opponents of the Equal Rights Amendment, claim or believe that the Amendment would require all states to legalize homosexual marriages. Very simply stated, the theory of this argument is that to deny a man or woman the right to marry another person of his or her sex is to discriminate on the basis of sex.

On the other hand, several leading proponents of the Amendment, including Senators Birch Bayh and Professor Thomas I. Emerson of the Yale Law School, believe that the state laws which deny to men and women alike the right to marry persons of the same sex accord the equality of treatment between the sexes which the Amendment requires, and that the Amendment would not require recognition of the validity of homosexual marriage.

Possible solution: Although it is impossible to predict with complete certainty the outcome of this argument in the courts, two factors strongly suggest that the Amendment will not be interpreted to require states to recognize homosexual marriages. First, this question has already been litigated in the State of Washington under that state's Equal Rights Amendment. The Washington Supreme Court held that the Amendment did not invalidate Washington's law prohibiting homosexual marriages and expressly rejected the theory of the Yale Law Journal cited in reference no. 1 below. See Singer v. Hara, 11 Wash. App. 247, 522 P. 2d, 1187 (1974).

Second, Senator Bayh, the chief sponsor of the ERA in the Senate, stated in debate on the Senate floor that he and the other sponsors of the Amendment did not interpret it to require the legalization of homosexual marriages. His remarks, noted in reference no. 2 below, are extremely important because the United States Supreme Court, as well as all lower courts, traditionally place great emphasis on a chief sponsor's interpretation of an act when asked to ascertain its meaning or application.

Of course, it has always been true that if a particular state legislature wishes to allow homosexual marriages, it may do so, with or without an Equal Rights Amendment.

References

1. Comment, "The Legality of Homosexual Marriage," 82 Yale L. J. 573, 583 et seq. (1973).

2. For Senator Bayh's comments, see 118 Cong. Rec. Part 7, 9314 (daily ed. March 21, 1972).

3. Note, "Constitutional Aspects of the Homosexual's Right to a Marriage License," 12 J. Family L. 607 (1973).

4. Note, "Domestic Relations--Minnesota Marriage Statute Does Not Permit Marriage between Two Persons of the Same Sex and Does Not Violate Constitutionally Protected Rights," 22 Drake L. Rev. 206 (1972).

5. Note, "Heterosexuality: A Prerequisite to Marriage in Texas?," 14 So. Tex. L. J. 220 (1973).

LEGAL RIGHTS OF UNWED PARENTS

Legal problem: Under a series of 1972 United States Supreme Court cases, cited in reference no. 1 below, the constitutional rights of the natural fathers of children born out-of-wedlock have been expanded, as have their duties. In those decisions, the Court said or intimated that a natural father was denied due process of law where his child was given for adoption by the mother alone, with no opportunity afforded him to object or consent to the adoption. As a result, many state statutes allowing a natural mother alone to place a child for adoption have been rendered unconstitutional, as they arguably might have been by passage of the Equal Rights Amendment. Furthermore, the legality of completed adoptions has been cast in doubt where the express consent of the natural father was not obtained. Thus, existing state statutes in this area need extensive revision in light of the 1972 Supreme Court cases concerning the constitutional rights of natural fathers.

It is possible that the same result would have been achieved after passage of the Equal Rights Amendment, since the state laws rendered unconstitutional by the 1972 Supreme Court decisions were statutes which give one sex alone, mothers, the right to consent to the adoption of a child.

Statutory reform is needed to clarify this important area of family law and to remove from the law many states adoption provisions which are already unconstitutional.

Possible solutions: The National Commissioners on Uniform State Laws have drafted a Uniform Parentage Act which seeks to solve the problems presented by the 1972 Supreme Court decisions insofar as the rights of the natural father to consent to the adoption of his child are concerned.

178

Section 24 of the Act seeks to resolve the obvious dilemma: while a natural mother is almost always identified at the child's birth, the natural father rarely is. How, then, may the natural father's rights to consent equally with the mother to the adoption of his child be preserved? Section 24 of the Act attempts to reconcile and balance the conflicting interests and problems by providing for: (1) notice to all persons named by the natural mother as possible fathers of the child; and (2) a hearing which will allow them to claim custodial rights to the child and object to the adoption. If a person does not appear at the hearing, or appears and does not object to the adoption, the court decree allowing the child to be later placed for adoption makes it final and not open to challenge.

Because section 24 does make an explicit distinction between the rights of mothers and fathers of natural children based solely on the sex of the parent, it is possible that it also may be challenged under the Equal Rights Amendment. If it is, the question which will be determinative is whether making such a distinction is justified because of a "unique physical characteristic" of one sex, the physical ability to bear children, resulting in the consequent positive identification of the mother at birth. Under the analysis of the "unique physical characteristics" test contained in the Yale article,[11] it seems virtually certain that a court would hold that the distinction between mothers and fathers made in section 24 of the Uniform Parentage Act should be sustained.

Section 24 of the Uniform Parentage Act deserves widespread study and legislative adoption, both because of the importance of this question in family law and because it is an attempt to solve a question which, on its face, is one which may arise under the Equal Rights Amendment.

References

1. Stanley v. Illinois, 405 U.S. 645 (1972); Rothstein v. Lutheran Social Services of Wisconsin and Upper Michigan, 405 U.S. 1051 (1972); and Vanderlaan v. Vanderlaan, 405 U.S. 1051 (1972).

2. The Uniform Parentage Act, 9 Uniform Laws Annotated (1973 Supp. 1975).

3. Krause, "The Uniform Parentage Act," 8 Family L. Q. 1, 12-16 (1974).

---

11. For a more complete discussion of the "unique physical characteristics" test and its application, see the first chapter, The Equal Rights Amendment and the Constitution, above.

4. Brown, Emerson, Falk and Freedman, "The Equal Rights Amendment: A Constitutional Basis for Equal Rights for Women," 80 Yale L. J. 871, 898 (1971) discuss the "unique physical characteristics" test. The authors state that statutes which distinguish between persons on the basis of sex to determine the parentage of children are justified.

5. The Uniform Adoption Act, 9 Uniform Laws Annotated (1973).

6. Note, "Adoption--Consent--Abandonment and Failure to Support--Imprisonment Constitutes Abandonment Such as Is Contemplated by the Adoption Statutes So As to Dispense with the Consent of the Natural Father in an Adoption Proceeding for His Child, and Failure to Support Due to Imprisonment Dispenses with the Right of the Natural Parent to Object to an Adoption Proceeding for His Child," 4 St. Mary's L. J. 87 (1972).

7. Hession, "Adoptions After 'Stanley'--Rights for Fathers of Illegitimate Children," 51 Ill. B. J. 350 (1973).

8. Note, "Adoption Consent Rights of the Unwed Father in Oregon," 53 Ore. L. Rev. 531 (1974).

9. Note, "Putative Fathers' Rights in Adoption Proceedings," 39 Mo. L. Rev. 573 (1974).

10. Note, "Stanley v. Illinois: What It Portends for Adoptions in Montana," 36 Montana L. Rev. 137 (1975).

11. Note, "Rights of Putative Fathers in Custody and Adoption Proceedings--Washington's Law in Perspective," 9 Gonzaga L. Rev. 826 (1974).

12. Schafrick, "Emerging Constitutional Protection of the Putative Father's Parental Rights," 7 Family L. Q. 75 (1973); 70 Mich. L. Rev. 1581 (1972).

13. Tabler, "Paternal Rights in the Illegitimate Child: Some Legitimate Complaints on Behalf of the Unwed Father," 11 J. Family L. 231 (1971).

14. Note, "'Strange Boundaries' of Stanley: Providing Notice of Adoption to the Unknown Putative Father," 59 Va. L. Rev. 517 (1973).

15. Note, "Protecting the Putative Father's Rights After Stanley v. Illinois: Problems in Implementation," 13 J. Family L. 115 (1973-74).

16. Krause, "Equal Protection for the Illegitimate," 65 Mich. L. Rev. 477 (1967).

17. Smith, "Illegitimate Children and Their Fathers: Some Problems with Title 2," 5 Tex. Tech. L. Rev. 613 (1974).

SEX-DISCRIMINATORY ASPECTS OF GROUNDS FOR DIVORCE

Legal problem: Although many states have unique sex-discriminatory grounds for divorce which will become unconstitutional after passage of the ERA, only two sex-discriminatory grounds for divorce are common today. The first is pregnancy at the time of marriage by a man other than a woman's husband, which obviously discriminates against women. The second is nonsupport of a wife by her husband, which discriminates against men.

Possible solutions: Although most sex-discriminatory grounds for divorce could be cured by simply extending them to the other sex, such a solution would not be consistent with the trend of divorce legislation in the United States. That trend, of course, is toward "no-fault" divorce, for which the only ground is "irretrievable breakdown" or "irreconcilable differences" between the spouses.

Repeal of sex-discriminatory grounds and substitution of "no-fault" grounds is decidedly preferable to extending sex-discriminatory grounds to both sexes. The provisions of the Uniform Marriage and Divorce Act concerning grounds for divorce deserve widespread adoption.

References

1. Brown, Emerson, Falk and Freedman, "The Equal Rights Amendment: A Constitutional Basis for Equal Rights for Women," 80 Yale L. J. 871, 949 (1971).

2. Uniform Marriage and Divorce Act, 9 Uniform Laws Annotated, Secs. 302, 303 and 305 and comments thereto (1973).

3. "Symposium on the Uniform Marriage and Divorce Act," 18 S.D. L. Rev. 531 (1973).

SEX-DISCRIMINATORY ASPECTS OF LAWS RELATING TO THE DIVISION OF PROPERTY ON DIVORCE, CHILD SUPPORT AND ALIMONY

Introduction

The rising incidence of divorce is an undeniable fact in American society. In the decade from 1963 to 1973, the divorce rate doubled;[12] since 1973, the trend has accelerated.

Although the increased availability and acceptability of divorce may be liberating in some respects for some persons, divorce means economic hardship and privation for many ex-wives who are mothers--for it is they, rather than their ex-husbands, who are almost always given custody of children. Although the customary wisdom portrays wives' custody of children as a hardship on husbands, it is a fact that in 85% of child custody cases, the husbands expressly consented to their wives' legal and physical care of their children.[13]

Although physically and emotionally demanding on the women who are charged with the entire burden of raising children, such an arrangement sounds fair enough until one learns the facts about child support payments. As noted throughout this section, in 42% of all cases, husbands default entirely on court-ordered child support in the first year; by the tenth year after orders are issued, only two out of ten husbands are paying anything.[14] Because of the extreme difficulties involved in collecting support payments, most lawyers find it uneconomic to handle child support cases.

Thus, American women--brought up to believe that marriage and children were the ultimate achievement in life, and whose career ambitions were either stunted or nonexistent because they expected to be full-time wives and mothers, all too often find themselves divorced, unable to collect any child support whatsoever and working in a job market in which women face severe employment discrimination. It is a genuine tragedy shared in middle age by millions of women whose high school dream was a husband, three children and a nice house in the suburbs; and it is a tragedy severely worsened by present laws.

---

12. Monthly Vital Statistics Report, Provisional Statistics, Annual Summary for the United States, 1973. (HRA) 74-1120, Vol. 22 (13), June 27, 1974, at 9.

13. Nagel and Weitzman, "Women as Litigants," 23 Hastings L. J. 171, 189n. 47, citing W. Goode, After Divorce 311, 313 (1956).

14. Weitzman, "Legal Regulation of Marriage: Tradition and Change," 62 Calif. L. Rev. 1169, 1195 (1974).

It is in the areas of property division on divorce, child support and alimony, then, that the Equal Rights Amendment can have great effect, if it is taken as the mandate it is meant to be-- the achievement in our lifetimes of true equality under the law for men and women. To make that mandate a reality the law must be seen and used as an instrument capable of causing and aiding social change--for it is only imaginative legislation which can solve the family law problems of which we all are aware, but with which few are truly concerned.

Reference

O'Flarity, "Divorce Modern-Style," 8 Trial 15 (1972).

The Division of Property on Divorce

Legal problem: There is a widespread belief in the United States that alimony is a burden imposed on husbands and unfairly extracted by grasping wives. That belief can only be labeled a myth in light of undeniable statistics. In fact, alimony is awarded in less than 10% of all divorces, and even when awarded, is difficult to collect.[15] Because of that reality, the Uniform Marriage and Divorce Act places primary emphasis on the division of property on divorce, and in section 308 provides that "maintenance," the term used in the Act for what is now known as "alimony," may be awarded only in the circumstances specifically set forth in the Act. The Uniform Marriage and Divorce Act's approach to property division and maintenance is based, then, on the reality of the small role which alimony actually plays in divorce in the United States today.[16]

Under present law, in the forty-three separate property jurisdictions, a wife who has not worked for compensation during marriage has accrued no vested property rights in the earnings of her husband during that marriage. In many of those states, however, courts are given the power by statute to divide property owned by either spouse upon divorce "equitably" between both spouses.

---

15. Weitzman, "Legal Regulation of Marriage: Tradition and Change," 62 Calif. L. Rev. 1169, 1181, 1195 (1974).

16. The sex-based distinctions made in awards of alimony, which any revision of divorce law will have to take into account to bring the law into accord with the Equal Rights Amendment, are discussed below.

In the eight community property states, while each spouse
has by law a one-half vested property interest in all property
earned by either of them during marriage, in only two of those
states does the statute require a mandatory fifty-fifty
division of property upon divorce. In the six other community
property states, regardless of the vested ownership interests
which each spouse had during the marriage, courts also are
given the power to divide the community property "equitably"
between the spouses.

Because court-ordered child support payments are so
frequently defaulted upon, and because alimony plays no role in
most divorces, the question of property division on divorce is
of great legal and practical significance. What improvements
are possible in this area which is of such critical importance
for so many divorced women?

Possible solutions: Section 307 of the Uniform Marriage and
Divorce Act, as amended in 1973, concerns the division of
property upon divorce. The section contains two alternatives,
one drafted for separate property states and one for community
property states. Both alternatives, rather than simply directing
a court to divide property "equitably" upon divorce, set out the
precise factors to be considered in dividing property. Section
307 specifically states that marital misconduct is not to be
taken into account in apportioning property, and more importantly,
that the contribution of a spouse as a laborer in the home shall
be considered in making such divisions.

Thus, section 307 of the Uniform Marriage and Divorce Act
is unquestionably a better guide for courts in dividing property
upon divorce than is present law in most states. Three possible
improvements should be considered, however, before section 307
is adopted as it was amended in 1973.

1.   Definition of "marital property." Before its amendment
in 1973, section 307 defined the "marital property" which courts
were to apportion between the spouses upon divorce. The original
section 307 essentially adopted the definition of community
property to define "marital property" in both separate and
community property states. Because of the defects in the
separate property systems which are discussed extensively below
in the chapter on Marital Property Laws, section 307's original
definition of "marital property" is preferable to the revised
version. The text of section 307 as originally drafted is set
forth in relevant part in reference no. 14 below.

2.   Mandatory fifty-fifty division of property. Because
courts have such wide discretion in making property awards even
under section 307 of the Uniform Marriage and Divorce Act and
because, as a practical matter, it is almost impossible to have

184

awards of a trial judge reversed on appeal, some commentators
have suggested that a mandatory fifty-fifty divison of property,
directed by statute, would be preferable to giving discretion
to trial courts to make "equitable" divisions of property. If
the definition of "marital property" contained in section 307
before its revision were used, and mandatory fifty-fifty
division of the property were specified by statute, both wives
and husbands would be farily treated--and lawyers' skills and/or
a particular judge's "discretion" would be removed as factors
which influence the determination of this important question.

3. <u>Standards for evaluation of wife's contribution</u>. As
an alternative to a mandatory fifty-fifty division of property,
section 307 as amended in 1973 might be improved by drafting
standards for valuing a spouse's contribution as a domestic
worker. As the section now stands, it is a great improvement
over present law; but it still offers no guide to a judge for
determining the value of uncompensated domestic labor performed
during marriage. Because the value placed on such services
could be heavily influenced by a particular judge's outlook and
personal experiences, section 307 would be improved by the
addition of valuation standards to minimize these discretionary
and perhaps prejudicial factors.

4. <u>Divorce insurance</u>. Finally, much discussion has
recently centered upon the concept of divorce insurance as a
means of guaranteeing that married women who have spent their
lives working in the home receive adequate economic compensation
upon divorce. Several studies have been made of the feasibility
of divorce insurance. Although it may seem a radical idea today,
in fact, it is probably no more radical than was the idea of
workmen's compensation insurance fifty years ago. The system
would operate through either mandatory or voluntary contributions from all married persons. Those who divorced would receive
payments from the fund so established. In any thorough evaluation
of the problems of divorced persons, a study of divorce insurance
and means of effectuating it is certainly justified.

References

1. Uniform Marriage and Divorce Act, 9 <u>Uniform Law
Annotated</u>, Sec. 307; as amended in 1973 (1973 Supp. 1975).

2. Nagel and Weitzman, "Women as Litigants," 23 <u>Hastings
L. J.</u>, 189-191 (1971).

3. Weitzman, "Legal Regulation of Marriage: Tradition and
Change," 62 <u>Calif. L. Rev.</u> 1169, 1186 (1974).

4. See B. Babcock, A. Freedman, E. Norton and S. Ross, Sex Discrimination and the Law 721-729 (1975), for a discussion of divorce insurance.

5. See Note, "Implied Partnerships: Equitable Alternative to Continuing Methods of Post-Marital Property Division," 26 U. Fla. L. Rev. 221 (1974) for a theory of mandatory fifty-fifty division of property acquired by married persons who operate a family business. The author based his theory on provisions of the Uniform Partnership Act.

6. Note, "Income Tax Consequences of Equal Divisions of Community Property in California: Collins and the New Divorce Law," 4 U. San Fran. L. Rev. 392 (1970).

7. Neumark, "Property Rights in Divorce," 62 Ill. B. J. 242 (1974).

8. Sassower, "Matrimonial Law Reform: Equal Property Rights for Women," 44 N.Y. St. B. J. 406 (1972).

9. Bronstein, "No-Fault Divorce, Alimony, and Property Settlement," 45 N.Y. St. B. J. 241 (1973).

10. Sassower, "No-Fault Divorce and Women's Property Rights: A Rebuttal," 45 N.Y. St. B. J. 485 (1973).

11. Kay, "Making Marriage and Divorce Safe for Women," 60 Calif. L. Rev. 1683 (1972).

12. "Is There a Future for Separate Property?," 8 Family L. Q. 315 (1974).

13. Foster and Freed, "Marital Property Reform in New York: Partnership of Co-Equals?," 8 Family L. Q. 169 (1974).

14. Section 307 of the Uniform Marriage and Divorce Act, as it appeared before its amendment in 1973, provided in relevant part:

> a. In a proceeding for dissolution of the marriage . . . the court shall assign each spouse's property to him. It shall also divide the marital property without regard to marital misconduct. . . .
>
> b. For purposes of this Act, "marital property" means all property acquired by either spouse subsequent to the marriage except:
>
> (1) property acquired by gift, bequest, devise or descent;
>
> (2) property acquired in exchange for property acquired before the marriage or in exchange for

property acquired by gift, bequest, devise, or descent;

(3) property acquired by a spouse after a decree of legal separation;

(4) property excluded by valid agreement of the parties;

(5) the increase in value of property acquired before the Uniform Marriage and Divorce Act, 9 Uniform Laws Annotated, Sec. 307 (1973).

Child Support: Problems of Enforcement

Legal problem: The problems found in the area of child support are not primarily those of defining the parent from whom payment is due or the proper amounts of such payments,[17] but in the enforcement of child support orders. The enforcement problems most often encountered and which need to be dealt with in any revision of family law pursuant to the Equal Rights Amendment will be discussed below.

Noncompliance with Court-Ordered Child Support Payments

Legal problem: Weitzman, in "Legal Regulation of Marriage: Tradition and Change," 62 Calif. L. Rev. 1169, 1195 (1974), sets forth a table showing the probability of a divorced woman collecting the child support payments ordered by a court. That table shows that 42% of court orders are completely ignored in the first year after the order was entered. By the tenth year, 79% of the fathers against whom orders were entered are paying nothing.

---

17. Section 309 of the Uniform Marriage and Divorce Act establishes satisfactory standards for factors to be considered by a court in determining the amount of child support payments; the section deserves widespread adoption. See Uniform Marriage and Divorce Acts, 9 Uniform Laws Annotated, Sec. 309 (1973).

Thus, the problem of child support for divorced women is primarily one of collecting that support. The legal remedies now available for debts in general--judgment on a debt, execution (sale by a sheriff of the debtor's property) and/or garnishment of the debtor's wages--are sufficient for ordinary debts which are a single lump sum owing to the judgment creditor. In the area of child support, however, these traditional remedies are totally inadequate.

Judgments for child support can only be obtained for payments in arrears at the time of the court action. Thus, a wife seeking to enforce a child support order must bring a separate lawsuit each time enough arrearages have accumulated to justify it; she then attempts to collect on the judgment through garnishment of wages or a sheriff's sale of property. At a later date, when further support payments have been missed, she must begin the whole process again. The legal time and fees involved in this procedure are extremely burdensome. When compounded by the common problems of husbands who have moved to another jurisdiction and husbands who have very little property or wages from which execution or garnishment can be obtained, the result is that most child support payments are eventually, if not immediately, defaulted upon. Thus, divorced mothers--who are granted custody of their children in 95% of the cases (85% with the husband's full agreement)--are left with the entire economic burden of rearing the couple's children.[18]

Possible solution: When the statistics are examined, it is obvious that the traditional remedies for the enforcement of debts are largely ineffective in the area of court-ordered support payments. Given this reality, and the likelihood that little change will be forthcoming in this pattern, Nagel and Weitzman have suggested that serious consideration be given to amending the Social Security Act to cover the children of middle-income divorced parents as beneficiaries under the Act or under state assistance programs.

A second and simpler approach, suggested by women in New York, would be to provide by statute for a payroll deduction for court-ordered child support payments. Under this plan, the employer would send a check to the wife at regular intervals in the amounts withheld from the husband's salary under the child support order. Such a procedure, which would be very similar in operation to present garnishment laws, appears to provide the best solution to a very difficult problem encountered by many divorced persons raising children.

---

18. In fact, Weitzman's table also shows that legal action is never taken at all against most husbands who are in noncompliance with child support orders. Given the difficulties of collecting judgments after they have been obtained, this lack of legal action is understandable.

188

To correct what is a major inequity in current society--
produced in part by the inadequacy of traditional debt
collection rules designed for lump sum debts when applied to
the unusual problem of child support payments which continue
over many years--some far-reaching solution is essential. An
effective answer to this question, one of immense importance
for millions of women, must be found and enacted into law when
state statutes are revised to comply with the Equal Rights
Amendment.

References

1. Comment, "Child Support in Missouri: The Father's
Duty, the Child's Right and the Mother's Ability to Endorse,"
36 Mo. L. Rev. 325 (1971).

2. Kelly, "Collecting Support for Children in Divorce
Cases," 44 Fla. B. J. 142 (1970).

3. Zumbrun and Parslow, "Absent Parent Child Support:
The California Experience," 8 Family L. Q. 329 (1974).

4. Foster and Freed, "The Long Arm to Catch Pappy,"
8 Trial 23 (Sept.-Oct. 1972).

Child Support Liability is Not Uniform in All States

Legal problem: All states in the United States have now
adopted the Uniform Reciprocal Enforcement of Support Act
(URESA) or some variation of it. However, URESA only provides
for the enforcement of support duties as those duties are
defined under the law of the state in which the spouse owing
the duty of support is found. Therefore, in order to make
URESA fully effective, the law of each state must impose
similar duties of support. If that is done, parents who move
to a different state will be under the same or similar support
duties there which they were under in the state in which the
order was originally entered; the support order can then be
enforced in the second state under URESA.

Possible solution: This problem is soluble by widespread
adoption of the Uniform Civil Liability for Support Act,
approved by the Conference of Commissioners on Uniform State
Laws in 1954. That Act has not been widely adopted, but it
must be in order to make URESA fully effective. However,
because section 3 of that Act imposes a different duty of
support on women than section 2 imposes on men, section 3 will
have to be revised to meet the requirements of the Equal Rights
Amendment.

References

1. Note, "'Un-Uniform' Reciprocal Enforcement of Support Act," 9 J. Family Law 325 (1970).

2. Comment, "Enforcement of Support Obligations: A Solution and Continuing Problems," 61 Ky. L. J. 322 (1972-73).

3. Comment, "Extradition and the Runaway Pappy," 2 Tex. Tech. L. Rev. 81 (1970).

Support Duties of Unwed Natural Fathers to Their Children

Legal problem: Unwed natural fathers are legally obligated to contribute to their children's support. However, a system of establishing paternity is needed in order to make those support duties meaningful.

Possible solution: Natural fathers are obligated by law to support their children if their paternity has been established. The Uniform Parentage Act, also discussed above, was drafted for precisely this purpose--to serve as an established and orderly means of determining fatherhood. If that Act is widely adopted, natural fathers liable for the support of their children can be legally identified. If the widespread reforms of support duties are not made, adoption of the Uniform Parentage Act would help somewhat to carry out more effectively the current laws and enforcement mechanisms in regard to liability for the support of children born to unmarried parents.

References

1. Uniform Civil Liability for Support Act, 9 Uniform Laws Annotated (1973).

2. B. Babcock, A. Freedman, E. Norton and S. Ross, Sex Discrimination and the Law 706 (1975).

3. H. Clark, The Law of Domestic Relations 200-206 (1968).

4. Weitzman, "Legal Regulation of Marriage: Tradition and Change," 62 Calif. L. Rev. 1169, 1195 (1974).

5. Nagel and Weitzman, "Women as Litigants," 23 Hastings L. J. 190-191 (1971).

6. The Uniform Parentage Act, 9 Uniform Laws Annotated (1973 Supp. 1975).

7. Krause, "The Uniform Parentage Act," 8 Family L. Q. 1 (1974).

8. Houle and Dubose, "Nonsupport Court Hearings: Constitutionality of Statutory Requirements," 14 N.H. B. J. 165 (1973).

9. For the suggestion concerning payroll deductions for court-ordered child support payments, see S. Ross, The Rights of Women 232 (1973). A model bill has been drafted by the New York City Chapter of the National Organization for Women; the author cited here states that a copy of the bill may be obtained by writing to Betty Berry, 541 East 20th Street, Apt. 7C, New York, N.Y. 10010.

10. Krause, "The Bastard Finds His Father," 3 Family L. Q. 100 (1969).

11. Gray and Rudovsky, "The Court Acknowledges the Illegitimate: Levy v. Louisiana and Glona V. American Guarantee & Liability Insurance Co.," 118 U. Pa. L. Rev. 1 (1969).

12. Note, "Illegitimacy: Equal Protection and How to Enjoy It," 4 Ga. L. Rev. 383 (1970).

13. Note, "Support of Illegitimate Children in Missouri," 13 St. Louis U. L. J. 311 (1968).

14. Note, "Constitutional Law--Equal Protection--Bastards--Illegitimate Children Have a Right Equal with That of Legitimate Children to Require Support by Their Fathers," 1 St. Mary's L. J. 146 (1969).

15. Note, "Family Law: Child Support for Illegitimates," 43 U. Mo-Kan. City L. Rev. 105 (1974).

Alimony

Although, as we have seen, alimony is awarded in less than 10% of all divorces, several aspects of it today are sex-discriminatory and will be unconstitutional after passage of the Equal Rights Amendment.

First, under present law in many states, alimony is awarded only to wives and is payable only by husbands. Second, awards of alimony are based, in many instances, on concepts of "fault" in the conduct or break-up of the marital relationship. Third, alimony almost always ceases upon the wife's remarriage. Finally, because in many states alimony is payable only by husbands, men alone are subject to criminal sanctions for nonpayment of alimony. In all of these aspects, alimony as it is known today is sex-discriminatory. Statutes which conform to the Equal Rights Amendment must include the following provisions.

Availability to Both Wives and Husbands

This, of course, is the first requirement of any equal system of alimony awards. However, to say that alimony should not be awarded on the basis of sex does not necessarily mean that it should not be awarded at all, or that the practical differences in the life situation of the spouses and the manner in which each has spent his or her married years cannot be taken into account in determining the amount of alimony due, and from whom. The widely-praised maintenance section of the Uniform Marriage and Divorce Act, section 308, meets all the requirements of the Equal Rights Amendment and takes into account the practical situations of many married women who have spent their adult lives out of the salaried labor force. Set out in reference no. 6 below, it deserves wide consideration and adoption.

One improvement which needs to be made in section 308 is to provide that in making maintenance awards, a court should consider not only the length of time necessary for an unemployed divorced spouse to obtain education and training, but also the necessary costs which would be incurred, including tuition and any day care costs for children.

References

1. Wasser, "Spousal Support and the Wife's Desire and Ability to Work," 8 J. Beverly Hills B. Ass'n. 23 (Mar.-Apr. 1974).

2. Note, "Alimony: Recognition as a Civil Effect in Putative Marriages," 20 Loyola L. Rev. 372 (1973-74).

3. Ehrlich, "The New Deal on Alimony," 8 Trial 22 (Sept.-Oct. 1972).

4. Note, "Constitutional Law--Divorce--Pendente Lite Awards--Counsel Fees--Costs--Alimony--Effect of Equal Rights Amendment," 8 Akron L. Rev. 171 (1974).

5. Comment, "The Support Law and The Equal Rights Amendment in Pennsylvania," 77 Dick. L. Rev. 254 (1972).

6. Section 308 of the Uniform Marriage and Divorce Act provides:

 a. In a proceeding for dissolution of marriage or legal separation, or a proceeding for maintenance following dissolution of the marriage by a court which lacked personal jurisdiction over the absent spouse, the court may grant a maintenance order for either spouse only if it finds that the spouse seeking maintenance:

  (1) lacks sufficient property, including marital property apportioned to him, to provide for his reasonable needs, and

  (2) is unable to support himself through appropriate employment or is the custodian of a child whose condition or circumstances make it appropriate that the custodian not be required to seek employment outside the home.

 b. The maintenance order shall be in such amounts and for such periods of time as the court deems just, without regard to marital misconduct, and after considering all relevant factors including:

  (1) the financial resources of the party seeking maintenance, including marital property apportioned to him, and his ability to meet his needs independently, including the extent to which a provision for support of a child living with the party includes a sum for that party as custodian;

  (2) the time necessary to acquire sufficient education or training to enable the party seeking maintenance to find appropriate employment;

  (3) the standard of living established during the marriage;

  (4) the duration of the marriage;

  (5) the age, and the physical and emotional condition of the spouse seeking maintenance; and

  (6) the ability of the spouse from whom maintenance is sought to meet his needs while meeting those of the spouse seeking maintenance.

Fault Not a Basis for Award of Alimony

Alimony is often awarded today to punish a guilty husband or is withheld from a wife who has erred. To the extent that alimony serves as compensation for the years many wives spend out of the labor force performing uncompensated domestic work, continuation of the "fault" concept in alimony or maintenance awards will deprive wives of what is in effect "back pay" for work already performed, and will arguably be unconstitutional under an Equal Rights Amendment.

If sections 307 and 308 of the Uniform Marriage and Divorce Act were widely adopted, the present practice would be abolished; both sections specifically state that "misconduct shall not be taken into account" in determining either the division of property or the amount or duration of maintenance awards.

References

1. Note, "Family Law--Marriage Dissolution--First Decision by Nebraska Supreme Court under Nebraska's New No-Fault Marriage Dissolution Statutes Leaves Uncertain the Question of Whether Fault Is to Be Excluded from the Post-Dissolution Determinations of Alimony and Property Settlement," 7 Creighton L. Rev. 369 (1974).

2. Note, "Property, Maintenance and Child Support Decrees under the Uniform Marriage and Divorce Act," 18 S.D. L. Rev. 559 (1973).

3. Hofstadter and Levittan, "Alimony--a Reformulation," 7 J. Family L. 51 (1967).

4. Note, "Alimony--The Next Step," 9 J. Family L. 200 (1969).

5. Comment, "Substitutes for Alimony: A Review of Methods for Providing Periodic Support Payments Subsequent to Divorce," 20 Baylor L. Rev. 314 (1968).

6. Comment, "Alimony, Property Settlement and Child Custody under the New Divorce Statutes: No-Fault is Not Enough," 22 Cath. U. L. Rev. 365 (1973).

7. Note, "Divorce--Alimony--Under Iowa's No-Fault Dissolution of Marriage Procedure Evidence of the Conduct of the Parties which Tends to Place Fault for the Marriage Breakdown Must Be Disregarded as a Factor in Awarding Property Settlement or Allowance of Alimony or Support Money," 42 <u>U. Cinn. L. Rev.</u> 127 (1973).

8. Note, "Does No-Fault Divorce Portend No-Fault Alimony?," 34 <u>U. Pitt. L. Rev.</u> 486 (1973).

Alimony or Maintenance Awards After Remarriage

Under current practice, a wife's remarriage terminates alimony payments, and a husband's remarriage often serves as a reason to reduce the amount of alimony owed his former wife. Again, to the extent that alimony serves as pay for uncompensated work performed during marriage, to end alimony upon remarriage will, in many instances, serve to discriminate against a wife who worked without pay in her former home.

Section 308 of the Uniform Marriage and Divorce Act contains no provisions concerning remarriage as a factor governing the length of time during which maintenance should be paid. States should adopt that section as drafted, and courts should interpret it strictly and without reference to existing practice.

References

1. Note, "Domestic Relations--Increase or Decrease of Permanent Alimony and Child Support--Granted Without the Necessity of Showing a Change in the Circumstances of Both Parties," 3 <u>U. Balt. L. Rev.</u> 328 (1974).

2. For a discussion of the concept of alimony as "back pay," <u>see</u> H. Clark, <u>The Law of Domestic Relations</u> 200-206 (1968).

Criminal Sanctions for Nonpayment of Alimony

Like the criminal nonsupport statutes mentioned above, the laws of most states provide for imprisonment of husbands who fail to make court-ordered alimony payments. However, even if criminal sanctions were made sex-neutral, it is possible that because men will be the sex most often ordered to make maintenance payments, retention of imprisonment laws which bear much more heavily upon men that women could be challenged as laws "neutral on their face, but discriminatory in impact." Further, many commentators believe that the sanction of imprisonment for nonpayment of either child support or alimony should be abolished.

This question should be studied both in light of the possible constitutional problems of imprisoning members of only one sex and in terms of the practical difficulties which wives encounter trying to collect child support maintenance awards.

If the procedure of withholding court-ordered amounts from paychecks suggested above were adopted, it is clear that criminal sanctions for nonpayment of child or spousal support should be removed.

References

Willging and Ellsmore, "The 'Dual System' in Action: Jail for Nonsupport," U. Tol. L. Rev. 348 (1969).

Some additional references concerning the subject of divorce and alimony include:

1. B. Babcock, A. Freedman, E. Norton and S. Ross, Sex Discrimination and the Law 692-706 (1975).

2. Uniform Marriage and Divorce Act, 9 Uniform Laws Annotated, Sec. 308 (1973).

3. H. Clark, The Law of Domestic Relations 200-206 (1968).

4. Nagel and Weitzman, "Women as Litigants," 23 Hastings L. J. 171, 189 (1971).

5. Comment, "The Economics of Divorce: Alimony and Property Awards," 43 U. Cinn. L. Rev. 33 (1974).

SEX-DISCRIMINATORY ASPECTS OF LAWS RELATING TO CHILD CUSTODY

There are several distinct legal problems which relate to the custody of children. Each will be described briefly here and possible solutions to each will be set forth.

Judicial Preference for Mothers in Custody Proceedings

Legal problem: It is a well known fact that in the 15% of custody cases which are contested, some judges give preference in custody matters to mothers solely because of their sex; this usually happens when the children are of "tender age." Such a judicial practice is a form of state action which violates the Equal Rights Amendment.

Possible solution: Section 402 of the Uniform Marriage and Divorce Act adopts a sex-neutral standard for determination of the custody of children; it outlines specific factors under which a court should make custody decisions rather than leaving the standard a simple and vague "best interests of the child."

As drafted, section 402 is adequate, but the comments to that section are disappointing. The comments indicate that "the preference for the mother as custodian of young children, when all things are equal, for example, is simply a shorthand method of expressing the best interests of children."

It is precisely this attitude which violates the spirit and possibly the letter of the Equal Rights Amendment. In order to avoid application of such a standard by judges, it is suggested that a sentence be inserted in section 402 which states expressly that the sex of a parent is not relevant to determinations of custody, and that custody decisions should be made solely in accordance with the sex-neutral factors listed in the section itself.

References

1. Comment, "The Father's Right to Child Custody in Interparental Disputes," 49 Tul. L. Rev. 189 (1974).

2. Note, "Domestic Relations--New Colorado Statutes Govern Procedure in Contested Child Custody Cases," 40 U. Colo. L. Rev. 485 (1968).

3. Leavell, "Custody Disputes and the Proposed Model Act," 2 Ga. L. Rev. 162 (1968).

4. Note, "Domestic Relations--Child Custody: Statutory Preference in Favor of the Mother is Not Applicable in Proceedings to Modify a Prior Custody Order," 6 Tulsa L. J. 176 (1970).

5. Note, "Paternal Custody of Minor Children,"
5 Memphis St. U. L. Rev. 223 (1975).

6. Note, "Child Custody: Preference to the Mother,"
24 La. L. Rev. 881 (1974).

Adultery or Misconduct of a Mother Will Often Cause a Court to Deny Her Custody, While a Father's Similar Conduct Will Not Bar Him from Receiving Custody

Legal problem: The sexual double standard prevalent in our society is often reflected in custody decisions which deny custody to mothers who have committed adultery, even though the children know nothing of the relationships and are close to the mother.

In contrast, fathers who have engaged in the same conduct are not necessarily considered unfit solely for that activity. Application of different standards regarding fitness for custody of children solely because of the sex of the parent violates the Equal Rights Amendment.

Possible solution: Section 402 of the Uniform Marriage and Divorce Act represents a major improvement over most current state law or practice in this regard. The section states explicitly that "the court shall not consider conduct of a proposed custodian that does not affect his relationship to the child." Because this problem is most definitely one which arises under the Equal Rights Amendment, adoption of section 402 should include the quoted sentence.

References

1. Note, "Custody Awards: Standards Used When the Mother Has Been Guilty of Adultery or Alcoholism," 2 Family L. Q. 384 (1968).

2. Callow, "Custody of the Child and the Uniform Marriage and Divorce Act," 18 S. D. L. Rev. 551 (1973).

3. Note, "The Lesbian Mother: Her Right to Child Custody," 4 Golden Gate L. Rev. 1 (1973).

Custody Rights of Natural Fathers

Legal problem: In Stanley v. Illinois, 405 U.S. 645 (1972), the United States Supreme Court held that an unwed father was denied due process where he was not given a hearing before being declared an unfit father. As discussed above, the rights of natural fathers have recently been expanded by the Court. Many state statutes related to the custody of children do not conform to the constitutional rights which natural fathers now have. Such statutes should be revised to clarify this important area of law.

Possible solution: A partial solution to the custody rights of natural fathers is contained in the Uniform Parentage Act which sets out means by which a father wishing to obtain custody may establish the fact of his parentage. The Act deserves widespread adoption.

As discussed more fully above, the question of the custody rights of natural fathers, as opposed to natural mothers, is one which arguably--although not truly--arises under the Equal Rights Amendment. Therefore, consideration of the Uniform Parentage Act is justified in any legislative action taken pursuant to the Amendment to avoid litigation on the question.

References

1. Note, "Persons--Custody of Illegitimates," 17 Loyola L. Rev. 459 (1970-71).

2. Marcus, "Equal Protection: The Custody of the Illegitimate Child," 11 J. Family L. 1 (1971).

3. Note, "Constitutional Law--A Dependency Hearing Which Would Deny an Unwed Father Custody of His Child on the Death of Its Mother without Reference to the Father's Fitness as a Parent Is Violative of Due Process and Equal Protection," 4 Loyola U. L. J. (Chicago) 176 (1973).

4. Harkins, "Putative Father's Visitation Rights," 19 Clev. St. L. R. 549 (1970).

5. Note, "Custody Rights of Unwed Fathers," Pacific L. J. 922 (1973).

6. Note, "The Impact of Stanley v. Illinois on Custody Proceedings for Illegitimate Children: Procedural Parity for the Putative Father?," 3 N.Y. U. Rev. L. & Soc. Change 31 (1973).

7. Note, "The Plight of the Putative Father in California Child Custody Proceedings: A Problem of Equal Protection," 6 U. C. D. L. Rev. 1 (1973).

8. Note, "Family Law: Rights of Illegitimate Children, Rights of Unwed Fathers," 1973-74 Ann. Survey Am. L. 233.

9. Note, "Constitutional Rights of a Putative Father to Establish His Parentage and Assert Parental Rights," 58 Marq. L. Rev. 175 (1975).

10. Note, "Family Law--Putative Father Denied Custody under Restrictive Interpretation of His Rights," 9 U. Richmond L. Rev. 384 (1975).

11. Note, "Constitutional Law--Right of Unwed Father to a Fitness Hearing Prior to State Imposition of Wardship Over His Illegitimate Children," 7 Suffolk U. L. Rev. 159 (1972).

12. Note, "Stanley v. Illinois: The 'Legitimate Birth' of the Out-of-Wedlock Father's Right to Be Heard at Custody Proceedings," 2 Capital U. L. Rev. 149 (1973).

Under Present Law More than One State May Take Jurisdiction to Determine the Custody of a Child

Under the prevailing conflict of laws rule in most states, presence of the child and one parent in the state is sufficient to give the courts of that state jurisdiction to enter orders regarding custody of the child. Such orders will often conflict with orders entered by another state which had jurisdiction while the child was present there. These rules result in "child-snatching" and blatantly contradictory orders from courts of different states concerning the custody of the same child. While the conflicting jurisdiction of different state courts in child custody matters is not within the purview of the Equal Rights Amendment, it is a problem which causes great harm to children and much disruption in family life. As such, this issue should be considered in any legislative package on family law, particularly since the National Conference of Commissioners on Uniform State Laws has drafted a Uniform Child Custody Jurisdiction Act which solves the problem described above. That Act has been adopted in several states since its approval by the Conference in 1968; its widespread enactment would go far to alleviate this problem. In the major legislative revision which will accompany the Equal Rights Amendment in state legislatures, consideration of this problem, which has such serious impact on many families, seems justified.

200

References

1. Bodenheimer, "The Uniform Child Custody Jurisdiction Act: A Legislative Remedy for Children Caught in the Conflict of Laws, 3 Family L. Q. 304 (1969); 22 Vand. L. Rev. 1207 (1969).

2. Hudak, "Seize, Run, and Sue: The Ignominy of Interstate Child Custody Litigation in American Courts," 39 Mo. L. Rev. 521 (1974).

3. Note, "Jurisdiction in Child Custody Awards," 5 Willamette L. J. 171 (1968).

4. Note, "Conflicting Custody Decrees: In Whose Best Interest?," 7 Duquesne L. Rev. 262 (1968-69).

Additional references regarding the custody of children include:

1. Uniform Marriage and Divorce Act, 9 Uniform Laws Annotated Sec. 402, and comments thereto (1973).

2. B. Babcock, A. Freedman, E. Norton and S. Ross, Sex Discrimination and the Law 706-713 (1975).

3. K. Davidson, R. Ginsburg and H. Kay, Sex-based Discrimination, 271-277 (1974).

4. Stanley v. Illinois, 402 U.S. 645 (1972).

5. Uniform Parentage Act, 9 Uniform Laws Annotated (1973 Supp. 1975).

6. Krause, "The Uniform Parentage Act," Family L. Q. 1 (1974).

7. The Uniform Child Custody Jurisdiction Act, 9 Uniform Laws Annotated (1973).

Chapter Five

LABOR LAWS

Table of Contents

14—88228

INTRODUCTION

The Equal Rights Amendment will affect state labor laws in three important ways. First, the Amendment will invalidate the state protective laws still effective for employers of less than fifteen employees, not covered by Title VII of the Civil Rights Act of 1964. Passage of the Amendment will, therefore, put all employers in the country on an equal footing as to the conditions of employment they must provide for male and female employees. Also, the Amendment will provide the occasion for the enactment of legislation which has been needed for many years-- protection against discharge for employees who do not wish to work overtime.

Second, the Amendment should reverse the Supreme Court's 1974 decision in Geduldig v. Aiello, 417 U.S. 484, in which the Court held that state unemployment insurance statutes did not have to provide coverage for pregnancy and pregnancy-related disabilities. For millions of American working women, this single result of the ERA's passage will be of tremendous importance.

Finally, the Amendment will provide an additional remedy-- a suit for damages in federal courts--for sex discrimination by state or local governments acting in their capacities as employers. The only significant remedy presently available is under Title VII, which contains a 180-day time limit within which complaints must be filed. Thus, although the Amendment will not impose new duties on state governments, it will give aggrieved employees an additional remedy which does not have the stringent time limit of Title VII.

THE EQUAL RIGHTS AMENDMENT AND PROTECTIVE LABOR LAWS

History of State Protective Labor Legislation

Until 1973, the influential AFL-CIO opposed passage of the Equal Rights Amendment. The organization based its stand on its desire to maintain the validity of state protective labor legislation which applied only to women. The union believed the Amendment would invalidate those statutes.

In fact, as the AFL-CIO recognized in 1973, Title VII of the Civil Rights Act of 1964 had already had enormous impact on the very statutes which the AFL-CIO claimed to be trying to preserve. To understand the history and current status of state protective labor legislation, it is necessary to review briefly two earlier Supreme Court cases which led to sex-discriminatory labor laws.

In the early years of the twentieth century, the American labor movement struggled in state legislatures across the country to obtain restrictions on maximum work hours and to obtain passage of minimum pay legislation. In New York State, a maximum hours law which applied equally to men and women workers was finally enacted; in Lochner v. New York, 198 U.S. 45 (1905), however, the Court held that statute an unconstitutional infringement upon due process rights of freedom of contract. The decision was a serious setback for the labor movement.

Because Lochner had invalidated labor laws of more general application, leaders of the movement then attempted to obtain state protective labor legislation which applied to women workers only. A measure of success was achieved in some states, and maximum hours laws which applied only to women employees were enacted.

These laws were also challenged; but, in Muller v. Oregon, 208 U.S. 412 (1908), the Supreme Court held that the inferior physical capacities and social position of women entitled them to be grouped in a special class with only a "minimum rational basis" needed to justify such laws. Thus, Muller v. Oregon ushered in an era which saw the passage across the country of state protective labor legislation.

Such laws, which will be discussed in more detail below, provided for minimum wages, overtime pay, rest periods, chairs, and a prescribed day of rest. All of these benefited only women workers. Other such statutes provided that women could work only a maximum number of hours per week; could lift only certain weights; were excluded from night work and from certain hazardous occupations, such as mining; and could not work for a statutorily-specified period before and after childbirth. For the American labor movement, these statutes represented many years of lobbying in state legislatures and hard-won victories in which union leaders took justifiable pride.

In 1964, Congress included Title VII in the Civil Rights Act enacted that year; that statute was to have profound effects upon state labor laws. Title VII, as originally drafted, prohibited discrimination by employers on the basis of race, religion or national origin. Sex was not included or considered until a Congressperson from Virginia, Representative Howard Smith, stood up on the floor of the House during debate and moved that sex be included in the prohibitions of Title VII. Although Representative Smith's motives can be doubted,[1] as passed by the Congress in 1964, Title VII provides:

---

1. Representative Smith was adamantly opposed to the entire Civil Rights Act of 1964, and there is almost unanimous agreement that his move to insert sex into Title VII was done either as a joke or in an effort to have the entire Title defeated on the floor of the House.

204

> It shall be an unlawful employment practice for an employer . . . to fail or refuse to hire or to discharge any individual, or otherwise to discriminate against any individual with respect to his compensation, terms, conditions, or privileges of employment because of such individual's race, color, religion, sex or national origin. (42 U.S.C. Secs. 2000e et seq.)

In amendments to Title VII enacted in 1972, Congress extended coverage of the Act to all private employers with 15 or more employees and to the state and federal governments as employers.

Also in 1972, the Equal Employment Opportunity Commission (EEOC), the federal agency charged with the enforcement of Title VII, issued guidelines concerning the effect of Title VII on state protective labor laws. The EEOC's authority to issue regulations which affect state laws is based on the supremacy clause contained in article VI of the United States Constitution. It provides:

> This Constitution and the laws of the United States which shall be made in Pursuance thereof; and all Treaties made, or which shall be made, under the Authority of the United States, shall be the Supreme Law of the Land; and the Judges in every State shall be bound thereby, anything in the Constitution or Laws of any State to the Contrary notwithstanding.

Under the supremacy clause, regulations or guidelines issued by a federal agency pursuant to that agency's authority to enforce a federal statute are "the supreme law of the land," just as the statute itself is. Any valid federal regulation or guideline, therefore, overrides state laws to the contrary.

The EEOC guidelines affecting state protective labor laws require that an employer covered by the Act extend to male employees benefits which had previously been provided through state laws only to women and that they completely ignore restrictions which operate to the detriment of women. The 1972 EEOC guidelines, then, which are discussed in more detail below, have already accomplished, with regard to employers covered by Title VII, precisely what the Equal Rights Amendment will do insofar as sex-discriminatory protective state labor laws are concerned.[2] They have already either extended to men or invalidated the sex-restricted protective labor legislation which by its terms applies to women workers only. However, the Equal Rights Amendment will still be beneficial in the area of state labor laws.

First, as to employers not covered by the Act--those with less than 15 employees--the Equal Rights Amendment will extend or invalidate the existing state protective labor legislation which, by its terms, applies to women only. Thus, with passage of the Amendment, all employers, regardless of the number of employees, will be placed on an equal footing as to the conditions of employment for both male and female workers.

Second, the Amendment will provide the impetus for states to amend statutes which remain on their books but which, in effect, have been either repealed or substantially amended by the 1972 EEOC Regulations.

Finally, the Amendment should provide support for the passage of state statutes which would prohibit employers from discharging any employee who refused to work over a certain number of hours per week. See the section on restrictive labor laws applying to women only, below, for a discussion of this important issue.

With this brief historical introduction, a discussion of specific state protective laws, the 1972 EEOC Regulations and the impact of the Equal Rights Amendment on each type of protective labor statute follows.

---

2. Both Title VII and the Equal Rights Amendment affect state labor laws. However, the manner in which each reaches state laws in the case of the extension of benefits rather than invalidation is different. Title VII operates indirectly upon state laws, as a result of its regulation of employment discrimination; it does not actually revise state laws. On the other hand, the Equal Rights Amendment affects state protective labor laws directly; both extension and invalidation of such statutes would therefore be relevant to all subsequent similar cases. For a more detailed discussion of this issue see footnote 107, in Brown, Emerson, Falk and Freedman, "The Equal Rights Amendment: A Constitutional Basis for Equal Rights for Women," 80 Yale L. J. 871, 926 (1971).

Extension of "Benefits" Provided in State Labor Laws to Cover Men

Minimum Wage and Overtime Pay Provisions

Legal problem: Many states still retain statutes which require that a minimum wage for each hour worked and a premium rate for hours worked over a fixed number of hours per week be paid to women employees. While an employer is free, of course, to pay male employees the same minimum wages and premium pay for overtime, many state laws do not require employers to do so.

These common provisions have already been invalidated by Title VII as to employers covered by the Act. Under the Equal Rights Amendment, they will be unconstitutional as to all employers.

Possible solutions: In Hays v. Potlatch Forests, Inc., 465 F. 2d 1081 (8th Cir. 1972), a federal appeals court held that the provisions of Title VII required that an Arkansas overtime statute which applied only to women be extended to cover male employees also.

Shortly thereafter the EEOC issued guidelines under Title VII. Those guidelines provide in pertinent part:

> 3. A number of states require that minimum wage and premium pay for overtime be provided for female employees. An employer will be deemed to have engaged in an unlawful employment practice if:
> (i) it refuses to hire or otherwise adversely affects the employment opportunities of female applicants or employees in order to avoid the payment of minimum wages or overtime pay required by state laws; or
> (ii) it does not provide the same benefits for male employees.[3] (emphasis added)

The principle of the 1972 EEOC guidelines, as well as that which would be applied under the Equal Rights Amendment, is twofold. First, laws which by their terms now apply only to women are extended to men as well. Second, laws which are now applicable to women only, but which place burdens or restrictions upon them, are invalidated.

---

3. 29 C.F.R. Sec. 1604.2(b)(3) (1972).

Thus, because the benefits of minimum wage and overtime pay have, since 1972, been required by Title VII to be given to both male and female employees of all employers covered by the Act, the logical solution for a state legislature to follow after passage of the Equal Rights Amendment would be to extend coverage of these provisions to employees of both sexes.

However, if a state legislature does not act after passage of the Equal Rights Amendment, the analogy provided by the 1972 EEOC guidelines and the Potlatch case make it virtually certain that any court asked to consider the effect of the Amendment upon a statute which confers such benefits on women only would extend those benefits to men also. Nevertheless, to avoid litigation after passage of the Amendment, legislation should be drafted and enacted which specifically extends these state laws to employees of both sexes.

References

1. B. Babcock, A. Freedman, E. Norton, and S. Ross, Sex Discrimination and the Law 282 (1975).

2. L. Kanowitz, Women and the Law 185 (1969).

3. Brown, Emerson, Falk and Freedman, "The Equal Rights Amendment: A Constitutional Basis for Equal Rights for Women," 80 Yale L. J. 871, 927 (1971). It should be noted that this article was written before adoption of the 1972 EEOC Regulations on this subject.

Statutes Requiring Special Rest Periods and Special Physical Facilities

Legal problem: Many state statutes in effect today require that employers provide special lunch and midday breaks for women employees and special physical facilities, such as couches in women's restrooms. The guidelines promulgated by the EEOC under Title VII require that the benefits of such statutes be extended to male employees also, unless an employer has a "business necessity" reason which precludes doing so. The Equal Rights Amendment would require that such statutes be extended to all employees without regard to the doctrine of "business necessity" contained in the Title VII guidelines.

208

Possible solutions: The 1972 EEOC Guidelines concerning statutes requiring special rest periods and special physical facilities provide:

> 4. /A/s to other kinds of sex-oriented state employment laws, such as those requiring special rest and meal periods or physical facilities for women, provision of these benefits to one sex only will be a violation of Title VII. An employer will be deemed to have engaged in unlawful employment practice if:
>
> (i) it refuses to hire or otherwise adversely affects the employment opportunities of female applicants or employees in order to avoid the provision of such benefits; or
>
> (ii) <u>it does not provide the same benefits for male employees. If the employer can prove that business necessity precludes providing these benefits to both men and women, then the state law is in conflict with and superseded by Title VII as to this employer. In this situation, the employer shall not provide such benefits to members of either sex.</u>[4]
> (emphasis added)

The "business necessity" exception to the principle of the extension of benefits to members of both sexes was written into the Guidelines to provide for very unusual situations, such as continuous assembly line manufacturing processes, where, if an employer were required to give all employees a 15-minute rest period twice a day--a common state provision applicable to women only--the employer's entire business could be seriously injured. The Commission most emphatically did not intend the "business necessity" exception to be construed to include cost or inconvenience to the employer as acceptable reasons for not giving benefits to either sex. The exception will, however, undoubtedly cause further litigation over the scope of its meaning.[5]

Although the courts have, in somewhat unusual decisions, explicitly refused to apply the quoted EEOC guidelines, it seems clear that after passage of the Equal Rights Amendment the principle of the extension of benefits to both sexes will require courts to follow the EEOC guidelines with the exception of the "business necessity" doctrine. Legislatures in particular states may feel that certain manufacturing situations--such as those envisioned by the EEOC when it adopted the "business necessity"

---

4. 29 C.F.R. Sec. 1604.2(b)(4) (1972).

5. For an elaboration of the doctrine of "business necessity" see Diaz v. Pan American World Airways, 442 F. 2d 385 (5th Cir. 1971); and Wilson v. Sibley Memorial Hospital, 340 F. Supp. 686 (1972).

doctrine--require that a very narrowly-defined exception to
required employee benefits be made. If so, that exception will
have to be drafted and enacted by statute. It cannot be
developed through case law under the Equal Rights Amendment.
For this reason also, then, it is important that state
statutes be thoughtfully revised after passage of the Amendment;
these problems should not be left to litigation.

References

1. B. Babcock, A. Freedman, E. Norton and S. Ross,
Sex Discrimination and the Law 282-287 (1975).

2. Cases decided after the 1972 Guidelines were issued
which refuse to apply those Guidelines include: Burns v. Rohr
Corp., 346 F. Supp. 994 (S.D. Cal. 1972); and Homemaker's, Inc.
v. Division of Industrial Welfare, 356 F. Supp. 1111 (N.D. Cal.
1972). In Steelworkers' Local 1104 v. U.S. Steel Corp., 4 FEP
cases 1103 (N.D. Ohio 972) aff'd, 479 F. 2d 1255 (6th Cir. 1973),
an appellate court affirmed a district court decision which held
that women employees were not entitled to back pay for lunch
breaks required by state law. The employer gave men the same
lunch breaks but paid them for that time because, under the
law, men could be interrupted during that half hour for work.
The court held that the employer had complied in good faith with
state law and that back pay was not due. For a criticism of
the decision, see B. Babcock, A. Freedman, E. Norton and S. Ross,
Sex Discrimination and the Law 286-287 (1975).

3. For an excellent description of case law under
Title VII from 1964 to 1971 see Note, "Developments in the Law--
Employment Discrimination and Title VII of the Civil Rights Act
of 1964," 84 Harv. L. Rev. 1109, 1195-1241 (1971).

4. Herbert and Reichel, "Title VII and the Multiple
Approaches to Eliminating Employment Discrimination," 46 N.Y.U.
L. Rev. 449 (1971).

The Invalidation of Restrictive Labor Laws Which Apply to Women Only

Maximum Hours Limitations

Legal problem: It will be remembered that the legislation
involved in both Lochner v. New York and Muller v. Oregon,
discussed above, absolutely prohibited employers from allowing
employees to work more than a certain number of hours per week.

210

Well into the twentieth century, such legislation was a primary goal of the labor movement because of the sweatshop conditions which were commonplace in many industries.

Thus, maximum hours legislation, even though applicable only to women, was thought to be of great benefit at the time it was enacted. During the last twenty years, however, maximum hours legislation has harmed women much more than it has helped them. Many employers who need trained employees to work more than forty-eight hours a week--a common limitation in state maximum hours legislation--refused to hire women because the law prohibited them from working more than the legally established number of hours. In addition, the legislation harmed those women who did obtain work because of the generally available premium pay for overtime which male employees could earn, but which was unavailable to women because of the maximum hours limitation.

While originally conceived of as a "benefit," maximum hours legislation cannot be simply extended to both sexes neutrally as other "benefit" laws can. Many businesses, such as the auto industry in nonrecession times, need workers for more than forty-eight hours a week. Further, many workers both want to work and need the extra money which overtime work at premium pay provides. Therefore, to place an absolute prohibition on any employee working more than a certain number of hours a week, in good economic times, would be impossible for industry and very unsatisfactory for the many employees who want to work the extra time to earn premium pay.

On the other hand, employers are, under present law, free to discharge or fire employees who refuse to work overtime. This issue received national attention in 1973 when the United Auto Workers made the employee's right to refuse to work overtime without being fired a prime bargaining point in their contracts with automobile manufacturers.[6]

Maximum hours legislation was entirely invalidated by the 1972 EEOC Guidelines, and has also been invalidated by federal courts which have considered the issue, with respect to employees covered by the Act. The 1972 EEOC Guidelines relating to this issue provide:

   1. Many States have enacted laws or promulgated administrative regulations with respect to the employment of females. Among these laws are those which prohibit or limit the employment of females, e.g., the employment of females in certain occupations, in jobs

---

6. For a description of the UAW-Chrysler negotiations on this point, see B. Babcock, A. Freedman, E. Norton and S. Ross, Sex Discrimination and the Law 281-282 (1975).

requiring the lifting or carrying of weights exceeding
certain prescribed limits, during certain hours of the
night, for more than a specified number of hours per
day or per week, and for certain periods of time before
and after childbirth. The Commission has found that
such laws and regulations do not take into account the
capacities, preferences, and abilities of individual
females and, therefore, discriminate on the basis of
sex. The Commission has concluded that such laws and
regulations conflict with and are superseded by
Title VII of the Civil Rights Act of 1964. Accordingly,
such laws will not be considered a defense to an otherwise established unlawful employment practice or as
a basis for the application of the bona fide occupational qualification exception.[7]

Courts which have considered the issue since 1971 have been in
almost unanimous agreement with the guideline provisions. The
leading case in the area is Rosenfeld v. Southern Pacific Co.,
444 F. 2d 1219 (9th Cir. 1971), which invalidated California's
ten-hour a day maximum hours legislation applicable to women
only. Other cases which have followed this decision are cited
in reference no. 4, below. The EEOC Guidelines, coupled with
the many court decisions on this issue, have had a tremendous
impact. Between 1964 and 1973, only one state, Nevada, had not
made a major change or exclusion in its maximum hours law.
Many changes were made by Attorney Generals' rulings or state
legislative amendments.[8]

The Equal Rights Amendment would make such legislation
unconstitutional. However, the Amendment should provide the
impetus for state legislatures to enact new and creative laws to
replace the outdated maximum hours legislation, rather than
simply invalidating the legislation, as Title VII has done for
employers covered by that Act.

Possible solutions: Commentators who have studied this
problem uniformly suggest that it be solved by enactment of
statutes in each state which explicitly provide that employees
of either sex may not be discharged for refusing to work more
than a statutorily-established number of hours per week. Such
statutes would allow employees who wish to earn extra money and
work overtime to do so; but those employees who value free time
more than extra money would not be penalized.

---

7. 29 C.F.R. Sec. 1604.2(b)(1) (1972).

8. See, for a list of the states which had changed maximum
hours laws in some way by 1973, B. Babcock, A. Freedman,
E. Norton and S. Ross, Sex Discrimination and the Law 271 (1975).

212

In the absence of such positive legislation, the unquestioned effect of the Equal Rights Amendment will be to invalidate totally all maximum hours legislation for all employers. This area, then, offers one more example of the ways in which the Amendment can provide a positive and beneficial impetus to reform laws which have been defective for many years, but which have not been studied in depth.

References

1. L. Kanowitz, Women and the Law 184 (1969).

2. Brown, Emerson, Falk and Freedman, "The Equal Rights Amendment: A Constitutional Basis for Equal Rights for Women," 80 Yale L. J. 871, 933 (1971).

3. B. Babcock, A. Freedman, E. Norton and S. Ross, Sex Discrimination and the Law 268-277 (1975).

4. Cases other than Rosenfeld which have invalidated maximum hours laws include: Kober v. Westinghouse Electric Corp., 325 F. Supp. 467 (W.D. Pa. 1971); Garneau v. Raytheon Co., 323 F. Supp. 391 (D. Mass. 1971); and LeBlanc v. Southern Bell Tel. and Tel. Co., 333 F. Supp. 602 (E.D. La. 1971).

Weight-lifting Limits for Women Employees

Legal problem: Many state statutes provide that women employees cannot lift more than a specified number of pounds while working. These laws, also enacted as protections for women workers, often act to their detriment because employers refuse to hire women on the ground that they may, often or occasionally, have to life weights in excess of that allowed by state law.

Such laws have been invalidated for employers to whom Title VII is applicable and will be unconstitutional under the Equal Rights Amendment.

Possible solutions: As to weight-lifting limits, the EEOC Guidelines, quoted above, also invalidate laws and regulations that limit or prohibit employing women in jobs requiring lifting weights above a certain limit. The guideline has been followed in numerous cases, a few of which are cited in reference no. 2, below.

The Equal Rights Amendment would also invalidate state laws which prescribe, according to sex, the weights which persons can lift. Under the Equal Rights Amendment, as under Title VII, individual ability must be the determining factor for the weight-lifting limits ascribed to any particular employee. Thus, weight-lifting limits cannot be established by sex; however, weight-lifting limits can be imposed for jobs if the weight-lifting requirement is sex-neutral. In other words, applicants of both sexes must be allowed to demonstrate their ability to meet the requirements of the job.

In addition, weight-lifting or other physical or strength-related skills must be closely related to the actual requirements of a job so that they do not serve as barriers which effectively exclude women from jobs for which the requirements imposed are clearly not necessary. Compliance with the ERA and Title VII could easily be circumvented if weight limits were not scrutinized carefully to see that they were actually needed in the particular job for which they were established.

References

1. B. Babcock, A. Freedman, E. Norton and S. Ross, Sex Discrimination and the Law 268-277 (1975).

2. Cases which have invalidated the weight-lifting requirement under Title VII include: Rinehart v. Westinghouse Electric Corp., 3 FEP cases 851 (N.D. Ohio 1971); Local 246 Utility Workers' Union v. Southern Cal. Edison Co., 320 F. Supp. 1242 (C.D. Cal. 1970); and Richards v. Griffith Rubber Mills, 300 F. Supp. 338 (D. Ore. 1969).

3. The most famous case on weight-lifting limits is Weeks v. Southern Bell Tel. and Tel. Co., 408 F. 2d 228 (5th Cir. 1969), in which the federal appeals court under Title VII invalidated Southern Bell's weight-lifting requirement for a particular job, ordered Mrs. Weeks hired for it and ordered back pay.

Exclusion of Women from Certain Occupations

Legal problem: In many states, women are excluded by statute from occupations considered "hazardous." Common statutory exclusions include mining, wrestling and bartending. Such statutory exclusions of women from occupations have been invalidated by Title VII for employers to which the Act applies and will be unconstitutional after passage of the Equal Rights Amendment.

Possible solutions: The only solution consonant with the Equal Rights Amendment is simply to repeal all laws which exclude any person from particular occupations based on that person's sex. These laws have also been invalidated by the 1972 EEOC Guidelines which specifically state that any statutes excluding one sex from a particular occupation are superseded by Title VII.[9] Such statutes should be repealed after passage of the Equal Rights Amendment or earlier.

Reference

B. Babcock, A. Freedman, E. Norton, and S. Ross, Sex Discrimination and the Law 271-277 (1975).

Statutes Providing that Women Cannot Work for Specified Periods Before and After Childbirth

Legal problem: Some states will retain statutes which prohibit women from working for certain specified periods before and after childbirth. Title VII has already invalidated these laws for employers covered by the 1964 Act. Further, these statutes have been invalidated by the Supreme Court decisions in Cleveland Board of Education v. LaFleur and Cohen v. Chesterfield County School Board, 414 U.S. 632 (1974). The statutes will also be unconstitutional under the Equal Rights Amendment.

Possible solutions: The 1972 EEOC Guidelines, quoted above, have invalidated, for employers covered by Title VII, state statutes which prohibit women from working for certain periods before and after childbirth without regard for the individual woman's desire or ability to work.

In 1974, these statutes were rendered wholly invalid by the Supreme Court's decisions in LaFleur and Cohen, above. In those cases, teachers challenged the constitutionality of school district rules which required maternity leave to begin four to five months before expected childbirth. The Court declared unconstitutional any rules which established arbitrarily-fixed maternity leave dates. The Court said that they were "conclusive presumptions" which did not allow an individual teacher to demonstrate that she was physically able to continue working longer than the arbitrarily fixed leave date. Thus, the LaFleur and Cohen decisions have also rendered unconstitutional, under present law, statutes and regulations setting arbitrary periods for maternity leave.

---

9. 29 C.F.R. Sec. 1604.2(b)(1) (1972).

They will also be unconstitutional under the Equal Rights Amendment. However, the Amendment will have broader application than the due process approach taken by the Court in LaFleur and Cohen. It will also have broader application than Title VII. Under the LaFleur and Cohen decisions, a statute requiring only pregnant women to prove that they are able to continue working could possibly withstand constitutional attack. Thus, LaFleur and Cohen would allow a state statute or a school board regulation to treat pregnancy differently than other temporary disabilities were treated. Such an approach would not be possible under the Equal Rights Amendment. The Amendment, as developed more fully in the following section, would require that pregnancy be treated the same as any other temporary disability; it would not be considered a "unique physical characteristic" which would justify different treatment for pregnant employees.

Thus, in this area, the Equal Rights Amendment will improve present law in two ways: it will prohibit the application of such statutes to any employees, not just those of employers of fifteen or more employees; and it will also render unconstitutional any distinction made by the state, through statutes or regulations, between pregnancy and other temporary disabilities, which the LaFleur and Cohen decisions do not. The Equal Rights Amendment will require the repeal of all such statutes.

References

1. Note, "Constitutional Law--Equal Protection--A Violation of Equal Protection Exists Where a Pregnant Teacher in a Public School System is Required to Take a Compulsory Maternity Leave without Showing that this Particular Pregnancy Interferes with the Performance of Required Duties," 38 Brooklyn L. Rev. 789 (1972).

2. Note, "Constitutional Law--Equal Protection--Mandatory Leave Rules for Public School Teachers," 50 N.D. L. Rev. 756 (1974).

3. Note, "Case of the Pregnant School Teachers: An Equal Protection Analysis," 34 Md. L. Rev. 7 (1974).

4. Note, "Mandatory Maternity Leave for Teachers--Now a Thing of the Past?," 3 Capital U. L. Rev. 323 (1974).

5. Note, "Constitutional Law--Mandatory Maternity Leave--Termination and Return Provisions of School Boards Violate the Due Process Provisions of the Fourteenth Amendment," 23 Drake L. Rev. 690 (1974).

EXCLUSION OF PREGNANCY FROM DISABILITIES WHICH ARE COMPENSATED UNDER STATE UNEMPLOYMENT INSURANCE

Legal problem: In Geduldig v. Aiello, 417 U.S. 484 (1974), the United States Supreme Court reviewed California's unemployment insurance program; under that program, virtually all California employees who had to quit work because of a health disability received unemployment insurance payments for twenty-six weeks. The only significant exclusion from the statute's coverage was disabilities related to pregnancy. The Court held that the equal protection clause did not prohibit the exclusion of normal pregnancies from the disabilities covered by an unemployment insurance program.[10]

The Equal Rights Amendment should have the effect of reversing Geduldig v. Aiello and requiring that state unemployment insurance programs compensate employees for all disabilities caused by pregnancies, whether normal or otherwise.

Possible solutions: It is clear from the majority opinion in Aiello that the Court applied only minimum scrutiny to the California unemployment compensation program which was challenged. In footnote 20, the only discussion in the majority opinion of the sex-discrimination issue, the Court said:

> Absent a showing that distinctions involving pregnancy are mere pretexts designed to effect an individous discrimination against one sex or the other, lawmakers are constitutionally free to include or exclude pregnancy from the coverage of legislation such as this on any reasonable basis, just as with respect to any other physical condition. (417 U.S. at 491.) (emphasis added)

As was discussed above in the first chapter, The Equal Rights Amendment and the Constitution, passage of the Equal Rights Amendment will at the very least insure that strict scrutiny is

---

10. For a discussion of the majority and the dissenting opinions in Geduldig v. Aiello, see the section on equal protection in the chapter on The Equal Rights Amendment and the Constitution, above.

the standard of review to be applied to sex-based
classifications.[11]

Under a strict scrutiny standard of review, which was
applied by the dissenters in Aiello, it is clear that an
exclusion based on pregnancy cannot be justified. As the
dissent noted, the cost of funding cannot be taken into account
in determining whether a classification is justified by a
compelling state interest.   In other words, when the strict
scrutiny test is applied, saving money for the state or for
employees cannot be justified as the compelling state interest
which legitimizes the exclusion of one class of persons. See
Geduldig v. Aiello, 417 U.S. at 495 (1974), citing Shapiro v.
Thompson, 394 U.S. 618 (1969) and Memorial Hospital v.
Maricopa County, 415 U.S. 250 (1974).

Under the most lenient standard of review which could
possibly be adopted by the Supreme Court under the Equal Rights
Amendment, it is clear that the dissent, rather than the
majority, in Aiello would prevail.

Further, although pregnancy is a "unique physical
characteristic"--which makes it sex-linked, not independent of
sex as the majority in Aiello claims--it does not meet or satisfy
the six factors which the Yale article sets forth. Although the
state, by excluding pregnancy from the disabilities which are
covered by its unemployment insurance program is, in fact,
dealing with a significant cost factor in the program, "less
drastic alternatives" are available which are not so costly as
to render them inapplicable here. In other words, the fifth and
sixth factors noted in the Yale article clearly outweigh the other
four. Those circumstances were acknowledged in the dissenting
opinion in Aiello, which noted that the district court, ruling
in favor of the women plaintiffs, had observed:

---

11. The majority attempts to state that pregnancy is not
linked to sex--that it is simply one physical condition which by
happenstance occurs only in women. See footnote 20, 417 U.S.
491. Even if one accepts the majority's incredible view that
pregnancy is not linked to sex, the statutory exclusion of
pregnancy from unemployment compensation benefits should be
analyzed as a law "neutral on its face, but discriminatory in
impact." Under that analysis, a statute which excludes
pregnancy clearly affects only women and no men. Thus, even in
light of the majority view that pregnancy is not sex-linked,
this analysis requires review of the statutes under the Equal
Rights Amendment.

See the first chapter, The Equal Rights Amendment and the
Constitution, above, for a discussion of statutes "neutral on
their face, but discriminatory in impact."

Even using /the State's7 estimate of the cost
of expanding the program to include pregnancy-related
disabilities, however, it is clear that including
these disabilities would not destroy the program.
The increased cost could be accommodated quite easily
by making reasonable changes in the contribution rate,
the maximum benefits allowable, and the other variables
affecting the solvency of the program. For example,
the entire cost increase estimated by defendant could
be met by requiring workers to contribute an additional
amount of approximately .364% of their salary and
increasing the maximum annual contributions to about
$119. (315 F. Supp. 792 at 798; cited in 417 U.S.
at 495.)[12]

Thus, the cost of including pregnancy in the unemployment
compensation program, a "less drastic alternative" than discriminating on the basis of sex, is not so great as to render that
solution unacceptable. It seems clear, then, that passage of
the Equal Rights Amendment should cause the Aiello decision to
be reversed.

As important as reversal of that decision will be, however,
equally important is the task of gathering statistics in each
state upon which a revised program can be based. Those
statistics should show how many women in a particular state
would be affected annually under the program when pregnancy is
a covered disability. They should demonstrate that covering
pregnancy is economically feasible, predicting the size of the
contributions needed from each employee to operate the expanded
program which will be required by the Amendment.

It might be noted that the Aiello decision has created a
strange anomaly. The EEOC, in its 1972 Guidelines, required
that employers covered by the Act treat pregnancy the same as
any other temporary disability under any health or temporary
disability insurance or sick leave plan.[13] Thus, when the state
is acting in its capacity as an employer, it must provide health
insurance plans which cover pregnancy and pregnancy-related
disabilities for women employees. However, under Aiello, a
state statute establishing a state unemployment compensation
program may exclude pregnancy from the list of covered

---

12. In the majority opinion, the Court noted that employees
were presently required to contribute 1% of their salaries, up
to a maximum of $85.00 annually.

13. 29 C.F.R. Sec. 1604.10 (1972).

disabilities. Thus, Title VII places the state, in its capacity as an employer, under a much more stringent duty than the Aiello decision imposes upon the state in its capacity as a lawmaker. Passage of the Equal Rights Amendment will end this anomaly.

References

1. Note, "Pregnancy and the Constitution: The Uniqueness Trap," 62 Calif.L. Rev. 1532 (1974).

2. Note, "Pregnancy without Penalty," 1 Civ. Lib. L. Rev. 31 (1973).

3. Note, "Sex Discrimination--State Disability Insurance Programs--Pregnancy-Related Disabilities--Equal Protection--Exclusion of Pregnancy and Childbirth Disabilities from State Disability Insurance Programs Does Not Violate the Equal Protection Clause," 3 Hofstra L. Rev. 141 (1975).

4. Comment, "Constitutional Law--Equal Protection--Exclusion of Pregnancy-Related Disabilities from State Unemployment Compensation Insurance Program Denies Equal Protection to Employees," 27 Vand. L. Rev. 551 (1974).

STATE GOVERNMENTS AS EMPLOYERS

Sex Discrimination in Employment

As noted above, Title VII has, since 1972, prohibited state governments acting in their capacities as employers from discriminating on the basis of sex. The Equal Rights Amendment will, in effect, duplicate that prohibition regarding sex discrimination by the state in employment.

However, as discussed at length in the section on admissions policies in the chapter on Education, above, and briefly summarized here, the Amendment will provide an additional remedy for persons who believe that a state government or any of its subdivisions--including public schools--has discriminated against them in employment on the basis of sex. Under Title VII, which is the only remedy now widely used for sex discrimination in employment by state governments,[14] a complaint must be filed with the EEOC within 180 days after the alleged discrimination took place. Failure to file within the prescribed time period acts to cut off an employee's or applicant's right to file a complaint.

Passage of the Equal Rights Amendment will give aggrieved employees or applicants the right to bring suits in federal courts for damages under the provisions of 42 U.S.C. Sec. 1983. The time period within which those suits must be brought, however, is determined by the applicable state statute of limitations for the particular type of suit. One federal district court held that any suit brought within five years could be heard because that was the applicable statute of limitations for contract suits in that state. See Green v. McDonnell Douglas Corp., 463 F. 2nd 337 (8th Cir. 1972). Thus, the Equal Rights Amendment will add an important new remedy--one without the very strict 180-day time limit contained in Title VII--for employees of state government who believe they have been the victims of sex discrimination.

References

1. The text in the section on faculty in the chapter on Education, above, contains numerous citations to cases holding that an independent cause of action exists under 42 U.S.C. Sec. 1983 for employment discrimination. In order to avoid repetition, this section has summarized the holdings described there.

2. See K. Davidson, R. Ginsburg and H. Kay, Sex-based Discrimination 799-804 (1974) for an analysis of the interplay between the remedies available under Title VII and those available under 42 U.S.C. Sec. 1983.

---

14. Some states do have state remedies for sex discrimination in employment. However, those statutes vary greatly from state to state in the strength of their enforcement provisions and available remedies. Further, the state agencies charged with enforcing such statutes differ markedly in competence and staffing. Therefore, state remedies for sex discrimination in employment are not treated here, both because no question under the Equal Rights Amendment is raised and because it is impossible to make generalities in this area. See K. Davidson, R. Ginsburg and H. Kay, Sex-based Discrimination 804-807 (1974), for a brief description of common inadequacies of such state procedures and commissions.

State Statutes Which Give Veterans' Preference in Employment by the State

Legal problem: Many states now have state personnel systems under which veterans of the United States armed forces are given bonus points or some other form of job preference when they apply for employment in state government. Because the armed forces are overwhelmingly male, such statutes are laws which are "neutral on their face, but discriminatory in impact" upon women, and will therefore be unconstitutional under the Equal Rights Amendment.

Possible solutions: As in the area of veterans' preference in admission to state schools, only two solutions seem possible here. First, veterans' preference statutes could simply be repealed entirely, leaving all applicants for state jobs to compete on their merits.

A second approach, which was enacted by the State of Washington in 1973 after that state adopted an Equal Rights Amendment to its state constitution, would be to broaden substantially the present veterans' preference statutes to include not only veterans but also their spouses. In this manner, a sex-neutral statute which benefited both sexes could retain the preference for veterans. Such an approach might be justified because of the substantial sacrifice many wives of men in the armed forces make while their husbands are in service. One possible objection, however, is that if both a veteran and his or her spouse apply for jobs with state government, both would get preferences under this approach--a double reward for service by only one of them.

Reference

For a brief discussion of the Washington revision and citations to the statutes, see Dybwad, "Implementing Washington's ERA: Problems with Wholesale Legislative Revision," 49 Wash. L. Rev. 571, 592 (1973).

STATE STATUTES UNDER WHICH BENEFITS ARE PAYABLE TO "WIDOWS" OR "DEPENDENT WIDOWERS"

Legal problem: Many state statutes--including pension funds; industrial or workmen's compensation insurance; employee benefits of common carriers; and teachers' retirement funds--contain provisions for benefits payable to the insured's "widow" in the event of the death of the insured. Other such statutes allow payment to a widower, but only if he can demonstrate actual dependency on his deceased wife at the time of her death.

Two Supreme Court decisions have already had the effect of making both of these common provisions unconstitutional under the equal protection clause. In Frontiero v. Richardson, 411 U.S. 677 (1972), the Court declared unconstitutional a federal statute which automatically gave a dependency allowance to wives of male Air Force officers but required husbands of female officers to prove their dependency before qualifying for benefits. In March 1975, the Court held in Weinberger v. Wiesenfeld, 95 S. Ct. 1225, that a provision of the Social Security Act which gave survivors' benefits only to widowed mothers and not to widowed fathers of dependent children, was a denial of equal protection. Thus, both types of state statutes are almost certainly unconstitutional under present law, as they will be under the Equal Rights Amendment.

Possible solutions: The only solution here is to amend all sections of state statutes which provide survivors' benefits only for widows to provide such benefits for "surviving spouses."

Statutes which require a widower to prove his dependency in order to gain survivors' benefits must be amended to either require all survivors to prove dependency or to do away with the requirement altogether. In light of the great cost of holding administrative hearings concerning actual dependency for every survivor of a person who had paid into some type of fund, the only practical solution would seem to be to repeal this type of statute altogether. If this were done, all surviving spouses would be eligible for benefits, regardless of dependence on the deceased person.

References

1. Both Frontiero v. Richardson and Weinberger v. Wiesenfeld are discussed at length in the equal protection section of the first chapter, The Equal Rights Amendment and the Constitution, above.

2. For a brief discussion of Washington's treatment of these types of statutes under a state ERA and citations to the statutes amended, see Dybwad, "Implementing Washington's ERA: Problems with Wholesale Legislative Revision," 49 Wash. L. Rev. 571, 592 (1973).

Chapter Six

MARITAL PROPERTY LAWS

Table of Contents

INTRODUCTION

On the day a woman marries, her financial situation is altered drastically by the marital property law of the state in which she and her new husband reside. If they live in one of the forty-three separate property jurisdictions,[1] her financial rights and responsibilities in the marriage, upon divorce, and upon her or her husband's death, will be governed by laws which are essentially the altered remnants of the Englist common law much as it existed soon after the Norman Conquest. If she and her husband reside in Washington, California, Arizona, New Mexico, Texas, Louisiana, Nevada or Idaho, the new wife's financial rights at all stages of her life will be governed by the marital property system known as community property, older yet than the common law system, and also substantially altered by legislative reforms to be described below.

These doctrines of property law, descended from concepts now approaching their thousandth birthday, have immense practical consequences for married women. As will be seen in the discussion which follows, the doctrines greatly affect a married woman's ability to obtain credit during marriage; the share of property acquired by either spouse during the marriage which each will receive in the event of divorce; a wife's ability to will property upon her death; and her right to property if she outlives her husband.

Marital property law, then, is not a dry, dusty field which is an exclusive preserve for property lawyers and judges. It is living law which vitally affects a basic aspect of every person's life--financial security. As such, the area must be studied and understood by all women--and it must undergo fundamental reform after passage of the Equal Rights Amendment.

GENUINE REFORM OF THE SEPARATE PROPERTY SYSTEMS

The Constitutionality of Separate Property Systems

Background of Separate and Community Property Systems

In the forty-three separate property jurisdictions, the legal theory under which married persons own property may be

---

1. The eight community property states are Arizona, California, Idaho, Louisiana, Nevada, New Mexico, Texas and Washington. Because the District of Columbia follows the separate property system, there are forty-three separate property jurisdictions in the United States.

simply stated. The earnings of each spouse after marriage retain precisely the status they had before marriage--as the separate property of the earning spouse, in which the other has no legal right or interest. Just as each has legal ownership of his or her earnings, each also has the sole right to contract with regard to those earnings, obtain credit based upon them and manage and control them. Similarly, all property brought to the marriage or inherited is the separate property of the owning spouse and under his or her sole management and control.

In addition to her right to ownership and control of any earnings or property she may have, a wife's financial rights in a separate property jurisdiction include the right to be supported by her husband in the fashion and manner he chooses. In return for this support, she is responsible for rendering the wifely services of keeping the house and tending any children the couple may have.[2]

Under the marital property law of the separate property jurisdictions, the only financial right of the wife who is not employed is the husband's duty of support. She has no legal interest or right to his earnings or what those earnings purchase, unless he deliberately makes a gift to her of some portion of his property by placing it in their names jointly or in her name alone.

The underlying theory of the separate property systems may be simply stated. In application, as we shall see, it becomes more complex.

In the eight community property states, a new wife's financial situation is quite different. If she is employed, her earnings, which before marriage were her separate property, become community property in which she and her husband each have a one-half ownership interest. Similarly, her husband's earnings after marriage become community property in which she has a one-half interest, regardless of whether or not she happens to be employed herself. Each of them will retain, as his or her separate property, any property brought to the marriage or inherited during it. The other spouse has no legal right or interest in this property, and the owning spouse has sole management rights over such property.

Insofar as ownership of property during marriage is concerned, then, the wife in a community property state is undoubtedly in a better position than her sister in a separate property jurisdiction. As far as management of community property is concerned, however, the situation in community

_____

2. See the chapter on Family Laws, above, for a discussion of the duty of support and the Equal Rights Amendment.

property states is not as simple. Until 1972, no community property state allowed wives to manage community personal property equally with their husbands, although some did allow them to manage their own wages. Since 1972, however, five of the eight community property states have converted to a system of equal management, giving the wife by statute the "equal right" to manage and control the entire community personal property. In Texas, a wife may control her own earnings and may jointly control the community property if her earnings are commingled with her husband's. In Nevada and Louisiana, a wife's right to management and control remains restricted or nonexistent.

What are the practical consequences of these two marital property systems which exist side by side in the United States today? Do their theoretical legal differences make any real difference in married women's lives? To answer the question, the operation of each property system at four important stages must be examined.

Property Rights During Marriage

In a credit-oriented society, the most important single aspect of a wife's financial rights during marriage is the ability to obtain credit. Through the use of credit, she may effectively enforce her husband's duty of support--which is otherwise totally unenforceable[3]--by purchasing needed items and deferring payment for them, or obtaining unsecured loans to make such purchases.

In October 1974, Congress passed the Equal Credit Opportunity Act, effective on October 28, 1975, which prohibits any creditor in the United States, whether a bank, savings and loan association, small loan company, retail merchant or other creditor, from discriminating in the granting of credit on the basis of sex or marital status.[4] The Act recognizes, however, the pervasive effects of state property laws upon a creditor's decision to extend credit. It specifically provides, among other things, that in making a particular decision as to whether to grant or deny credit, a creditor may consider the application of state property laws which affect an applicant's creditworthiness.

---

3. See section on the duty of child and spousal support in the chapter on Family Laws, for a discussion of the problem of enforcement of support rights in an ongoing marriage and the changes in present support laws which the ERA will require.

4. See 15 U.S.C. Secs. 1691 et seq. (Supp. Pamphlet No. 1, Feb. 1975).

What is the impact of the Equal Credit Opportunity Act on a wife's ability to obtain credit in separate and community property states?

In any of the forty-three separate property jurisdictions, whether a wife obtains credit under the new Act will depend on several factors. If she is employed, a creditor must evaluate her creditworthiness just as he would any married person's, male or female. However, because most women's incomes are lower than men's, the application of purely objective standards will not give the employed wife in a separate property jurisdiction the same amount of individual credit which the average employed husband would obtain. If an employed wife wishes to obtain a greater amount of credit, she may ask her husband to pool his income with hers in making the application and to expressly agree to be liable on any debts either of them incurs.

If the wife in a separate property jurisdiction is not employed--and over 55% of wives are not[5]--she may obtain credit only in one of two ways. In all credit transactions except those with retail merchants, her husband must sign an agreement stating that he will pay any debts she incurs. The credit so obtained will, then, not be hers, but her husband's.

The second means of obtaining credit for such wives is used only by retail merchants who, under certain circumstances, will open accounts for the wife alone for the purchase of "necessaries." Under the common law, and today, the doctrine of "necessaries" supplements the husband's duty of support by allowing merchants to extend credit to a wife for goods purchased without the consent of a husband and to hold the husband liable for the purchase price. However, because the doctrine is hemmed with legal uncertainties,[6] any individual creditor may justifiably refuse to extend credit under the doctrine, and thereby leave the unemployed wife in a separate property jurisdiction with only one means of obtaining credit--the express agreement of her husband to pay any debts created. For such wives, who are the majority of married women in the United States, the Equal Credit Opportunity Act is hardly a giant step forward. In fact, for them it represents no advance whatsoever in the critically important matter of obtaining equal credit.

---

5. During calendar year 1973, 42.8% of married women were employed outside the home. See Statistical Abstract of the United States 340 (1974).

6. See section below for a complete discussion of revisions the ERA will require in this doctrine.

After October 28, 1975, in the five community property states with completely equal management provisions for community personal property, a wife, whether employed or unemployed, may obtain credit on exactly the same terms and in exactly the same amounts as her husband may, without his signature or consent to any transaction. This is so because she has a one-half ownership of all the community property, which includes both his and her earnings, and has the legal right to manage and incur debts binding the entire community personal property, just as he does. Thus, if the community itself is creditworthy, she may obtain charge cards, retail charge accounts, or unsecured bank or small loans on precisely the same terms as her husband. The credit so obtained will be hers alone.[7]

The situation is not so happy for wives in Nevada and Louisiana. Because those states have not given them the same right to manage the entire community personal property which their husbands enjoy, they are in much the same position as is the unemployed wife in a separate property jurisdiction: they may be granted credit only with the express consent of their husbands, or through retail merchants' willingness to apply the doctrine of "necessaries" to their credit applications. In Texas, a wife must be employed in order to obtain credit independently of her husband. The unemployed wife is in precisely the same position as is the wife in Nevada, Louisiana or any separate property jurisdiction.

During marriage, then, the most important financial rights of a wife are those involving credit. The community property system, as recently amended in five states by the addition of equal management provisions for community personal property, unquestionably offers married women the best opportunity for obtaining credit on the same terms as their husbands.

Property Rights upon Divorce

As has been noted by a sociologist whose speciality is divorce and its impact on American life, the marital property laws of most of the United States assume that a husband and wife will marry only once and that they will stay married until they die.[8]

---

7. See 15 U.S.C. Secs. 1691 et seq. (Supp. Pamphlet No. 1, Feb. 1975); Proposed Regulation, 12 C.F.R. Sec. 202.5 (F) 40 Fed. Reg. 18183 (1975).

8. Weitzman, "Legal Regulation of Marriage: Tradition and Change," 62 Calif. L. Rev. 1169, 1200-1210 (1974).

In fact, American society has long since moved away from that model, as attested to by a staggering divorce rate. How does a wife fare upon divorce in separate and community property states?

Two property questions are involved in any divorce, in any jurisdiction--property division and the possible payment of alimony or child support ordered in the divorce decree.

Although it is a common belief that alimony awards are a component of most divorces, that belief is simply unfounded. In fact, as seen in the chapter on Family Laws, alimony is awarded in less than 10 percent of all divorces, and because alimony is deductible from the husband's income and includible in the wife's, payments which are actually for the support of children are often labeled "alimony" to lower the husband's income tax.[9] Thus, alimony is not a large factor to be considered in the property questions which arise upon divorce.

Child support, which is customarily awarded to a wife granted custody of children, is not as customarily paid. As discussed at length in the chapter on Family Laws, the record of child support payments actually made by husbands is a dismal one:

> 62 percent (of husbands) fail to comply fully with court-ordered (child support) payments in the first year after the order, and 42 percent do not even make a single payment. By the tenth year, 79 percent are in total noncompliance.[10]

Thus, with alimony awards infrequent and child support awards difficult or impossible to enforce, the question of the division of property owned by either spouse upon divorce is a crucial one for wives.[11] How does each marital property system deal with the problem?

Theoretically, in a separate property system, the spouse who has earned property is the sole owner of it. In those marriages--over 55% of all marriages--in which the wife does not work outside the home, the spouse who owns property upon divorce will necessarily be the husband. Even in those marriages where

---

9. Id. at 1186.

10. Id. at 1195.

11. Suggestions for improvement in collection of child support awards and in alimony are set forth at length in the chapter on Family Laws.

the wife is employed, the property she has accumulated is sure to be of less value than her husband's because of women's lower pay scales and the years even most employed women spend outside the labor force rearing children. Theoretically, then, upon divorce, property is divided according to which of the spouses owns it. Obviously, the separate property system gives a husband much-favored odds.

In fact, however, as noted in the chapter on Family Laws, there has been a trend in separate property states toward dividing property "owned" by husbands alone "equitably" between the spouses where specific legislation in a particular separate property jurisdiction allows it. In 1968, twenty-six of the forty-three separate property jurisdictions had statutes providing for such a division.[12] The theoretical harshness of the separate property systems has thus been mitigated by legislation in the majority of jurisdictions.

In community property states, although the statutes give each spouse a vested ownership interest in one-half of all community property, only two of the eight states require that such property be equally divided upon divorce.[13] In the six other states, the statutes allow a court in a divorce proceeding to make such division of the community property as it considers "equitable" under the circumstances. In particular cases, such statutes may work a hardship upon the wife, particularly in those states where fault is taken into consideration in dividing property upon divorce, but in the majority of situations the wife in a community property state is aided by the unstated presumption that community property belongs equally to the spouses, and should be divided equally upon divorce.

Upon divorce, then, while the differences between the two systems may be in fact less great than they are in theory, the basic premises of the separate and community property systems have a substantial effect on the divisions of property ordered. The basic premise of the separate property system, as we have seen, is that property is owned by the person who earned it during the marriage. In a community system, the basic premise is just the opposite: regardless of who earned property during marriage, it is owned equally by both spouses. With such premises as the starting points for courts asked to divide property "equitably" upon divorce, it seems inevitable that the

12. K. Davidson, R. Ginsburg and H. Kay, Sex-based Discrimination 248n. 31 (1974).

13. Those two are Louisiana and California. See Younger, "Community Property, Women and the Law School Curriculum," 48 N.Y.U. L. Rev. 211, 212n. 10 (1973).

wife in a community property state will receive a larger share of the property accumulated by either of the spouses during marriage than will the wife in a separate property jurisdiction.

An extreme example of the unfairness women may encounter under separate property systems is found in a New York case, where a husband divorced his wife after 22 years of marriage. Both husband and wife had worked during the entire marriage. For about 14 years before the divorce, they and their children had lived largely on the wife's earnings; during that time the husband, in his own name, invested heavily in what he said was a "crash program" for "our" later years. In dividing the property upon divorce, the court held that the investments were all the husband's separate property; the wife received nothing for having supported the family for some 14 years. See Wirth v. Wirth, 38 App. Div. 2d, 611, 326 N.Y.S. 2d 308 (1971).

With child support orders and alimony elusive promises at best, the matter of property division on divorce is one of paramount interest to wives in the United States. Improvements in the law concerning property division on divorce are discussed extensively in the chapter on Family Laws.

Property Rights of a Wife Who Predeceases Her Husband

Although the majority of American wives outlive their husbands, the amount of property owned at death by those who do not depends entirely on the property system of the jurisdiction in which the couple lived. If that jurisdiction adheres to a separate property system, the wife may will only property which she has acquired by her own labor outside the home, or which she inherited or was given. As we have seen, she has no legal interest in property earned or accumulated through her husband's labor, and no statutes exist which give her the right to will any portion of her husband's property if she predeceases him. Thus, those women who do not own property independently of their husbands or who are not employed during marriage die literally penniless in separate property jurisdictions, with no property whatsoever to leave to children, parents or others for whom they might wish to provide.

Women in community property states, by contrast, die owning one-half of the community property, and in all eight community property states have the right to will their halves of the community to whomever they choose. Very often, this right can make a real difference to a woman concerned about the care of children, parents or others.

For wives who predecease their husbands, then, the theoretical differences described at the beginning of this chapter have a real and important impact upon their ability to assure that

persons they care for receive property from them at their
deaths. As to this aspect of a married woman's financial life--
her ability to will property at death if she predeceases her
husband--the marital property law of the jurisdiction in which
a woman resides has immense practical effect.

Property Rights of a Wife Whose Husband Predeceases Her

The endless permutations of law concerning the property
rights of a wife whose husband has predeceased her make
generalization in this area difficult at best. However, it may
be said that in all but three separate property jurisdictions,[14]
either the common law protection of dower or a statutory
"widow's election" or "forced" share offer the surviving wife
some share of the separate property of her deceased husband.
Under these doctrines, the wife has a right to such property
regardless of her husband's wishes; he cannot totally "disinherit"
her. However, if he did provide for her by will, she must
choose, or "elect" between taking "under the will" or "against"
it under her dower or "forced" share rights.

In general, in those jurisdictions where a form of common
law dower is still in effect, the wife has the right to a life
estate interest in an amount varying from 1/3 to 1/2 of the
real property which her husband either owned at any time during
the marriage or died owning. A dower interest is only the right
to enjoy the property or its benefits for the lifetime of the
surviving wife, not an absolute ownership interest. The deceased
husband has the right to name those persons who will take the
property after the wife's death.

In those states having a "widow's election," also known
as a "forced" share of the deceased husband's estate, the wife
is given an absolute ownership interest in 1/3 to 1/2 of all
the husband's property which he owned at the time of death,
regardless of any provision in his will to the contrary.

Both these forms of protection for the widow constitute
implicit recognition of the major defect of the separate property
systems--their failure to compensate a wife for the services she
performed in the household during the marriage. In fact, both
common law dower and the more recent statutory "widow's election"

---

14. Those three are North Dakota, South Dakota and
Georgia. See Ryman, "A Comment on Family Property Rights and the
Proposed 27th Amendment," 22 Drake L. Rev. 505, 509 (1973).

provisions in effect affirm the concept of a community of
marital interest in property by ignoring the fact that such
property was technically "owned" during life by the husband
alone. As such, they can be faulted only in their assumption
that all marriages will last for the lifetime of the spouses,
and that wives who outlive their husbands will receive their
just share of the marital property at that time. When that
assumption fails--as it does in all marriages which end in
divorce rather than the death of the husband, or in which
the wife predeceases the husband--the separate property systems
offer at best a spotty and haphazard recognition of the wife's
labor during the years of the marriage.

In the eight community property states, the wife whose
husband has died is left with her one-half ownership interest
in the community's real and personal property. Her husband
is free, just as she is, to will his one-half interest in the
property to anyone he chooses.

In the four possible stages of a married woman's life--
during the marriage itself, at divorce, at her death before
her husband's, or at his death before hers--the community
property system consistently offers wives the opportunity for
ownership of greater amounts of property, and greater freedom
to deal with it. Its assumption of a community of marital
interest, and thus of a community of marital property, is more
consonant with the manner in which most couples view their
marriages, and it gives the woman who works in the home and
rears children both fair compensation for her labor and equal
dignity with her husband.

Constitutionality of Separate Property Systems under the
Equal Rights Amendment

Will the separate property systems be unconstitutional after
passage of the ERA as laws "neutral on their face, but
discriminatory in impact" upon married women?

Arguably, yes. These property systems in effect say to all
married persons "you own what you earn." In the factual setting
in which such systems operate, however, it is the men in the
society who are expected to fulfill the role of wage earners,
and women who are expected to remain in the home and care for
house and children, uncompensated by wages. Even if a wife does
work outside the home, the facts of the society in which she
must obtain employment mean that she will be employed at a lower
level than would be a comparable man; will be paid less; will
not advance as rapidly; and cannot expect to earn as much in
her working lifetime. In what sense, then, can these "neutral"
separate property systems be said to be truly neutral as
between husbands and wives? The systems are so established as

to reward the man who does only what society expects of him--
work outside the home--and to penalize the woman who also does
only what she has been raised to believe is expected of her--
work inside the home. It is arguable, therefore, that under
Supreme Court precedents, the separate property systems are
"neutral on their face, but discriminatory in impact," and should
be declared unconstitutional after passage of the Equal Rights
Amendment.[15]

While the legal answer cannot be certain at this point, the
equitable one is: a new system of marital property law should
be fashioned for the separate property jurisdictions to conform
to the spirit, if not the letter, of the Equal Rights Amendment.

Community Property As An Alternative to the Separate
Property Systems

One solution, of course, is to study seriously the
possibility of converting the entire United States to a form of
community property. It is possible, although far from certain,
that such a conversion could be accomplished constitutionally as
to all property now owned by married persons in the United States.
That possibility deserves the most serious and searching study.

First, if a change is made to community property which
affects only property acquired by married persons after the
effective date of the Equal Rights Amendment, this conversion--
one of the most important reforms ever to take place in
American law--will not be fully effective for thirty or forty
years. Thus, unless some means is found of converting all
property owned today by married persons to a form of jointly-
owned marital property, all such property in separate property
jurisdictions will retain its separate property status.

Second, a conversion to community property which affects
only property acquired after the effective date of the change
would mean that the forty-three separate property jurisdictions
would go forward under two systems of property law for many
years--a system of separate property as to that acquired before
the date of change; and a system of community property as to that
acquired afterwards. The complicated legal problems and tangled
litigation such a procedure would cause defy description.

---

15. For a full discussion of the theory of laws "neutral
on their face, but discriminatory in impact," see the first
chapter, The Equal Rights Amendment and the Constitution.

Thus, to make the Amendment fully effective in this vital area, every effort should be made to apply the new law to <u>all</u> property owned by married persons, whether owned now or acquired after the effective date of the Equal Rights Amendment.

Such a sweeping change may be possible because when marital property systems are analyzed, it will be seen that their effects are important in three primary respects: (1) as to creditors or other third parties who deal with one or both of the spouses concerning "family" or "community" debts during marriage; (2) between the spouses themselves at divorce; and (3) as to the surviving spouse when one of them dies.

If a statute were drafted which stated that as to each of these three aspects, property owned by either spouse which was acquired during the marriage would be treated as if it were owned by the spouses equally, the separate property systems now in existence would have been in effect converted to community property systems—and not just as to property acquired <u>after</u> the date of the change, but as to all property owned by married persons.

The obvious question is: why is such a procedure not violative of the fourteenth amendment due process clause which prohibits the states from taking a person's property without due process of law? Arguably, because the law in separate property states is, in constitutional terms, already so close to the proposed change, such a statute would not "take" property. The law in all separate property states now requires that a husband support his wife; many require that their property be divided "equitably" on divorce; and most give a surviving spouse a share of the property of the deceased spouse. A change in these three aspects might thus be only an affirmation of the rights the wife already has and a restructuring of the property relations in marriage so that the wife could enforce those rights, as she is frequently unable to do today.

For those interested in the question of the constitutionality of the change suggested, a more complete discussion is contained in reference no. 3 below.

It was said by Holdsworth, the English legal historian, that the problem of establishing an equitable system of married women's property rights is one of the most difficult in the entire field of private law. While that is undoubtedly true, the opportunity for reform which will come with ratification of the Equal Rights Amendment should not be lost. If the question is one of the most difficult, it is also one of the most important in family and property laws.

The minimal changes set forth in the section immediately following should not be accepted as satisfactory solutions to the age-old question of how a legal system should deal with the property rights of married women.

References

1. See Johnston, "Sex and Property: The Common Law Tradition, the Law School Curriculum and Developments Toward Equality," 47 N.Y.U. L. Rev. 1033 (1972), for an in-depth criticism of the effect on married women of the separate property systems.

2. For a complete discussion of reforms which the Amendment will require in the areas of divorce law, property division on divorce, child support and alimony, see the chapter on Family Laws, above.

3. Although to most lawyers, the notion of converting to a national community property system, and making that change as to all property owned today by married persons, as well as to all property acquired in the future, is a radical one, the idea has its precedents. Most important is California's experience with its "quasi-community property" system, which provides that separate property brought into California by persons who were formerly domiciled in a separate property state will be treated as if it had been acquired in California--i.e., as if it were community property. Thus, California has effectively made the change proposed here for all persons who move to California; the change has been repeatedly held constitutional under both the California and United States Constitutions. See Addison v. Addison, 62 Cal. 2d 558, 399 P.2d 897 (1965) and Cooper v. Cooper, 269 Cal. App. 2d 6 (1969), 74 Cal. Reptr. 439; see also the law review articles on this subject cited in reference no. 4 below.

As to the change proposed in this section, it is quite arguably not a "taking" within the meaning of the fourteenth amendment due process clause because many state laws already come so close to the proposed revision.

Concerning the first aspect discussed in the text, the rights of creditors or third parties to collect "family" or "community" debts, it will be seen below that the doctrine of "necessaries" and "family expense" statutes, currently in effect in all separate property jurisdictions, already allow creditors to reach the separate property of one spouse to pay for "necessaries" purchased by the other. To enact suggestion (1) above, then, would really only broaden the definition of "necessaries" and make the property of both spouses liable to creditors for them. Constitutionally, this is arguably not a very drastic change from present creditors' remedies in the separate property states--although it is a change which would drastically affect the ability of married women to obtain credit.

As to suggestion (2), the division of property on divorce, it would be legally simple to implement a system of division of property owned by either spouse which was acquired during marriage by enacting section 307 of the Uniform Marriage and Divorce Act as it stood before its amendment in 1973.

Before the 1973 amendment, section 307 provided in relevant part:

> (a) In a proceeding for dissolution of the marriage . . . the court shall assign each spouse's property to him. It shall also divide the marital property without regard to marital misconduct. . . .

> (b) For purposes of this Act, "marital property" means all property acquired by either spouse subsequent to the marriage except:

>> (1) property acquired by gift, bequest, devise or descent;

>> (2) property acquired in exchange for property acquired before the marriage or in exchange for property acquired by gift, bequest, devise or descent;

>> (3) property acquired by a spouse after a decree of legal separation;

>> (4) property excluded by valid agreement of the parties; and

>> (5) the increase in value of property acquired before the marriage.[16]

This definition of "marital property," it should be noted, is identical in all important respects to the definition of "community property" in community property states today.

It might also be noted that twenty-six of the separate property states already allow "equitable" division of property on divorce, regardless of which spouse legally "owned" it. Thus, the change proposed here is not a drastic revision of many states' present laws.

---

16. Uniform Marriage and Divorce Act, 9 Uniform Laws Annotated, Sec. 307 (1973).

Finally, as to suggestion (3), the rights of a surviving spouse in the property of the other, all but three of the separate property states already give either or both spouses a satutorily-fixed share in the other's property upon death. Simply changing the proportion of that share and the definition of the property of the deceased to which it applied should not render the change constitutionally defective.

Thus, the possibility which should be seriously considered to affect all these areas would be to enact the community property system in its most important aspects to replace the present separate property systems.

4. The following articles discuss the constitutionality of California's quasi-community property statutes and conclude, along with the courts, that the quasi-community property statute, which has the effect of "converting" separate property to community property when a couple moves to California from a separate property jurisdiction, is constitutional. See

(a) Schreter (now Kay), "'Quasi-Community Property' in the Conflict of Laws," 50 Calif. L. Rev. 206 (1962);

(b) Note, "Marital Property and the Conflict of Laws: Constitutionality of 'Quasi-Community Property' Legislation," 54 Calif. L. Rev. 252 (1966); and

(c) Note, "Retroactive Application of Legislation Changing Inter Vivos Marital Property Rights," 54 Calif. L. Rev. 266 (1966).

MINIMAL REFORM OF THE SEPARATE PROPERTY SYSTEMS

Introduction

Beyond the basic assumption that only the earner of property legally "owns" that property, several important features of the separate property systems will be unconstitutional under an Equal Rights Amendment. The features most clearly in need of revision are set forth below.

Curtesy; Dower; and Wife's "Nonbarrable" or "Forced" Share

Legal problem: Curtesy and dower as they exist today in the United States are holdovers from law developed by the courts in England, known as the "common law." Generally, dower and curtesy in the United States are statutory provisions, intended to ensure that the surviving spouse will not be left unprovided for, if the spouse who died attempted to leave all his or her property to others by will. The right to dower or curtesy prevails over the rights of claimants under a will.

At common law, the widow had a right, known as dower, to a life estate in one-third of all lands which her husband owned at any time during marriage. A widower had a comparable right, known as curtesy.

In its contemporary common form in the United States, dower and curtesy generally give a surviving spouse the right to a life estate in 1/3 to 1/2 of the real property which his or her spouse owned upon death. In a vew few states, dower attaches to all real property owned by the husband during marriage; this means that even if the husband sold the property to a third party who did not know he was married, the wife has a life estate in that property.

A "life estate" in property means that the recipient gets only the use of the property, or income produced by the property, during the recipient's lifetime; it is not outright ownership of the property itself. The recipient of the life estate cannot, for example, sell the property itself, but she or he does own any income from it. In some states, dower is an interest in one-half of the husband's lands and curtesy is an interest in one-third of the wive's lands.

Some states have enacted what is known as a "nonbarrable" or "forced share" for wives only to replace dower rights. This statutory share generally gives the wife outright ownership of a portion of her deceased husband's property, rather than the life estate in real property which she would receive under common law dower. Existing "nonbarrable" or "forced share" statutes will be unconstitutional under the Equal Rights Amendment, if they give such a share only to wives and not to husbands.

Possible solutions:

"De-sexed" Dower Rights

About sixteen states have enacted what is popularly known as "de-sexed dower." This statutory reform of dower rights gives both spouses equal interests in a portion of the entire estate of the decedent when one spouse survives the other.

The Uniform Probate Code, drafted by the Conference of Commissioners on Uniform State Laws and adopted in nine separate property states as of January 1, 1975, gives the survivor a one-third interest in the "argumented estate" of the deceased spouse, and thus in effect adopts a form of "de-sexed dower."[17] Both "de-sexed dower" and the provisions of the Uniform Probate Code are formally sex-neutral and probably will be constitutional under the ERA.

Since these rights attach only to property owned at death, some commentators have suggested that both "de-sexed dower" and other nonbarrable share systems could be improved if some provision were made to prevent a spouse from giving property away, either outright or in trust, during his or her lifetime. Such gifts, because they reduce the amount of property owned at death, reduce the other spouse's dower or "nonbarrable" or "forced" share rights. Obviously, since men own most of the property in separate property states, and since 85% of wives outlive their husbands, women are the persons who are hurt most by such gifts before death. In order to protect against reduction of the property to which dower, curtesy or a statutory share apply, most proposals for reform have suggested that both spouses be required to consent to large gifts of the other's property or to gifts of certain types of property.

The Uniform Probate Code deals with the problem of gifts from the decedent's estate through the definition of the "argumented estate" contained in section 2-202. That section simply includes in the decedent's "estate" of which the survivor takes one-third any gifts exceeding an established amount to which the survivor did not consent in writing.

Elimination of All Forms of Spousal Protection at Death

A second approach suggested to equalize dower, curtesy and a wife's "nonbarrable" or "forced" share is simply to do away with all forms of protection for a surviving spouse. In fact, three states, North Dakota, South Dakota and Georgia, provide neither husbands or wives with a statutorily-protected legal interest in the other's property at death. The idea behind this approach is that the statutes cause complicated accountings; make otherwise valid conveyances of property invalid in a few states; and are simply not needed in most instances because spouses commonly do provide for each other. While this solution would be formally neutral in that it would give neither spouse

17. See Uniform Probate Code, Sec. 2-201, 8 Uniform Laws Annotated (West 1973).

242

a legal interest in the other's property upon death, it might well be attacked as a provision "neutral on its face, but discriminatory in impact." If one sex will be hurt by the lack of such protection, it will be women, since under the law of the separate property states, women acquire much less property than their husbands and thus arguably need the statutory guarantee of a fixed legal interest in the property of their husbands upon their husbands' deaths.

Increase in Amount and Property to Which "De-sexed" Dower Applies

Yet a third solution would be that suggested above as a partial means of converting the separate property systems to community property: extension in all jurisdictions of the "nonbarrable" share to all property acquired during marriage and an increase in the amount of such share to 1/2, rather than the present 1/3. This approach would in effect institute the community property system in separate property states upon either spouse's death.[18]

Which of these, or any other possible approaches, would be preferable is beyond the scope of this Commentary. Whatever the solution, however, the problem should be treated as an inherent part of the establishment of a new and more equitable marital property system in the United States. It should not be viewed as a legal question separate and independent from the totality of marital property law--because, in truth, it is not.

References

1. See Ryman, "A Comment on Family Property Rights and the Proposed 27th Amendment," 22 Drake L. Rev. 505 (1973), for a complete description of the precise form of spousal protection at death in effect in every state of the United States in 1973.

---

18. The Uniform Probate Code provides for the survivor to take a one-third interest in the "argumented estate" of the decedent. If this amount were increased to one-half, the Code would provide an acceptable model in this regard. See, Uniform Probate Code, Secs. 2-201 and 2-202, 8 Uniform Laws Annotated (West 1973).

2.   See L. McDonald, Fraud on the Widow's Share (1961) for a description of the problem of gifts before death to defeat a nonbarrable share and possible solutions.

3.   For the view that there is no need today for any form of spousal protection at death, see Plager, "The Spouse's Non-Barrable Share: A Solution in Search of a Problem," 33 U. Chi. L. Rev. 681 (1966).

4.   Johnston, "Sex and Property: The Common Law Tradition, The Law School Curriculum, and Developments Toward Equality," 47 N.Y.U. L. Rev. 1033, 1079-1083 (1972).

5.   Note, "Protection of the Surviving Spouse: The Demise of Dower and Curtesy and the New Oregon Probate Code," 6 Willamette L. J. 449 (1970).

6.   Johnson, "Abolition of Dower in Virginia: The Uniform Probate Code as an Alternative to Proposed Legislation," 7 U. Richmond L. Rev. 99 (1972).

7.   Note, "Abolition of Dower: An Occasion for Re-examining the Surviving Spouse's Rights in Illinois," 3 Loyola U. L. J. (Chicago) 94 (1972).

8.   Curry, "Intestate Succession and Wills: An Analysis of Article 2 of the Uniform Probate Code and the Law of Ohio," 34 Ohio St. L. J. 114 (1973).

The "Necessaries" Doctrine

Legal problem: In twenty-one states, the common law doctrine of "necessaries" still exists as a concomitant of the husband's duty to support the wife. Under that doctrine, merchants may sell to the wife articles which are "necessaries" and collect the purchase price from the husband. In these states, no corresponding liability for wives exists for articles purchased by husbands; therefore, the doctrine of "necessaries" will be unconstitutional under the Equal Rights Amendment.

Possible solution: Aside from the far more preferable approach of revising the entire structure of marital property law in the separate property states, one means of imposing formal equality in this area would be for states to adopt the newer "family expense" statutes which twenty-two separate property jurisdictions now have. Under a "family expense" statute, either spouse is liable for items, defined in the statute as items of "family expense," which are purchased from a merchant

244

by the other spouse. The "family expense" statutes are by their
terms sex-neutral; therefore, they would also fit the revised
dual duty of support which will be necessary after the ERA. The
chapter on Family Laws contains a thorough discussion of the
duty to support and needed changes there.

While "family expense" statutes provide a statutory
definition of "family expenses," it should be noted that only
court decisions define, often after the fact, what items are
"necessaries." Therefore, any particular merchant is fully
justified in refusing to extend credit to a wife who wishes to
purchase goods in reliance on the latter doctrine since if the
husband disputes his liability for the goods purchased, they may
or may not be held by a court to have been "necessary" to that
particular family's lifestyle and needs. For this reason,
although the doctrine is sometimes used by retail stores, it
does not offer married women a reliable means of establishing
credit without their husbands' consent, and it will not do so,
even after the effective date of the Equal Credit Opportunity
Act.

References

1. Gates, "Credit Discrimination Against Women: Causes
and Solutions," 27 Vand. L. Rev. 409 (1974).

2. See Annotation, "Necessaries Furnished Wife--
Liability," 60 A. L. R. 2d 7, for a summary of the problems
merchants face if they rely on the doctrine of "necessaries"
in extending credit to married women.

3. See H. Clark, The Law of Domestic Relations 186 (1968),
for a discussion of "family expense" statutes.

4. Note, "The Connecticut Family Expense Statute: Conn.
Gen. Stat. Sec. 46-10," 44 Conn. B. J. 259 (1970).

Tenancy by the Entirety

The estate of tenancy by the entirety is a form of joint
property ownership between husbands and wives. Originally
developed in fourteenth century in England, it is still found in
the property law of some twenty-two states today. In twelve of
those states, a creditor of one of the spouses alone who has gone
to court and gotten a judgment cannot collect the judgment from
the spouse's interest in any property held by the spouses as
tenants by the entirety until the nondebtor spouse has died,

survived by the debtor spouse. If the debtor spouse dies first, the creditor cannot collect at all from property which had been held by the spouses in this form of ownership. For that reason, if property, whether real or personal, is held by married persons as tenants by the entirety, creditors asked to extend credit to one of them will request the signatures of both if tenancy by the entirety property is put up as collateral.

Thus, in many states, the very existence of this form of property ownership substantially inhibits the granting of credit to married persons. However, because tenancy by the entirety is an estate found only in separate property states-- where, as we have seen, property is "owned" by the spouse who earns it--a husband is more likely than a wife to have other assets or a larger income upon which to obtain credit. Thus, the estate probably harms married women more than married men.

A second and more obvious problem is that in some states the husband alone has the sole right to "manage" property held by him and his wife as tenants by the entirety. Also, some courts have held that all rents gained from leasing property held in tenancy by the entirety belong to the husband. Both of these rules will clearly be unconstitutional after passage of the Equal Rights Amendment.

Possible solutions: Tenancy by the entirety is in effect a variation of joint tenancy, which is a form of property ownership by two or more persons who may or may not be married. Since creditors can collect against a joint tenant's interest in a joint tenancy just as they can against any other property, spouses do not encounter the same difficulty in borrowing against their interest in joint tenancy property as they do in borrowing against their interest in property held as tenants by the entirety. Also, a spouse can, at will, sell his or her interest in a tenancy by the entirety without the consent of the other spouse. For these reasons, some have suggested that tenancy by the entirety be abolished; many states have already done so.

If that is not desired, at the very least the legal incidents of the estate of tenancy by the entirety must be reformed by:

1. making it possible in all states for creditors to collect debts immediately after judgment from the interest of each spouse in property held as tenants by the entirety;

2. specifically providing that both husband and wife have the right to manage any property held as tenants by the entirety; and

3. giving the spouses an equal interest in all rents from such property.

246

References

1. Johnston, "Sex and Property: The Common Law Tradition, the Law School Curriculum and Developments Towards Equality," 47 N.Y. U. L. Rev. 1033, 1083-1089 (1972).

2. Note, "Real Property--Tenancy by the Entirety in Real Property during Marriage," 47 N.C. L. Rev. 963 (1969).

3. Note, "Wife's Right to Rents from Tenancy by Entirety," 24 Wash. & Lee L. Rev. 353 (1967).

4. Craig, "Analysis of Estates by the Entirety in Bankruptcy," 48 Am. Bankr. L. J. 255 (1974).

COMMUNITY PROPERTY SYSTEMS

Introduction

As noted earlier, eight states of the United States[19] adhere to the community property system to determine the property rights of married persons. Under that system, all property brought to the marriage, inherited or given to either spouse during the marriage is the separate property of that person. The other spouse has no right, title or interest in such property, and only the owner may manage and control it. The earnings of either spouse during marriage, however, are community property, in which each has a one-half ownership interest, regardless of which of them actually earned the money. Because of this feature, the community property system is a more just system of marital property law than is the separate property system followed in the other forty-two states and the District of Columbia.

All the community property states, except Louisiana and Nevada, have revised their laws quite drastically since 1967; most of the changes were made in order to "equalize" sex-discriminatory provisions in the older statutes. Because of these recent modifications, many in those states may believe that their community property laws will not need revision after passage of the Equal Rights Amendment. However, as will be seen below, there are many important questions which were left unresolved by the recent reforms in those six states. Thus, passage of the Equal Rights Amendment should cause further reform and improvement in the community property law of all eight community property states.

---

19. Arizona, California, Idaho, Louisiana, Nevada, New Mexico, Texas and Washington.

Community Property and the Equal Credit Opportunity Act

In October 1974, Congress passed the Equal Credit Opportunity Act, effective October 28, 1975.[20] That Act prohibits any creditor in the United States from discriminating on the basis of sex in any aspect of a credit transaction. As noted earlier, in the five community property states[21] in which wives have completely equal power to manage and control the community property, the Equal Credit Opportunity Act will, for the first time, give unemployed married women a means of obtaining credit in their own names, without their husbands' consent, and to the same extent as their husbands. The only criterion which a creditor may ask a wife who works in the home to meet when she applies for credit in one of those five states after October 28, 1975, is whether the community itself (the two spouses as a unit) is creditworthy—the amount of assets and obligations outstanding.[22] If it is, she may obtain a Mastercharge, Bankamericard, retail charge account, small loan, bank loan or any other form of credit exactly as her husband could. For the first time, a partial solution will be at hand to one of the most pervasive and troubling problems in family law—that of support in the ongoing family, discussed at length in the chapter on Family Laws. For this reason alone, adoption of community property as a system of marital property law might be considered in separate property jurisdictions.

There are, of course, sex-discriminatory aspects of the law of the community property states which will become unconstitutional after passage of an Equal Rights Amendment. Those features, as well as others which would improve the community property systems' treatment of married women, are discussed below.

---

20. 15 U.S.C. Secs. 1691 et seq. (Supp. Pamphlet No. 1, Feb. 1975).

21. Arizona, California, Idaho, New Mexico and Washington.

22. See Proposed Regulations, 12 C.F.R. Sec. 202.5(f), 40 Fed. Reg. 18183 (1975). The Equal Credit Opportunity Act is found at 15 U.S.C. Secs. 1691 et seq. (Supp. Pamphlet No. 1, Feb. 1975).

248

References

1. _See_ Younger, "Community Property, Women and the Law School Curriculum," 48 N.Y.U. L. Rev. 211 (1973), for an in-depth critique of the sex-discriminatory aspects of community property law.

2. Krauskopf and Thomas, "Partnership Marriages: The Solution to an Ineffective and Inequitable Law of Support," 35 Ohio St. L. J. 558 (1974).

3. Kulzer, "Property and the Family: Spousal Protection," 4 Rutgers Camden L. J. 195 (1973).

4. A general reference work concerning community property is W. De Funiak and M. Vaughn, Principles of Community Property (2nd ed. 1971).

Management of Community Property

Legal problem: In Louisiana and Nevada, wives are prohibited by statute from managing the community property in which they have a vested one-half ownership interest.[23]

In Texas, section 5.22 of the Texas Family Code in effect prohibits a wife from managing any portion of the community except her own wages. As to those, she has sole management and control.[24] The Texas management scheme, while not as blatantly sex discriminatory as those in Louisiana and Nevada, could well be challenged as a law "neutral on its face, but discriminatory in impact." What it says to Texas wives is that if they want to manage any property, they must earn it--even though they own one-half of the community property. Thus, the Texas management system will quite possibly also be unconstitutional under the Equal Rights Amendment.

---

23. In Louisiana, a wife may not manage even her own earnings because they are community property. In Nevada, a wife may manage her own earnings if they are expended "for the support" of the family. Such a statute appears very difficult to apply.

24. As of the date of this publication, the Texas statute provided that a husband or wife had sole control of his or her own earnings unless they were placed in the same account with the other's earnings (known in community property law as "commingling"). If that happens, the spouses have "joint" control over the property.

Possible solutions: Five community property states, Arizona, California, Idaho, New Mexico and Washington, have recently enacted completely equal management provisions for community personal property. These five states follow a partnership theory of community personal property management: either spouse alone may manage, control, dispose of or encumber the entire community personal property, just as partners may under the explicit provisions of the Uniform Partnership Act and the common law of partnership.

Several of these states have had equal management provisions in effect since 1973, with no reported problems. Thus, the solution for Louisiana, Nevada and Texas is legislative adoption of a truly equal community property management system, based on analogy to the rights of business partners.

References

1. "Community Property: Symposium on Equal Rights," 48 Tul. L. Rev. 560 (1974).

2. "Section 5.22 of the Texas Family Code: Control and Management of the Marital Estate," S.W. L. J. 837 (1973).

3. Bingaman, "The Effects of an Equal Rights Amendment on the New Mexico System of Community Property: Problems of Characterization, Management and Control," 3 N.M. L. Rev. 11, 36-55 (1970).

4. N.M. Stat. Ann. Sec. 57-4A-8 (1953) (Supp. 1975).

5. McKnight, "Texas Community Property Law--Its Course of Development and Reform," 8 Cal. Western L. Rev. 117 (1971).

6. Note, "Community Property: Male Management and Women's Rights," 1972 L. & Soc. Order 163.

7. Cross, "Equality for Spouses in Washington Community Property Law--1972 Statutory Changes," 48 Wash. L. Rev. 527 (1973).

8. Cross, "The Community Property Law in Washington," 49 Wash. L. Rev. 729 (1974).

9. Young, "Joint Management and Control of Community Property in Idaho: A Prognosis," 11 Idaho L. Rev. 1 (1974).

250

10. Note, "California's New Community Property Law--Its Effect on Interspousal Mismanagement Litigation," 5 Pacific L. J. 723 (1974).

11. Huie, "Divided Management of Community Property in Texas," 5 Tex. Tech. L. Rev. 623 (1974).

12. Note, "Equal Management and Control under Senate Bill 569: 'To Have and to Hold' Takes on a New Meaning in California," 11 San Diego L. Rev. 999 (1974).

13. Note, "Equal Rights and Equal Protection: Who Has Management and Control?" 46 So. Cal. L. Rev. 892 (1973).

14. Olds, "Conveyances by Married Women in Texas," 8 Houston L. Rev. 677 (1971).

Characterization of Debts As "Separate" or "Community"

Legal problem: In no community property state except New Mexico does there exist a statutory definition of "separate" and "community" debts. Nevertheless, in all these states, the law as to what property may be reached to satisfy a particular debt is drastically different depending on the characterization of the debt itself as "separate" or "community."

In general, creditors may reach assets belonging to the community (husband and wife) to satisfy community debts; but, to satisfy a separate debt, creditors may be able to reach only the separate property, if any, of the spouse who created the debt, or in some states, the debtor spouse's separate property plus his or her one-half interest in the community property.

While the lack of definitions of "separate" and "community" debts may not seem serious, it is rendered important by passage of the Equal Credit Opportunity Act. Creditors who are not sure that a wife is contracting a "community" debt, which may be satisfied from all community property, may use that uncertainty as an excuse for refusing credit where it is due. Thus, to make equal credit a reality with as little litigation as possible, all community property states should define "separate" and "community" debts by statute, rather than leaving those important definitions to the vagaries of case law.

Possible solutions: In 1973, the New Mexico legislature enacted a new community property statute which is more comprehensive than any other state's community property law. That statute defines the character of debts contracted by each spouse before, during and after marriage. Because virtually all contract debts created by married persons are defined as community debts, and because the statute then opens as much property as possible to the collection of community debts, wives in New Mexico theoretically stand to gain more than wives in any other state from passage of the federal Equal Credit Opportunity Act.

References

1. Equal Credit Opportunity Act, 15 U.S.C. Sec. 1691 (d) (Supp. Pamphlet No. 1, Feb. 1975).

2. N.M. Stat. Ann. Secs. 57-4A-4 and 57-4A-5 (1953) (Supp. 1975).

3. Bingaman, "The New Mexico Community Property Act of 1973: A Commentary and Quasi-Legislative History," 5 N.M. L. Rev. 1 (1974).

4. Note, "Liability of the Husband for the Contractual Obligations of His Wife--Louisiana Legislation and Jurisprudence," 30 La. L. Rev. 441 (1970).

5. Note, "Community Property--Community's Liability for Husband's Antenuptial Debts," 20 Loyola L. Rev. 355 (1973-74).

6. Note, "Creditor's Rights and the Community of Gains," 34 La. L. Rev. 874 (1974).

7. Note, "Federal Tax Liability of the Wife for Community Income Earned by the Husband," 32 La. L. Rev. 471 (1972).

8. Note, "Income Tax--Louisiana Wife's Liability," 17 Loyola L. Rev. 767 (1970-71).

Debt Collection

Legal problem: Beyond the problem of the characterization of a particular debt as community or separate, Nevada and Louisiana retain unequal provisions for the collection of debts from the property of husbands and wives. The entire community property is liable for the husband's debts, but none of it is liable for the wife's. On the other hand, the wife's separate property is not liable for any portion of the community's debts, while the husband's entire separate property is liable.

Possible solution: No problem has been encountered in the other six community property states which have recently enacted equal debt collection provisions. However, it should be noted that the broader the class of property which is liable for community debts, the more likely creditors are to extend credit to either spouse to create community debts.

References

1. Younger, "Community Property, Women and the Law School Curriculum," 48 N.Y.U. L. Rev. 211, 236-238 (1973).

2. Ellis, "The Effect of the New Mexico Equal Rights Amendment on Debt Characterization and Collection," N.M. L. Rev. 61 (1972).

3. N.M. Stat. Ann. Secs. 57-4A-4 and 57-4A-5 (1953) (Supp. 1975).

4. Bingaman, "The New Mexico Community Property Act of 1973: A Commentary and Quasi-Legislative History," 5 N.M. L. Rev. 1 (1974).

Character of Property As Separate or Community When Spouses Are Separated but Not Divorced

Legal problem: Two legal problems are present here. The first is simple. In Louisiana and Nevada, whose community property systems are still untouched by legislative reform, the wife's earnings become separate property when the spouses are living separately; the husband's earnings remain community property in which the wife has a one-half interest. Obviously, such a statute can be amended to treat the spouses in a formally neutral manner by making the earnings of both either separate or community when they separate.

In New Mexico a statute provides that the earnings of both remain community when the spouses separate unless they agree in writing to the contrary.[25]

In California and Washington, however, the earnings of both become separate property the moment the spouses physically separate. Although undoubtedly drafted to avoid federal income tax liability for the other spouse's income after separation, these statutes may be further examples of laws which are "neutral on their face, but discriminatory in impact." When a couple separates, the wife in almost all instances takes responsibility for any children; thus, she is often prevented from working at all or may be able to work only part-time. Her husband's earnings,

25. N.M. Stat. Ann. Sec. 57-4A-2 (1953) (Supp. 1975).

meanwhile, which were community property while they lived together, become his separate property in which she has no interest. Even when children are not involved, in a society in which the average wage of working women is 57% that of working men,[26] a rule under which married persons' income automatically becomes separate property upon physical separation will leave the wife with less property than her husband. For these reasons, then, the California and Washington solutions, while simpler from an income tax standpoint, create hardships for married women and should be reconsidered.

Possible solution: The solution to both the Nevada and Louisiana problems, as well as the Washington and California situations, is to declare by statute that upon separation the earnings of married persons remain community property unless the spouses agree by contract that they are separate property.

Reference

Younger, "Women, Community Property and the Law School Curriculum," 48 N.Y.U. L. Rev. 211, 229-230 (1973).

The Community Property "Widow's Election"

Legal problem: For estate tax reasons, a husband in a community property state may wish to make a will which forces his surviving widow to "elect" or choose between: (1) taking a life estate in the entire community property under his will, which means that the widow receives only the income produced by the property during her lifetime rather than outright ownership of it; or (2) taking her one-half of the community property as the absolute owner. The choice for the widow, then, is between being the beneficiary of a trust she does not own, but from which she receives all the income produced by both hers and her husband's half of the community property, or owning her one-half of the community outright. Because substantial federal estate tax savings are possible through use of the "widow's election" will or trust device, it is widely used in planning large estates in community property states.[27]

---

26. Women's Bureau, U.S. Department of Labor, Highlights of Women's Employment and Education 2 (1974) (1973 data).

27. Because the federal estate tax is imposed only on estates of $60,000 or more, the gross community estate must be $120,000 or more before either the bushand's or wife's estate will be subject to federal estate taxes. For this reason, the "widow's election" is used only in planning relatively large estates.

Although a wife can put her husband to a "widower's election"--which makes the doctrine sex-neutral and thus constitutional under the Equal Rights Amendment--the situations in which a wife would be in an economic position to do so have been relatively rare to date. To ensure that policy considerations underlying the "widow's election" are taken into account, this question should be treated by statute in any general revision of community property laws after passage of the Equal Rights Amendment.

Possible solutions: Although either spouse can today put the other to an "election," and thus effect large tax savings, there is a policy argument which can be made against the existence of even a sex-neutral "election" device.

Most women outlive their husbands. If put to an "election" which their husbands have told them is a good tax savings, almost all will choose to take under the will and forego their one-half outright ownership of the community property. However, taking under a "widow's election" means taking the property as the beneficiary of a trust which is managed by an independent trustee. Thus, the widow loses control of the property, and must live on income from investments which the trustees think are wise.

It is possible, then, that retention of the "election" device after passage of the ERA will have the unintended effect of coercing widows into living as beneficiaries of trusts managed by others rather than as managers of property which they own in their own right. Because of this result, and because statistics demonstrate that 85% of wives outlive their husbands, it can be argued that perpetuation of the "widow's election" after passage of the Equal Rights Amendment will, regardless of the tax savings possible, tend to prevent women from having the opportunity to manage property and investments themselves.

References

1. Younger, "Women, Community Property and the Law School Curriculum," 48 N.Y.U. L. Rev. 211, 241 (1973).

2. Wren, "The Widow's Election in Community Property States," 7 Ariz. L. Rev. 1 (1965).

3. Johanson, "Revocable Trusts and Community Property: The Substantive Problems," 47 Tex. L. Rev. 537 (1969).

4. Johanson, "Revocable Trusts, Widow's Election Wills and Community Property: The Tax Problems," 47 Tex. L. Rev. 1247 (1969).

5. Halbach, "Community Property 'Widow's Election' and Some of Its Surprise Counterparts," 107 Trusts & Estates 1164 (1968).

6. Note, "Widow's Election As an Estate Planning Device in Washington," 43 Wash. L. Rev. 455 (1967).

7. Lane, "The Widow's Election As a Private Annuity: Boon or Bane for Estate Planners?," 44 So. Cal. L. Rev. 74 (1970).

8. Note, "California Inheritance Tax in Widow's Election Cases: Taxation in the Twilight Zone," 5 Sw. U. L. Rev. 165 (1973).

9. Kahn and Gallo, "Widow's Election: A Return to Fundamentals," 24 Stan. L. Rev. 531 (1972).

Division of Community Property on Divorce

Legal problem: While the law in all community property states unequivocally vests a one-half ownership interest of all community property in each spouse, only two of those states require that upon divorce each spouse be given his or her vested ownership intrest. The other six allow a court to apportion community property "equitably" as the court's view of the circumstances dictates. Thus, wives or husbands often receive less than one-half the community property on divorce, with the remainder going to their respective spouses.

Possible solutions: The obvious solution is to require by statute that courts divide community property equally upon divorce, as the vested property right each spouse has in the property would seem to require.

While this solution seems preferable to giving courts broad discretion, it would be helpful to know in what ratios courts in community property states in fact apportion property and upon what factors such apportionment is based. Since no study of such decrees exist, however, it is preferable for legislatures to require a mandatory division now, as was suggested above in the chapter on Family Laws, rather than to wait for such studies before taking action.

References

1. Younger, "Women, Community Property and the Law School Curriculum," 48 N.Y.U. L. Rev. 211, 241-245 (1973).

256

2. Note, "Military Retirement Benefits As Community Property," 25 <u>S.W. L. J.</u> 340 (1971).

3. Note, "Military Retirement Benefits As Community Property: New Rules from the Supreme Court?," 24 <u>Baylor L. Rev.</u> 235 (1972).

4. Note, "The Wife's Community Interest in Her Husband's Qualified Pension or Profit-Sharing Plan," 50 <u>Tex. L. Rev.</u> 334 (1972).

5. Comment, "California's Divorce Reform: Its Effect on Community Property Awards," 1 <u>Pacific L. J.</u> 310 (1970).

6. Comment, "Retirement Benefits and the Right to Reimbursement," 11 <u>Houston L. Rev.</u> 960 (1974).

7. Note, "Marital Property--The Enhanced Book Value of Separately Owned Close Corporation Stock May Be Subject to Community Claims," 6 <u>Tex. Tech. L. Rev.</u> 259 (1974).

8. Curry, "Partitioning Community Property," 2 <u>St. Mary's L. J.</u> 219 (1970).

9. Note, "Retirement Pay: A Divorce in Time Saved Mine," 24 <u>Hastings L. J.</u> 347 (1973).

10. Note,"The Unsettled Question of the Military Pension: Separate or Community Property?," 8 <u>Cal. Western L. Rev.</u> 117 (1971).

<u>"Quasi-community Property"</u>

Legal problem: All of the community property states located in the western half of the United States have experienced much greater population growth in the last twenty years than has the country as a whole. Many of the persons who move to these states are middle-aged or retired, and have lived in separate property states all their lives. Thus, if the wife did not work for compensation during the marriage, all property will be the separate property of the husband. Under the rule in effect in most community property states, increases in the value of separate property during marriage are separate, not community, property. An all too common situation is that of a couple whose sole assets, acquired in a separate property state, are the husband's separate property. When they move to a community property state, all increases in the value of those assets will remain the husband's separate property, in which his wife has no legal interest. The only means by which a wife can obtain any property rights after such a move is through her own earnings or those of her husband. If they are retired, all property will remain the husband's separate property.

The problem can become severe upon a husband's death. If the couple had remained in a separate property state, the wife would have been protected by the dower or "forced" share laws in effect in most of those states; under those laws she would automatically be given a 1/3 or 1/2 interest in some portion of her husband's separate property. In a community property state, however, she has no dower rights because under a community system, wives are assured of ownership of one-half of the community. The wife who has moved from a separate property state, then, will have neither a dower interest in her husband's separate property nor any interest in community property (assuming they have acquired no community). If her husband is unaware of this legal situation, and either dies without a will, or leaves his property to children, the wife will have little or no property upon his death.

In families where most or all of the property is the wife's separate property, the husband will find himself in the same dilemma.[28]

Possible solutions: California, inundated by migrants from separate property states, has led the way in this area of law by adopting what is known as "quasi-community property." Under California law, any property owned by persons who have moved to California which would have been community property if they had lived in California when it was acquired is treated as community property at divorce or upon the death of either spouse.

The Uniform Probate Code in sections 2-201 et seq. also contains provisions which effectively establish "quasi-community property" in community property states at the death of one spouse through an "elective share" system. Although some believe that this portion of the Code has technical defects which need further study, certainly it and the California statute both offer better protection to a spouse moving to a community property state late in life than does no statute at all.

All community property states should adopt some form of "quasi-community property" statute in any revision of property laws pursuant to an Equal Rights Amendment. Unquestionably, such a statute should follow the California model and provide for the establishment of "quasi-community property" upon divorce as well as upon death.

---

28. A complicated legal problem also exists when spouses move from community property states to separate property states. That problem, however, does not have the potential for harm to wives which its counterpart, discussed in this section, does. It is therefore not treated in the text although some of the references included below deal with it.

References

1.   Uniform Probate Code, 8 Uniform Laws Annotated, Secs. 2-201 et seq. (1973).

2.   Cal. Civ. Code Sec. 4803 (1970).

3.   Bodenheimer, "Community without Community Property: The Need for Legislative Attention to Separate Property Marriages under Community Property Laws," 8 Cal. Western L. Rev. 381 (1972).

4.   Note, "Selected Community Property Problems of the Migrant Spouse," 7 Family L. Q. 433 (1973).

5.   McClanahan, "Property Problems of the Migrant Client: A Statutory Solution," 111 Trusts & Estates 950 (1972).

6.   Note, "Property Problems of the Peripatetic Client," 5 Real Prop., Probate & Trust J. 526 (1970).

7.   Wiley, "Community Property in a Common Law State," 21 Prac. Lw. 81 (1975).

Earning Capacity As an Assest of the Community

Legal problem: When a marriage ends in divorce and the amount of the community's assets is determined for division between the spouses, the earning capacities of the spouses are seldom considered. It is generally a husband whose earning capacity has been increased during the years of marriage by a wife's responsibility for home and children; wives also often support their husbands' educations and pay for family expenses by working outside the home while the husbands develop their own careers to their fullest potential. Thus, rule which ignores the earning potentials of spouses upon divorce harms wives more than husbands. This judicial doctrine in community property states is arguably a rule which is "neutral on its face but discriminatory in impact" and it will possibly be unconstitutional under the Equal Rights Amendment. Even if not unconstitutional, however, the rule undoubtedly operates to the detriment of married women, and should be changed by statute to improve the community property sytem.

Possible solution: Only one solution seems feasible. That is to declare by statute that "earning capacity developed during marriage" is a property asset of the community which must be valued upon divorce in dividing property between the spouses.

The problem, of course, is not in stating the rule, but in properly valuing earning capacity in particular cases. However, because situations will vary so greatly, the only workable statutory solution would seem to be to declare the rule simply, and let lawyers argue and judges decide the amounts to be awarded in individual cases.

References

1. This is a question which will be increasingly litigated. A New Mexico wife recently lost in her attempt to have her husband's license to practice medicine declared a community asset; see Muckleroy v. Muckleroy, 84 N.M. 14, 498 P. 2d 1357 (1973). In California, however, a wife succeeded. There the court determined that part of her husband's law practice was the property of the community; see In Re Lopez, 38 Cal. App. 2d 93, 113 Cal. Rptr. 58 (1974).

2. Note, "Domestic Relations--Goodwill of a Professional Practice Acquired after Marriage Is Held to be Community Property in the State of Texas," 2 Tex. So. U. L. Rev. 383 (1973).

3. Note, "Interest of the Community in a Professional Education," 10 Cal. Western L. Rev. 590 (1974).

Property Problems of Persons Who Marry a Wealthy Spouse

Legal problem: Although not a problem of equal rights, this is one of the defects of the community property system which should be legislatively corrected in any general revision of community property laws pursuant to the Equal Rights Amendment. The problem may be simply stated: in all but three community property states, increases in the value of separate property after marriage remain the separate property of the owning spouse. If one spouse is very wealthy, and therefore neither works, the other spouse will obtain absolutely no property rights during marriage; all increases in the value of the wealthy spouse's property will be that spouse's separate property.

Even if the nonwealthy spouse is employed, he or she will be injured: his or her earnings will be community property, in which the wealthy spouse will have a one-half ownership interest, while in five of the eight community property states the nonwealthy spouse will obtain no interest whatsoever in the increases in value of the other's property.

260

Although this problem affects only a small percentage of the population, the effect on those few is severe and can cause great hardship. Legal remedies are relatively simple; therefore, some legislative solution should be included in any general revision of property laws pursuant to the Equal Rights Amendment.

Possible solutions: Two solutions are possible here. A rule that all increases in the value of separate property after marriage are community, not separate, property could be adopted. This is in fact the original Spanish law of community property, and it is followed today in Louisiana, Idaho and Texas. In those community property states, the nonwealthy spouse gains a one-half interest in all increases in value of the other's property after marriage.

A second solution would be to copy the "nonbarrable" or "forced" share system in effect in many separate property states, discussed at length above, which gives either spouse an interest in the separate property of the other upon death. If this solution is chosen, it should cover both the circumstances of divorce after a given number of years of marriage and that of the death of the wealthy spouse.

References

1. K. Davidson, R. Ginsburg and H. Kay, Sex-based Discrimination 158-171 (1974).

2. W. de Funiak and M. Vaughn, Principles of Community Property 71 (2d ed. 1971).

TABLE OF CASES

INDEX

COMMUNITY PROPERTY SYSTEMS (cont'd)
      Separate property, 225-226, 259-260
      Separate property systems, converted to, 235-239
      Separation, characterization of property upon,
          252-253
      States which operate under, 161, 225, 246
      Theory of, 226-227, 231, 234
      Wealthy spouse, problems of, 259-260
      Widow's "election", 253-254

COMPENSATORY AID
      Constitutionality of, under ERA, 39-41

CONSORTIUM
      ERA, effect of on rights of recovery, 168
      Generally, 168-169

CONSPIRACY
      Husband and wife, 106

CONTRACEPTION
      U. S. Supreme Court case, (Eisenstadt v.
          Baird), 51

CREDIT
      See Community Property Systems; Equal Credit
          Opportunity Act; Separate Property Systems

CRIMINAL OFFENSES
      See also Judicial Process; Juveniles; Prisons;
          Prostitution; Sexual Assault
      Alimony, non-payment of, 194
      Child support, non-payment of, 33, 181
      Conspiracy, husband and wife, 106
      Sex crimes, 104-105

CURRICULUM
      See Education

CURTESY
      See Dower and Curtesy

CUSTODY OF CHILDREN
      See Child Custody

DAY CARE CENTERS
      ERA "requirement", 156
      University provided, 150

DEATH
      See also Dower and Curtesy; Forced Share Statutes
      Statistics comparing men and women, 241, 254
      Widows' property rights, 233-234
      Wife's right to will property, 233

DIVORCE
      Alimony, 190
      Child custody, see Child Custody
      Child support, see Child Support
      Insurance, 184
      "No-fault", 159, 180
      Property division, 182-186, 229-232
            Domestic labor, valuation of, 184, 193
            Misconduct or fault considerations, 183,
                  193, 231
      Sex-discriminatory grounds for, 180
      Statistics, 157, 181

DOMESTIC WORK
      See Uncompensated Domestic Labor

DOMICILE
      Children, 174
      ERA, effect of, 172
      Women
            Married, 172
            Students, 172

DORMITORIES
      Prisons, 68
      Privacy, right of, 34
      Schools, 139-140

272

EDUCATION AMENDMENTS OF 1972
    See Title IX

EEOC
    See Civil Rights Act of 1964 -- Title VII

EIGHT AMENDMENT
    Prisons, cruel and unusual punishment, 69

EMPLOYMENT
    Compensation for widows and widowers, 221-222
    Conditions of,
        Generally, 206-215
        Hours, maximum, 209-212
        Maternity leave, 11, 147, 214-215
        Over-time, 206-207, 210, 211-212
        Physical facilities, 207-209
        Rest periods, 207-209
        Wages
            Minimum, 206-207
            Women's compared to men's, see Wages
        Weight-lifting limitations, 212-213
    Exclusion of women, 213-214
    Graduates, hiring of, 152
    Insurance, 13, 202
    Legislation
        ERA, effect on, 204-209, 212, 213, 215
        Protective labor laws, 202-205, 207
        Sex-discriminatory, 202-203
    Maternity leave, 11, 147, 214-215
    Military, 15
    Part-time teachers, 152
    Public schools, 144-148
    Racial discrimination, 32
    Salaried, for women outside the home, 156, 208
    State government, 219-220
    Teachers, part-time, 152
    Title VII
        See Civil Rights Act of 1964 -- Title VII
    Title IX
        See Title IX
    Unemployment compensation, 216-219
    Veterans, preference for in state government, 221
    Work release programs in prisons, 73

284

SODOMY
>   Prostitutes, male, 100-101
>   Statutes, 105
>>   Compared to rape, 86-87

STATE ACTION
>   Equal Rights Amendment, 21-22
>   Fourteenth Amendment, 21-22
>   Government subsidies as, 114
>   Institutions and organizations
>>   Banks, 25-26
>>   Educational institutions, private, 24, 114
>>   Extra-curricular organizations, 135-136
>>   Insurance companies, 26-27
>>   Private clubs, 27-28
>>   Public schools, admissions policies of, 117-118
>>   Religious institutions, 24-25
>>   State facilities, right of sex-restricted groups to use, 137-138
>   Tests applied under, 22-24
>>   Public function, 23
>>   Significant state involvement, 22-23

STATUTES "NEUTRAL ON THEIR FACE, DISCRIMINATORY IN IMPACT"
>   Alimony, non-payment of, 194
>   Athletics, 75, 124-125, 128, 132
>   Community property management statutes, 248
>   Concept defined, 31-33
>   Divorce, division of property upon, in community property states, 256
>   Earnings, of spouses after separation, 252
>   Forced share statutes, 242
>   Marriage, common-law and putative, 167
>   Prisons, 70
>   Prostitution statutes, 100-102
>   School admissions, 120-121
>   Separate property systems, 234-235
>   Sexual assault cases, 98

STATUTORY RAPE
>   See Sexual Assault

UNIFORM PARENTAGE ACT
    Adoptions, 177-180
    Child custody, rights of natural fathers, 198
    Child support, duties of natural fathers, 189
    ERA, effect of, 178

UNIFORM PARTNERSHIP ACT
    Community property systems, analogy to, 249

UNIFORM PROBATE CODE
    Application, 240-241

UNIFORM RECIPROCAL ENFORCEMENT OF SUPPORT ACT (URESA)
    Enforcement of child support, 188

"UNIQUE PHYSICAL CHARACTERISTICS"
    Children, women's ability to bear, 178
    Factors establishing, 36-37
    Generally, 31, 35-38
    Pregnancy, 35-37, 133, 143, 216-219
    Sexual assault statutes, 86-87

UNIVERSITIES
    See Education

URESA
    See Uniform Reciprocal Enforcement of Support Act

VETERANS AND VETERANS' PREFERENCE STATUTES
    See Armed Services; Education; Employment

VOCATIONAL SCHOOLS
    See Education

WAGES
    See also Employment; Uncompensated Domestic Labor
    Women's compared to men's, 158, 228, 230,
        234, 252-253, 258

88630—886 11/75 Reprint 1,500 OSP